Date Due

DEC 22 68			

THE NARRATIVE POEMS OF
MARK VAN DOREN

By Mark Van Doren

THE
NARRATIVE
POEMS
OF
MARK VAN DOREN

HILL AND WANG • NEW YORK

63962

First Edition September 1964

Manufactured in the United States of America
by American Book–Stratford Press, Inc.

CONTENTS

JONATHAN GENTRY

(1931)

Jonathan Gentry

I
OHIO RIVER
1800

Jonathan Gentry, with an English heart
Broken in two high places that must heal;
Jonathan Gentry sailed, and told the sea-winds:
"Your meadows are green with salt and endless anger,
What you look down on, flying, is flat death.
I could have died too, sea-winds, sea-winds,
I could have bled too long from either bruise.
But over the American mountains
The American meadows wait.
Broad with good breath,
Sea-green with only grass,
And heaving with God's promises to men,
The American meadows, faint from so long calling,
Still bring their voice to me. Here now I have it"—
Holding his heart—
"And here it makes loud music for the mind
To feed on and be wrapped with and grow well.
Already, winds, I smile at my forgetting
Figure and name that in the suit of friendship
Stole my white love at midnight from a room;
And bursting the door outward, burst two chambers

3

High in my side where he and she had been.
No, no—not quick to close. It has been empires.
Or has it been a fly's life in the sun?
But in good time the meadow-song
Came, and I straightway heard;
And straightway come."

Standing among the taut ropes and the seamen,
Courteous like a knight with hidden wounds—
In the deep, shaded center still they flowed
And solemnized his glances, till each smile
Came out of him as gentle as abstracted—
Jonathan Gentry sailed,
And told at last the sea-gulls:
"Shore-birds,
Dwellers upon the dead edge,
Criers above the white line of salt and beaten sand around the
    world,
Wing watchers
Sick of an old sameness—
Gulls, it was not you I sailed to see.
Lead me to land and go again,
Ruefully rising, rising,
Desolate up and up, forever behind me.
Birds of an old world,
My eyes are shaped for newness, and for wings
Of paradise above an inland river.
Over the inland mountains it commences,
And flows a thousand miles
Along the meadows of the mind:
Deep in my heart I hear it round the bends,
Taking new thought of bluff and ripple and pool;
Dreaming among the flats;
Rousing, rousing again;
Then pulling in daylong peace—nightlong, daylong pulling—
Past gentle and old gigantic and thoughtful trees.
Birds of the salt beak,

4

Line-criers,
My taste is all for freshness, and for free
New-going wings above an inland valley."

So land, and stripling cities
Aproned from the sea.
So coaches, carts, and cobblestones and faces,
And doors that shut and opened as he waited—
A week, a month he waited—
Then the long jolting out of Philadelphia,
West and a little north, and west again.
Like a tired tortoise,
Clambering up old slopes of rock and weed
To nothing at the top, then down and on
And on and up once more, and on and down,
Went the filled wagon.
Jonathan Gentry rode, or walked and rested,
Over the endless hills, and told the driver:
"No, I am never weary. No, I am going
Only for curious reasons. Yes, I am married.
No, I am going alone"—till the driver spat,
Reaching an end of words. But hairy eyes
Still crawled the length of Gentry, and a tongue
Rolled in its cheek unwillingly confined.
The couple from New England with their baby
Talked in a tavern once, before the fire,
Of where the new land was, and how they went there
Hoping to find a country young as milk.
Jonathan Gentry loved them, and he whispered:
"Yes, we are done with oldness, done with men
Pressing too hard upon us"; but they stared,
And Gentry ever after smiled alone.

One more mountain lay there,
Looking the other way, and Gentry said:
"Nothing will ever move you, nothing make you
Turn your old head to see who comes so late.

All of it in your eyes! You have it all there,
And had it when there were no men to weep.
You had it when there were no women either:
Women to weep and laugh and run away.
Is it a world ancient beyond all error?
Is it too young to know? And will it know?"
The horses leaned;
The wagon, gritting its last gravel,
Groaned, and they zigzagged up.
Too steep, the driver said, and so they rested
Where a bright spring, refusing to go further,
Tumbled down past them backward, laughing loudly
At labor and all good purpose. But they left it,
Took a long breath and toiled, and wound thrice more
Right upward, till the trees
Opened; the mountain stopped; and all their faces
Fell on the broad Ohio, soft below.

Like a white dream this beautiful of rivers
Lay in its forest folds, and if it moved there
None of them knew it now. They too were moveless—
High, little gods of momentary stone—
They too were dreams the mountain dreamed, old father
Of flocks of dreams that circled each day and fell.
When they could see again they wept and wondered,
Turned to each other and chattered, and wiped their eyes.
But Gentry's eyes had nothing for the others.
They still were stone as the path tilted down,
Dragging the jolted wheels;
They still were fixed on air as the slow road
Slanted all day and night,
And another infinite night,
Crookedly down to the clearing and into the town
Where smoke rose, and houses of new logs
Huddled away from hills;
They still were sightless eyes until he wandered,
Leaving the unhitched horses tossing their hay,

To a smooth bank and stood there, while the river
Moved at his feet, and moving, brought more water
That followed and flowed and followed, and stopped in eddies
Only to go again.
So Gentry stood and trembled, and his eyes
Melted, and his mind
Entered the faithful flood.

Nine days the hammers rang, the sledges thudded,
Saws whined, and swarming men along the shore
Fitted the fragrant timbers of an ark
That floated on the tenth day and received them—
The couple from New England with their baby,
A preacher with a brown beard and a brood
Whose mother lay in Maryland under a hill,
Two men with silver watches and cigars,
A blue-eyed woodsman swinging gun and fiddle,
Twelve boatmen, lanky-jawed; and Jonathan Gentry.
Then came the bags and bundles, and the stove,
And chairs tied two together, and the beds;
Then, timorous in their ropes, the seven sheep
The preacher could not leave, the fiddler's pig,
Two heifers, and two Jerseys big with milk.
The creatures in their stout pen at the stern
Bawled as the bugle blew; the cabin people
Crowded the clumsy bow, and the languid boatmen,
Languid no more this morning, heaved at the sweeps.
The flat craft, swinging slowly into the middle,
Moved to a dwarfish music; for the woodsman,
Climbing the cabin ladder, scraped his bow
Thinly upon the strings; it came back thinly
And sadly now to the shore as the sawmen shouted,
And down at the stern the sheep called faintly too.
But the small music, rising between the mountains,
Moved as the long oars moved; and when they ceased,
The ark come full to the current, wavered on
Like the lost voice of birds.

7

Over the mountains, boys,
Into the land of grass;
Down the big river, boys,
Stand up and pass.
  With a heave-la-ho,
  And a heave-la-hum,
  Bend and go
  Till kingdom come.

One time there was Adam,
One time there was Eve.
Can it come again, boys?
What do you believe?
  With a heave-la-ho,
  And a heave-la-hum,
  Bend and go
  Till kingdom come.

Eden's up ahead, boys,
And the golden age.
Not a lawyer there, boys,
Or parson in a rage.
  With a heave-la-ho,
  And a heave-la-hum,
  Bend and go
  Till kingdom come.

No one's very bad there,
And no one's very good.
It's the promised land, boys,
Land of livelihood.
  With a heave-la-ho,
  And a heave-la-hum,
  Bend and go
  Till kingdom come.

And children in a low line by the shore
Stretched like a fringe of weeds, and would have hailed them;
But nothing could be heard beyond small cries
And piping little laughter, that the ring
Of axes in the forest and deep bells
Of happy-throated dogs, and idle screams
Of jays and red-birds mingled with and lost.
More settlements; and Gentry,
Straining his eyes and ears, would have beheld
Joy on the new-born faces, and heard songs
Never before let loose from mouths of men.
But still it was too far; so he was left
To his own shining thoughts, and to the river;
While on the shore young men and women lounged,
Envying him that floated like the summer—
Suspended a long season out of time—
Envying him the soft air and the clear,
Unchanging gentle current, south and south.
Storms came; windy rain beat up the water,
And thunder from the hills
Dropped down as if to break them, boat and all.
But sun came always after, and he said
This only was to prove the land was old;
Longer ago than men it had a voice—
And used it now, remembering. If a gorge
Threatened them in the night, and rapids roared,
And the tired boatmen cursed like evil birds,
Gentry in the morning smiled and found
The smooth way only smoother, south and west.
And now the days were longer, and the trees
Taller along the shore, and thicklier hung
With vines and ranging moss; and now the river,
Rounding the great slow bend, went west and west.
But Gentry now was done with his own thoughts,
That, living too long inward, drooped a little,
Dying unless he spoke.

10

The preacher with the brown beard, praying loudly,
Ceased, and sending his circle of children off,
Turned a big face toward Gentry: "Brother in trouble,
Brother in mortal need of the touch immortal,
What of our days ahead? What night has cast them
Into your face's shadow, that no smile
Lightens, and no morning may expel?
Tell me; for your silence is a load
Like sin upon us all, and thwarts us all."
Gentry, as if awakened out of years
Of stiff and standing sleep—startled a little—
Frowned; but when he thought of the humming woodsman,
And thought of the pair of men that even now
Smoked at the other rail and hung white hands
With rings upon them over the roughened wood,
Smiled:
"Brother? But not in trouble are we brothers.
What burden could bear these down?"—watching the rail—
"What night? And what of the fiddle? We move in song.
The days ahead are waiting, and their brows
Are bland with perfect ignorance of our past.
Sadness is forgotten here; we bring
No seed of it to sow in any meadow."
But the small eyes in that big face looked shrewdly,
And the brown-bearded mouth said "Nevertheless
Something is sore inside you, something is hard,
Moveless and smooth like stone." So Gentry thought:
"He can be told"; and told of the man and woman
Lost in a London moment; but concluded:
"All of it left me lightly when I landed;
Nothing remains of them I have forgiven—"
"Forgiven!" the preacher groaned, and bit his beard
In anger at a word so mildly made;
"Forgiven! You were not just to end it so.
Evil sometimes is monstrous, and calls out
For monstrous good to take it by the throat.

You should have stayed and salted with your wrath
Such love-wounds, such red flowing mouths of hell!"
Gentry, in mingled shock and pale dismay,
Knew that the others heard, and turned to see
Wry, empty grins twist over the rail and down.
The two men there bowed promptly, and one said:
"Now that you know we listened, let us argue
Half of the sermon sound. You might have stayed;
But not to do as much as one weak deed.
You could have stayed and lived. It didn't matter.
Nothing was new in that. Nothing is new
In anything men can manage; and this world
We poke through now is no calves' pasture either.
Isn't it so, musician?" For the fiddler,
Mending his bow, had wandered along to hear.
He kept a kindly eye on Jonathan Gentry—
Standing in sudden trance—and picked his strings
Mock-soberly a while before he sang:

> Over the mountains, boys,
> What came you for to find?
> Look ahead and see, boys,
> And never look behind.
>> Bend and go,
>> Then stop and stay
>> And get you ready
>> For the Judgment Day.

> Over the mountains, boys,
> You'll work as hard as ever;
> Except the very lazy;
> Also the very clever.
>> Bend and go,
>> Then stop and stay
>> And get you ready
>> For the Judgment Day.

Over the mountains, boys,
We're starting in again;
And what eternal pity
We're doing it with men.
    Bend and go,
    Then stop and stay
    And get you ready
    For the Judgment Day.

Over the mountains, boys,
What came you for to find?
It soon will be the same, boys,
As though you looked behind.
    Bend and go,
    Then stop and stay
    And get you ready
    For the Judgment Day.

The mountains fell away, and now the full unconscious river
Slowlier moved west, or idly slid along the south.
The bottoms opened farther, and little rounded hills
Divided where a northern stream washed a muddy mouth;
But over warm forests, beyond the mingled waters,
Turkey-buzzards floated in circles from the south.

Watching them tilt and spiral, Gentry said:
"These are the birds I dreamed of, yet their slow wings
Mock me, as if to say I knew too much,
Dreaming of Eden then, and know too little,
Dreaming of Eden now. Slow birds,
Wind-sleepers,
Writers of lazy lines upon the sky,
You taunt me with your aimlessness, you tell me
Not to inquire the meaning in an up-sloped invisible wing-stroke,
Not to demand the purpose of a plume.
Therefore you high drones,
You lofty, tongueless inlanders

13

Cutting a higher circle as I talk,
I ask you nothing more, but only ask
Of men henceforth, and women. They must answer."

So day by day, the still shores drifting past,
Off to the north and south, and the great sycamores
Sunning themselves in patches where no shade
Darkened their silver sides, and turkey-buzzards
Counting the indolent hours and losing the count,
They told him, one by one, wherefore they stood there
Riding upon his river.

The pale-nosed pair behind their long cigars
Grew solemn now in praise of bottom soil.
They came to see their hundred thousand acres,
Bought with a piece of paper months ago,
And take its virgin measure. Was he buying?
A bargain there. They talked of the Muskingum,
Scioto, and Miami beds of salt,
Of iron that could be floated on these waters
Down to the mouths of coal mines, and of mica
Glittering underground for picks to take.
They talked, and Gentry listened; yet his thoughts
Turned even while they talked upon the preacher:
Perhaps he had a reason one could hear.

But all he got was thunder from the beard—
Broom of the Lord, that went to sweep the west
And cleanse it for the righteous feet to come.
No dance, if this could help it, of bright heels
Of change across those meadows; no loose growth
Of loveliness unpruned, and innocent vine.
This son of wrath was marching with a face
Furious against old sin, and bound to find it
Planted upon the prairies with the spring;
But stamping would destroy it, and strong hands
Would follow, sowing winters of old faith.

He saw a country filled with stiffened feet
That trampled flowers in rhythm with cold bells
Ringing beyond the mountains through all time.

No hope in him, said Gentry; or in these—
The couple from New England passing by
Almost without a question. Yet he asked it,
And once again was quieted with a stare
Half timid and half proud, as now the husband
Bragged of the hard days gone and of the new ones
Flowing ahead like honey, in whose hive
A boy might feed, and not a father fail;
While Gentry thought of little burrowing beasts—
Two marmots and their young one—nosing westward
Into a thicker pasture they had smelled.

The woodsman, taken last, was short of words.
He only came to try the river once
And see what kind of people floated on it.
Somewhere along Kentucky he would change
And work his way upstream again by fall.
The fall was when he got his little living
In Pennsylvania woods with trap and powder.
No house had ever held him. "But the pig?"
He took it for an old friend who was married
And lived on part of an island farther down.
He said he chiefly came to see the river.
He knew the songs but hadn't heard them sung
On water. What he wanted was the water,
With people going on it mad as mice.
And he would tell them so, and scare them home,
If he were some one better than a fiddler.
The fiddle fooled them all; the cat was belled.
"But you," he said to Gentry, "I can talk with.
You are the maddest of them all. You look
For something that was never in the world.
It wasn't where you lived and you grew thoughtful.

It won't be where you will live either, Mister.
Not that I mind such madness. Do you see?
I like it. I am only walking, talking;
Waiting till you say your say yourself."
He winked, and Gentry let him pull the others
Round them in a ring, as if to hear
A peddler, or a hatless politician.
So when they all were there, Gentry began
Half talking to himself; yet half to them.

The sun was soon to set upon the full, unconscious river;
It came along the water now, wide and ripple-red.
The long, low shore lines sagged with the silence;
Not a bird sounded, settling into bed;
Not a wave went there, so steadily they drifted
Down the middle water, cool and straight ahead.
A dozen people standing, small in the twilight.
This the final river? These the waiting dead?

"Sleep-walkers,
River-mates,
Ohio-blinded, groping two by two
For ever and ever onward, westward, penned in a careful ark;
Mountain-swarmers,
Valley-finders,
Drift-logs and meadow-men with pollen in your eyes;
We are the shades of an old race;
These are the final ferries down the dark stream
That may flow into morning; and may only
Deeper and deeper drop into the night.
Creatures crated together
And floating out of an old time;
Remnants,
Dream-passengers,
We go perhaps unto the death of deaths.
You—and you—and you—have spoken easily
Of a new life, a clear day

16

Dawning this side the mountains, a flowered field
Waiting for men to walk it and be dusted
Angel-wise with powder of pure gold.
But you I tell—and you—that time is old;
Time withers even now upon its stalk,
Waiting with us the planted end,
Leaning to watch us die. And we shall die,
Raft-riders,
Ark-fugitives,
Unless we fall like rain upon the dry,
Wide harvest of burnt death that spreads and spreads,
Licking the borders of this valley now.
Chosen people,
Noah's men,
What use to bring the old world on our backs,
What beauty in baggage here?
When the dove flew,
And the rainbow rested high on the steaming hills,
What gain from an Ark that opened and let forth
Stale fools,
Fortunate knaves:
Creatures the same as ever creatures were?
When the crow flies,
And the shores draw near to receive us, lords of the land,
What good if we step not forth new men,
New minds in the cool of a day untouched of time?
The American meadows wait,
But not for us if we come there
Unchanged, unbright, and unanointed.
They were not made, I hear them cry,
To be another width of waste: the weary edge of a tramped
    range
Already weary and too wide.
And so they wait for us to choose,
And multiply, and plant the choice
Within a million minds to come, and some day reap—
Some day reap death?

17

Who now says death?
Who now has the worm in his heart, who dares
Step forth and carry contagion?
Who knows?
I knew my grief, then stumbling here
Knew my great hope; and have it still.
Who now has more?
Who now sees harvests ahead of men not hollow, not stuffed
    white husks, not snake-skins left on a rock, not moth-shells,
    fragile as amber, found on trees?
Who knows, and says to go on?
Who feels? Who sees?"

No answer; but the sun upon the full, unconscious river
Spread a sudden purple; then the empty west.
The people moved away now as dumbly toward the cabin
As sheep before a shepherd, driven into rest.

Not a whisper told him, tall by the low bow,
What his mind desired; nor could he hope to hear.
All he had was silence, slipping up the river,
All he had was night, lapping from the rear.

All the silent night had, and the endless river,
Was something small and dark there that floated like a leaf;
And others coming after it; but not a sign to say now
Whither they were drifting, or whether into grief.

Not a whisper told the sky whether green or brown,
Whether these were spring-drift or offal of the fall.
Only up from one of them, hidden down the dark stream,
Rose a tiny wailing, drowsy over all.

It rose upon the soft tide of stillness flowing by,
Came a little way along, and then as quickly ceased.
This is what it said against the night above the river;
This is what it sang before it died beneath the east:

18

Over the mountains, boys,
Come long lonesome way.
Morrow morning, boys,
Be a different day.
    Go sleep now
    And shut your eyes;
    Let whatever
    Got to rise.

Over the mountains, boys,
Don't know where to go.
Morrow morning, boys,
Some us bound to know.
    Go sleep now
    And shut your eyes;
    Let whatever
    Got to rise.

Over the mountains, boys,
Can't see far ahead.
Morrow morning, boys,
Maybe dark and dead.
    Go sleep now
    And shut your eyes;
    Let whatever
    Got to rise.

Over the mountains, boys,
End old river road.
Morrow morning, boys,
Lift a different load.
    Go sleep now
    And shut your eyes;
    Let whatever
    Got to rise.

II
Civil War

The sun upon two generations falling
Fell on the bones of Gentry, in a grave
No wider for their being prophet's bones,
No longer for the length inside the eyes.
The ark had paused; the waters had gone on;
Gentry, moving northward over land,
Had found the flowery prairies in the spring;
And forty flowery springs, with forty winters,
Had made him an old man whose prairie children
Forgot him in a grave that was too small
To hold so large a hope, however silent.
Silence was all he had between himself
And seven sons who loved the present time,
And, laboring the green ground, had other sons
Who loved another present.
                Yet in one
Was something like a memory remaining
After the mind had closed, some nerve surviving
Out of a body otherwise put by.
Jonathan Gentry Third had eyes within him,
And a slow tongue, deep rooted in the heart,
That grew not out but up, and wrapped the brain.

Jonathan Gentry Third this winter morning
Waited upon no dawn, but in the stillness
Climbed the dark stairs and found his brother, and shook him.
"Charlie, it's time."
The boy in the cold bed laughed. "I heard you coming;
I knew by the army shoes, the iron slippers.
Anyone else up yet?"
"No, and you mustn't wake them. Come to the barn.
I'll have the horses ready. And be fast.
They say the train won't wait a half a minute;
They'll call the roll and miss us, and go on."

20

Powdery snow had drifted in the night
Like sand against the door, that opened groaning—
Opened and suddenly shut with a windy shriek.
The harnessed horses, nosing the warm hay,
Lifted a pair of faces to the lantern
And blinked as if they knew the narrower face—
Big in a mist of breath now, but they knew it—
The dark-eyed face that came along and spoke:
"Yes, Prince, yes, Billy,
Time for us to go;
Time for team of horses now to take a team of men;
Time for them to leave you home and ride so far away
There won't be any horses there as good as you, as you—"
He stroked the pair of noses as he talked,
Then dropped his hand again; and dropped his voice:
"Star face,
Bald face,
Gentle and sideward eyes, and coats furry with cold,
Warm necks and shoulder-skin, and belly and tender flank,
Warm hearts, pounding on, pounding on,
Prince Boy, and Dappled Billy,
Wait for us and keep the farm,
Keep it well and warm for us, and keep yourselves, and wait."
Holding their heads as if they had not heard,
They let themselves be led to the sleigh; then, starting,
Beat a monotonous music on the shrill,
White ground to where the boy at the opened gate
Stood yawning.

The crusted road before them in the first light
Had lines of black upon it, of old ruts;
But all the way was smooth for them in the robes,
And day came on them merrily as they passed
Two houses set together among barns.
This was the day; and one of the houses knew it,
For out of an upper window a hand fluttered,
The fringy curtains trembled, and a face,

21

Small in the snowy distance, watched them go;
And watched an arm of Jonathan wave slowly.
Charlie looked straight forward, playing his white breath
Smokily into the wind; but soon he stopped that.
"What did she have to say last night especially?
Anything fit to tell?" He grinned, and Jonathan
Tried to be careless too as he answered "No."
"Didn't she even send me her goodbye?"
"Yes; she said to take good care of Charlie.
But now be still and drive awhile, or talk—
Well, if you have to talk, begin with the war."
"I would, if I knew anything about it.
You are the politician—you begin."
But Jonathan said nothing, and the miles
Slid quietly beneath them on to town.

The engine had grown quiet with its waiting;
Out of the clumsy funnel, like a flower,
A curl of smoke was held beyond escaping,
And hung with all the people on the hour.

The Nineteenth Illinois was soon to waver
Down the unfinished track ahead and south;
But now the captain put aside his saber,
And many a girl was giving him her mouth,

And many a girl was weeping at a window,
And many a soldier's face within was red;
The little town boys kept their arms akimbo
And marched; or stiffly tumbled, playing dead.

There was an ancient woman who had squinted
All morning up and down, and counted caps.
And there were Prince and Billy, nearly winded,
Waiting another driver, gone for wraps.

Jonathan and Charlie stood together
Inside the foremost window of the train;

22

One beheld the horses at the tether,
But one beheld the boys, and laughed again,

And laughed to see the hats, so high and silky,
That moved upon the heads of solemn men.
"Our engine is a man," he said, "or will be,
And one of these can make the funnel then."

The engine bell rang suddenly;
Steam was roaring somewhere up ahead;
Over the dead-white field beyond the depot
Went the brown shadow of smoke.
There were commands, a settling into place;
The town increased its voice, and women crying
Ran with the started coaches; then the whistle,
Smothering voice and bell; and then a silence.
The silence was of watching eyes, and lasted
Only as long as glances go unseen.
But when the people turned upon each other,
Quietness all at once again—and the singing,
Down the long track,
Of soldiers:

> The girls we left at home, sir,
> Are very warm and kind;
> There won't be any smile ahead
> To match the tear behind;
> But John Brown's eyes, sir,
> Are lying cold and blind,
>   And we must stay
>   Until they see
>   Old America
>   Stand free.
>
> The land that we have left, sir,
> Is where content was born;
> There won't be on a southern field

Such green and yellow corn;
But John Brown's eyes, sir,
Lie fallow and forlorn,
  And we must stay
  Until they see
  Old America
  Stand free.

All of us that go, sir,
Want to come back together;
There won't be any rebel camp
With fellows of our feather;
But John Brown's eyes, sir,
Are lonely in this weather,
  And we must stay
  Until they see
  Old America
  Stand free.

Should a brother fall, sir,
And not come home again,
There won't be any rebel ear
To hear complaining then.
John Brown's eyes, sir,
Look out of dying men,
  And we must stay
  Until they see
  Old America
  Stand free.

The train went on, the wooden coaches creaking
Endlessly past the farms that lay in the white day
Scattered beyond all gathering; save for a village
That huddled along the tracks, then opened again,
Losing itself in a blank no mind could measure.
Inside the soldiers, finishing their song,
Fell to a round of talk, and some of them tramped

So merrily up the aisle beside the brothers,
Charlie could sit no longer, and he joined them.
Jonathan followed his voice awhile, then lost it,
Mingled among a dozen not so clear.
Jonathan sat alone. He too would join them—
Soon he would be there, saying a hundred hellos—
But now he sat alone by the pictured window,
Letting the whiteness whirl inside his eyes
Until there came a death of sound and color.
Only the white was there for color, and only
The click of the frozen rails for sound; and only
Jonathan in the world to see and hear.

Click, click, clickety click, clickety clickety clickety click,
Click, click, click, click, clickety clickety click;
Prince, Prince, Billy and Prince, Agatha, Agatha, Agatha Rowe,
Barn, road, bin, tree, Charlie O Charlie come home;
Agatha, Charlie, Billy and Prince, timothy, timothy, timothy
    tops,
Spring, summer, winter, fall, Jonathan, Jonathan Gentry;
Agatha, Agatha waving her hand, goodbye goodbye goodbye in
    the night,
March, April, May, June, and summery summery corn;
Three things, a triple of things, I had and I haven't, I had and
    I haven't,
Agatha, Agatha, home, and Charlie—but there'll be Charlie, I
    still have Charlie;
Charles, Charles Gentry and brother, answer to roll call, Gentry
    and brother,
Where is the boy his brother would keep? Under the cotton fast
    asleep;
No one to wake him? Yes, I can wake him, shake him, wake
    him, take the boy home,
Home, home, by Agatha's window, Agatha come right down;
Spring, summer, winter, fall, Charlie and Jonathan Gentry;
Click, click, clickety click, clickety clickety clickety click,
Click, click, click, click, clickety clickety click.

"Twenty-five miles already," Charlie informed him,
Coming back suddenly now with a green cigar.
"Jon, you're the politician; you begin
And tell me what the war so far's about.
That song—is that the reason we are going?
Four hundred thousand fighting for a blind man?"
"The war's about as many things, my boy,
As there are men to think of it, and women.
There are as many wars as there are leaves
On trees, and who can say what leaves are for,
Or which of all that hang there is the true leaf?
John Brown hangs there, and many that are marching
Go beneath a corpselight, with madness in their eyes.
I think the war is not about a man, though,
And least of all about another man
They hope to hang in a sour apple tree—
The sooner then the better; yet his breath
Would sweeten it, and half of us would cry.
I think it isn't either about black heads
That bend all day in the cotton, and come home
To pitiful beds, and bleed from a dirty blow.
The war is about ourselves, and what we love.
Harry Camargo couldn't stand his wife,
And so he went the first month, and he marches
With a charmed life and shines among the faithful:
Happy because it's treason to come home.
And there was Ira Benjamin; his law books
Leaned a little crazier every day;
He went and is an officer, and hopes
Jeff Davis won't be caught for ten more years.
Some of the boys here go because the going
Is wonderful in itself, for they have heard
Songs sung, and light was bright along a barrel.
The war is about ourselves: you, Charlie, and me.
We go because we love the land we live on;
Somehow or why—I mean to find out how
Down there in the other land, the bitter country—

It's threatened, the way we live, the first idea.
The man that I was named for—not our father—
Came west with some new country in his mind:
Each place a gentle kingdom—that's the way
He lived it in his mind; and it could die,
And will die if we lose. But we'll not lose.
Every man a year from now will enter
His kingdom, north or south, and sit with wisdom
Safely upon the center of a world
Where kingdoms are as many as the men
To rule them and be wise in the slow way
Good farmers from the end of time were wise.
The war is about ourselves, Charlie, ourselves."
"It may be so for you," said Charlie, waiting
More than his usual moment for the words;
"But not for me. You want to know my reason?
Only that you were going, and I couldn't—
I couldn't—Jon, do you want a cigar like this?"
They rose and found the fat boy with the tray,
And puffed among the others, or walked back
To feel the swaying platform, and to count
The curves that now came oftener; for hills,
Snowy and small, began around them here.
They said they knew the train was getting south.

They knew it even better when the sheds
Of workmen gone for winter slept in snow,
And piles of ties, with rusting tall machines,
Waited upon the season. Here the rails
Ended, and here the ending afternoon
Was darkened by low orders to fall in.
Down a grey road they marched, the column stumbling
Over uprooted lumps of ice and mud;
Down a long way they went, with not a sign now
Of people in any world; and some of them said
They soon would reach the river, the Ohio.
But just before the full of darkness fell,

27

Barns loomed like little mountains on the right;
Sheep bawled, and lantern light across the snow
Showed a wide doorway opening into rest.
They climbed the ladders laughing, and found hay
Like feathers underfoot—or so they said
Who but the night before in papered rooms
With curtains and washed covers had lain down—
And laughed again, and rolled their blankets round them.
There was some talk and tumble, but it ceased,
And night took up its watch under the rafters.
It waited above the rafters, too, and farther
Beyond than any could know; but here, unheard,
Invisible in sweet darkness, lay the hundred.

The barge that bore them next day over the river
Touched earth a little eastward of a town
Whose children, black and white, came out to watch them:
The dark ones standing backward of the rest,
Haltingly up a hill, but all grown silent;
Though soon they chattered loudly in the cold
As first the column formed and then departed
Down the old eastern road. The chatter, rising,
Followed upon the wintry air a way,
Then met the soldiers' singing; and died there.

> Over the river, boys,
> Come now and take a stand;
> Over the river, boys,
> In the strange land.
>> Hayfoot, strawfoot,
>> Tramp right through
>> And make one country
>> Out of two.

> Over the river, boys,
> Plenty of southern mud,

28

Mixed already, boys,
With northern blood.
   Hayfoot, strawfoot,
   Tramp right through
   And make one country
   Out of two.

Over the river, boys,
Buzzard, looking down,
Can't make up his mind
If that's John Brown.
   Hayfoot, strawfoot,
   Tramp right through
   And make one country
   Out of two.

Over the river, boys,
John Brown sure enough,
Playing with a buzzard,
Blind man's buff.
   Hayfoot, strawfoot,
   Tramp right through
   And make one country
   Out of two.

Over the river, boys,
Into the strangers' land.
We call them kin, but they
Misunderstand.
   Hayfoot, strawfoot,
   Tramp right through
   And make one country
   Out of two.

Over the river, boys,
Wait and hear them yell.
But there's enough blue heaven
To hold all hell.

Hayfoot, strawfoot,
Tramp right through
And make one country
Out of two.

On they went and left behind the cold, unconscious river.
On they went, and turned, and swung around a little hill.
The children watched the last man; then into their houses;
And now the flowing river worked its old unseeing will.

It flowed as it would always flow, without a thought of rivers
Sliding from the south to make it wider as it went.
It never saw the hidden country past the little mountain
That took the hundred in now, closing like a tent.

The river never knew of any valley, east or south,
Wherein a wintry wilderness of tents and greying men
Waited round a nightly fire, waited for the spring;
The river never sent a sigh for what would happen then.

No one standing here beside the cold, unconscious river,
No one could have seen the hidden country of the war.
But many a hill was posted there, and soon the time was coming,
The green and bleeding season death had lingered for.

On beyond the little hills Kentucky, Tennessee,
Cumberland, and Shenandoah nestled in their names:
Dark and ancient syllables, lords of an old language,
Lords of an old fire that long ago put out its flames.

They flickered in deep caverns now, perhaps as old as time,
But only rock was there to see, and cold and sleeping trees,
And meadows up from winding streams descended from the
    hills;
Meadows, and the campfires smoking over these.

It only was a little while that such a light would live;
A day would come again of darkened slopes and the cool grass,

30

With peace upon the mountain-heads, and silence in the plains.
But here a party tramped to reconnoiter up a past,

A file of teams was plodding there, and on the farthest pike
Guns glistened in the mud; a messenger rode forth;
He met another messenger; the bayonets stood still;
Then slowly on again, these newest comers from the north.

Slowly down the valley there to make another camp,
Light another square of fires, and wait upon the spring.
Winter wasted slowly now, but rain was in the air,
And birds; and thoughts, set upon a fearful thing.

In April, in Virginia, when the rain
Came softly, with a coolness like the breath
Of new-born haze upon the mountain-heads,
And mud was round the tents, and sentries coughed
Like sheep in a wet wood; on April evenings,
Charlie being gone three tents away—
The boy was restless, and the candles soothed him,
Dripping upon the blanket and the cards,
Shining upon the foreheads of new friends—
On April evenings Jonathan stayed in,
Reading a letter. He would light his torch,
Unfold the fingered sheets, and lose the world
In lines he knew already; but he read them.
He read them for the way they had of making
Daytime out of nighttime, and of turning
Half of the tent wall back: the northern wall,
Towards Agatha, towards home, the only home.

"Dear Jon:
I just saw Prince and Billy going by.
You wouldn't know them, they're so fine and fat.
The boy from town's too good to them almost.
You wouldn't say so, though. Too good to babies!
Half past ten, and I should think of dinner—

Jon, what do you and Charlie eat I wonder—
But now I won't awhile. Well, yesterday
Your father and my father walked and talked
Between here and the barn, and it was you—
I didn't see your father, I saw you.
And yet it wasn't you, for you are different—
More, being mine, and less too, being younger.
Then afterwards I thought I saw us two there,
A tiny girl and boy, held by the hand
Between them, and I had the oddest feeling,
As if we two were only parts of them.
And yet it's only you I am a part of.
I know it now so well. And so I guess
I felt that way because it was your father—
My father and your father. I was excited;
I had that happy heavy feeling here—
You can't see where, and wouldn't know—but, Jon,
All this is one more way to say I love you.
I love you, and I love you, and I ride
Quite often past your place. It's just the same—
House, barn, and little barn, and the wide walls
Of hedge around the fields—so cold and brown,
But the first thaw has softened them, and soon
I'll write of greenness everywhere, and wind
Like feathers, and the little building birds.
I went in once. Your mother let me read
What you and Charlie wrote her from Virginia.
She lives on letters, Jon, and so do I,
Though when they come I have to stop pretending
You're just a mile away from me, at home.
I do that all the time. I love you, Jon."

He read it every night, till others came—
Three of them tied together with brown string
And dropped somewhere in the mud, but he could read them—
And then he bound them all in a thin bundle,
Just thick enough to feel inside his coat,

32

And read them when he could. He even read them,
Hastily, for one nervous noisy hour,
The night the army moved; and Charlie laughed.
But it was frightened laughter.

                       Fierce commands,
Though spoken low, as if death walked and cursed them
Out of the corners of a whiskered mouth;
Commands that rang along, low on the ground
Like lightning laid on hills; the breathing of men
In fear, yet more in hurry, the father of fear;
And horses splashing by; and rifles clicking—
These cracked the tune of his mirth, these left him silent;
So when he spoke at last the words were husky.
"Well, Jon, we're off."

                   "All right, but we're together."
Both voices had a strangeness as they started.
Both big and little boy, the brothers Gentry,
Moved as the dark line moved, against the morning.
No singing now; but day in another valley,
Brightness under another noon, and rest,
And rumors that the war was farther away
Than ever—would it be there when they got there?—
And cooling water lifted out of wells
Behind the shuttered houses: then was song,
With Jonathan to join it, for he found
New lightness in his feet now, and he sang.

        Another damnation day, boys,
        Another damnation night,
        And maybe we don't come up, boys,
        And maybe we dassn't fight!
        Never you worry, Johnny Reb;
        Take a long breath and hold it tight.
          Yankee Doodle went down south
          To get him a stick of candy;
          He stuck it in his Sunday mouth
          And came home Doodle Dandy.

Another damnation ridge, boys,
And then the enemy's there.
Another damnation slide, boys,
Out of this mountain air.
Never you worry, Johnny Reb;
Look up and let us part your hair.
    Yankee Doodle went down south
    To get him a stick of candy;
    He stuck it in his Sunday mouth
    And came home Doodle Dandy.

Another damnation song, boys,
And then forever quiet.
Another damnation rumpus, boys,
Before the biggest riot.
Never you worry, Johnny Reb,
We got a tune, and you're to try it.
    Yankee Doodle went down south
    To get him a stick of candy;
    He stuck it in his Sunday mouth
    And came home Doodle Dandy.

Another damnation inch, boys,
And see them give a mile.
Another damnation hour, boys—
Eternity then awhile.
Never you worry, Johnny Reb;
Old John Brown'll rise and smile.
    Yankee Doodle went down south
    To get him a stick of candy;
    He stuck it in his Sunday mouth
    And came home Doodle Dandy.

A pair of peaceful mornings, and a pair
Of afternoons with houses going by,
And Jonathan to watch them, one by one.
They sat so idly there, and the red road

Went on so warm and winding, farm by farm,
That Jonathan half wondered where it was—
The evil, the cold danger. Not in houses;
Not in the budded hedges; and no barn,
Empty of beast and wagon, but looked long
At Jonathan, who looked and turned away.
So on the column tramped, and Charlie's feet
Ground the same dust as Jonathan's, or rested
Quietly by their side on grassy banks
Where honeysuckle gathered; and they talked—
Strange talk, compact of laughter and low fears—
But all the time in silence one was saying:
"The evil, the cold danger,
It isn't in these windows; it isn't in the weary way
These houses lie and look at us, it isn't
In any patient barn.
The country is good country, for I see
Good barns in it. Good barns,
Good boys, we used to say;
Good people all.
Good people, come and listen while I tell you—
Tell what? And who would listen?
And where are all the people gone today?
All fled? All fighting?
The fighting is to come. It will be strange,
Fighting this country of the harmless barns:
We're in it now, this country, and it lets us
Walk, and talk, and sleep, and wake, and sing.
We're in it, and the fighting hasn't happened.
It's strange, as if a dream
Dragged at my feet and made them very
Drowsy; a very
Dream."

So when it happened he was unprepared,
His mind and heart conversing in the shade
Of his wide-branching nature, murmuring there

While he stood dumbly by, and while the woods
They marched in—not the forest of his thought—
Rang with a sudden shot.
     Then a mad chatter
Of rifles ahead, and a pause, and the guard retreating.
They came where he could see them—a pale huddle
Of running and stumbling things—and now he heard
Commands along the column to deploy.
"Take cover! Corporal—corporal—cover your men!
Cover yourself, you fool!"
     The battle was on.
Jonathan by a low rock in a gulley,
With three strange men in blue beside him firing,
Tugged at his rifle too, as they had taught him,
And peered beyond the rock, and aimed, and trembled.
But all he saw was new green branches falling,
Leaves cut and floating down, and on the rock
Fresh ferns, the April growth, torn up and dead.
"Where's Charlie now!" The bullets coming over
Said nothing of any Charlie, and he looked
At nothing, left or right, but flying dirt,
And balls of smoke, and spreading legs of men
Who peered like him and fired, and maybe trembled.
"Where's Charlie? Where did they put him? Will he be
  careful?"
The questions all were useless, but he asked them,
And, asking them, lost count of the hot hours,
That ended now as suddenly as they came.
The woods ahead, no longer smoking trees,
Turned into men who leapt and yelled, advancing—
Advancing now, a grey and angry wave,
Foaming upon them. They could see the eyes,
The long hair and the hats; and they could fire,
And many of those could spin and tumble there;
But now they ceased to fire, and falling back,
Fled, for the day was lost.
     And more was lost.

36

Jonathan, remembering as he ran
How when the time for four to leave the rock
Had come and gone—how one of them had stayed there—
Jonathan, remembering his surprise,
Felt nothing now as his exhausted feet
Stumbled on corpses. Some of them were bleeding,
Some of them had no hands, or any eyes;
Some of them lay without a wound to show:
Boys in blue coats, asleep. He counted them,
Unconscious of the counting, till he came
To safety, and the camp, and the tired hundred.
"Where's Charlie!" Asking blindly, he was answered—
"Here, Jon!"—and fell to laughing over-loudly
As now the brothers fumbled for each other,
And found their hands, and wrung them, and sat down:
Both home without a scar, and weak as children.

Time rested then, while day on quiet day
Brought warmer, dustier weather; and brought there,
To Jonathan in his tent, another letter,
With maple leaves laid freshly in the fold.
"They were so green, and made so great a sound
The day I talked beneath them with your mother—
The end-of-May winds tried to blow them down,
At your house and at my house, but they stuck—
They stuck like me to you, if I do say so,
And sassed the wind as I would sass the war—
I would, but I am here and it is there,
Doing I don't know what to you and Charlie.
Some nights I dream I have it where my hands
Can wave it way away, and I can scold it,
And shame it for the thing it wants to do.
Then other nights I can't as much as dream;
I only lie there wondering what it wants,
And hoping it can't have it. All the having
Must be between you, Jonathan, and me.
The roads are dry, but not too dusty yet,

And the big cornfield downward from your house
Is perfect black, with long green lines upon it—
The baby corn. Your boy from town was plowing,
Yesterday when I rode the sorrel by,
And bragged about the stand. He'll keep it clean—
And keeps our Prince and Billy like a pair
Of dudes on Sunday. Do you think of church?
I don't. I think of Jonathan and Charlie,
Two boys that go as one, but they are different.
You are the whole, the rather solemn blackbird,
He is the wing, the red wing, by your side.
Goodbye, and fly away home. I love you, Jon."

He wrapped it with the others, and would read it
In its own turn by night; but once by day—
The morning of the day the dozen died—
He read it. For the twenty had been picked,
The skirmishers to clear the Afton road,
And Jonathan's and Charlie's names were there.
They had an hour till ten, the time of going.
Charlie had whistled, and the red-haired boy
He knew from Indiana had strolled over,
Laughing, as if to lay the ghost of danger
In such a day ahead, and such a duty.
But Jonathan, stone silent when he joined them,
Pressing the under pocket of his coat,
Laughed not at all, though Charlie thought he smiled.
At ten the party left in two divisions,
One for the right-hand fields and one the left.
At twelve they still were plodding, left and right—
Charlie among the woods now, where he walked,
Indian wise, from tree to sheltering tree
And listened for loud noises on the road;
But Jonathan, who led the right division,
Had only open meadows, where he hid,
With seven men behind him, under walls
Of rail and rock, with honeysuckle down them.

At twelve the woods were innocent; but now,
At very noon, with white light everywhere,
And warmth upon the meadows like a room
Wherein old people move and smile and nod,
Jonathan stopped.
                    The house and barn ahead
Were empty if the captain had been right;
But if he had been wrong those little windows,
High by the eaves, and staring at them now,
Commanded all this wall and had them covered.
He thought: but then the captain had been right,
Captains are always wiser than we know;
And there was a quick instant when he saw
House, fence, and barn as if they had been his,
Jonathan Gentry's, in another day,
Under a northern noon; as if he crept
Home now with cap and rifle to surprise
His people, who were clasping hands and weeping;
And Agatha was coming on her mare;
And Prince and Billy whinnied.
                                Then the sun
Told him. Something shone a dreadful moment
Out of that upper window on the left.
His house—but not his house—was armed against him:
Windows with bright eyes in them, of guns;
Bright hatred pointing down at him from home.
He crouched, and seven crouched, and missed the first
Wide shot. It hissed among the honeysuckle,
Flattening on a stone. But now a volley,
And one two three four skirmishers went down.
Another; then a yell from the sharp woods:
Charlie and they, the twelve good men, were coming.
"Hurry, my boy! For God's sake though be careful."
They came, and three of them fell; and now the fire
Dropped hotter upon the few, with no escaping.
And now the raid was ready.
                            So they charged;

39

And so the elder Gentry, turning to see
If one too young ran still among the rest,
Staggered and almost fell; but kept on running;
Then staggered again, and slipped into black water
Over his head, and floated among cool caverns
Down from the sun and down, and down, and down.

The stream that brought him back flowed on forever,
Swiftly and very smoothly, up and on,
So swiftly that it sickened him sometimes
And blurred the little picture of the sun
That hung in a square frame, the cavern's end.
Then he would have it bright again—burning
His buried eyes. But now the end was coming.
The current pulled more strongly at the last,
Sweeping him on so swiftly that he fainted
Just as the picture altered, and a window
Hung in its shining place.
                            He opened his eyes
Slowly, in a cabin, to the voice
Of an old man who came to him and said:
"Hello, my boy."
"Hello."
"They left you in July, and this is August.
The war went on and left you—"
                            "Where is Charlie?"
"Charlie?"
        "He's my brother. Was he—too?"
"A dozen altogether. They believed
Thirteen, but here you are. So I was right.
I don't remember such a name as Charlie."
"Maybe he—"
        "Yes, let's say so. Now be quiet,
And sleep again."
                He slept, and when he woke,
They talked; and many a sultry day they talked
Of how the house was his, the tall old man's,

40

And how it burned that day, and how the barns
And all the little buildings went but this:
"The mansion of the wronged," he smiled and said.
"Yet I myself had freed them. They were gone.
All of them here were gone but me. I stayed.
It was my house and ground, my little—kingdom."
He looked at Jonathan's eyes, that watched the word
Half fearfully, as if it were a spectre.
"Kingdom. It's your word; the only word
You gave me for a sign that I should like you.
You know I ought to hate you."
                              "Yes, I know."
"But how can distant kings destroy each other?
There is your kingdom. Here is mine; or was.
They didn't so much as run with the same rain.
Mountains and miles between them, and a river.
You lived on yours, I lived on mine, and only
A war like this could make us any different.
Yet hearing you I know we are not different.
You came for the same reason—fearing me—
That my three sons went—fearing you—and fought.
Each to preserve his kingdom, that was safe
Already. There was never any danger."
"But how could such a war be such a fool?"
"I wonder. Yet it was."
                      "Then where is Charlie?
Charlie has got to be somewhere alive.
He's got to, for I brought him, and he's guiltless!
Charlie—"
          "Now you ought to sleep again.
Be patient. Word comes slow, and in good time
The best of all good words—excepting home—
May come; it might be lame, and have to crawl."

He slept, and mended slowly; till the day
They heard some voices laughing at the door.
They opened it for Corporal Charles Gentry,

Who waved a stripèd sleeve in wide salute,
Then ran as small boys do unto their fathers.
"Sergeant Jonathan Gentry, I believe;
Hero of Afton Road, and"—then the tale
Of how the raid had ended, and of how
This old Virginian stayed against full orders.
"Now, sir, he'll go along if you'll allow him."
No word from the old man; but as they went
He stood, a single pillar of a house
That otherwise was level ashes, watching.

Charlie had brought a letter that began:
"Dear Jon, where are you now and can you hear me?
Not me so much as all these loving locusts,
Loving the trees and letting it be known
As nothing I can whisper lets you know.
They love the going summer, as I love
All going time—it's going, Jon, it's going,
The war is getting older every day.
There never was a war that wouldn't die.
I used to dread the growing old of seasons;
I died a little with them, and I knew
How hard it is to die when every morning
Meets you a little later, like a friend
Deserting you by gradual degrees.
It used to leave me heavy, and it leaves me
Heavy as ever now—but now I love it.
I loved your maples yesterday at noon,
Hung with the full of summer, holding on
For dear life; but there's something dear in death.
I speak of seasons, Jon, and afternoons
Dying of too much time. I love you, Jon."

Time dragged a weary foot along the far,
Thin edge of a spent summer, waiting now
On fall, and on another waste of winter.
It was an idle time, but Charlie bragged

42

Of battles still to be, or grumbled, laughing,
Because so many chosen men decayed
In a slow camp—corn rotting in good fields.
He knew they had been chosen by the fact
That here they were still laughing and alive;
He said they were elected to be missed
By any bullet coming. He was safe.
The sharpest rebel claw had never scratched him.
Jonathan believed him, though he said:
"Be careful, nevertheless; luck isn't a fool."
Jonathan, believing the bright lingo,
Had yet no faith in fortune; luck was lazy,
And tended only a few, and couldn't remember—
Luck certainly couldn't remember who were brothers.
They talked; and winter wandered down the hills,
And days went by uncounted, as if sheep
Should keep on coming after the eyes were closed.
They talked, or Charlie came with noisy friends
And cut the cards for poker, while the blanket
Warmed to the candle light, and spread its brownness
Under the waves of song—the doleful song.

<blockquote>

Four long, long, long,
Long and weary winter-years.
Told the war to stop, but thunder
Deafened him; he never hears.
 Dig a hole;
 Make a bed;
 Nothing now but
 Night ahead.

Four old, old, old,
Old and sorry summer times.
Told the war to weep, but he was
Busy with the Widow Grimes.
 Dig a hole;
 Make a bed;

</blockquote>

Nothing now but
Night ahead.

Four rainy, rainy, rainy,
Rainy, windy equinoxes.
Told the war it's wet, but he was
Yelling in the wood for foxes.
　Dig a hole;
　Make a bed;
　Nothing now but
　Night ahead.

Four long, old, rainy
Roads from here to there and home.
Told the war to pack, but he was
Playing on a paper comb.
　Dig a hole;
　Make a bed;
　Nothing now but
　Night ahead.

Time dragged a frozen foot along the far,
Thin edge of a spent winter, waiting now
On spring; and spring arrived, and letters came
To quicken the slow blood of time and man.
"Dear Jon: There is a newness in the wind;
Old age has died again, the mangy lion,
And where he laid him down a little lamb
Struggles to stand; he will, but now he wobbles,
And his thin knees are colder than he likes.
Nothing is here for him but folded grass
And black and broken weeds, but he is breathing
Sweetly against the ground, and grass will rise
Like rain to taste the sweetness and be tasted.
I know it, for my appetite is fed
On hope, that still is small, and hardly green;
But I can feel it growing, and I know

Why grass comes—it is wanted by the wind,
To taste of it, and in good time be tasted.
There is no need to tell you what I hope for.
Maybe it wouldn't come so quickly then.
You guess, and Charlie guess. I love you, Jon,
And you must let me see you soon, and soon."

In middle spring,
With battles all around them, but they held
A quiet hill, they waited;
In middle spring, one morning with the round,
Warm, life-bestowing sun
Their battle came:
Faintly at first,
Like horns of early hunters, moving trees
To frosty music, melancholy mirth;
Then louder, and less musical; and now
Full cry upon them, ranged along a wall
Midway within a forest down the slope.
Midway it struck them, and confounded most
Cool Jonathan, who listened and remembered
Nothing but one old man; and looked along
For no one now but Charlie in the line.
He found him with his eyes, and smiled; but turned
Full face to meet the monster, loose at last.
There was to be an end of it, and soon;
But while it breathed, the many-headed beast,
Its breath was to be hotter, and its reach
Longer, and the murder of its claws
More awful than the oldest there remembered.
Backward awhile the battle moved, and fell
On earthworks farther up the bleeding mountain;
Backward again, until on top they panted,
Firing like blind men—and so Jonathan,
Whose eyes were fixed on nothing as he fired,
Lost now from every soldier he had walked with,
Or talked with in a tent—through all that smoke,

And noise of ripping branches, and burst shells,
No Charlie to be seen. Then forward, slowly,
Down the wrecked hill they reeled; then swiftly, swiftly,
Howling in shrill pursuit; until the woods
Cleared, and the thing was over, and he heard
Wailing, as if the monster, deadly wounded,
Lay in the forest somewhere, lifting its heads
One after another, bloody, and spent, and blind.
The monster—but he paused.
The monster! His exhausted mind
Came back, and he could see; and he could hear
Men, crying men, bestrewn like colored birds,
Tumbling after a volley, brought to ground,
Wingless and still, or pitifully moving.
Men everywhere, and some without a sound.
Men everywhere—and where was Charlie Gentry?
Somewhere safe, he said; it was to be.
But when the searchers passed him he went with them,
And looked a long hour, and looked, and looked:
And found,
There in the middle morning, in a forest,
In spring, beneath a white,
High sun that warmed his back as he stooped over,
Death in a smiling boy—
Smiling right up and up toward nothing at all—
Death in a guiltless boy.

He lay as he had lain so long ago
That Jonathan remembered through a mist:
How the sun loved him, and he seemed to know,
And laughed at lady-bugs along his wrist;

And slept; and how the April afternoon
Went slowly over both of them at rest;
How Jonathan stood up, and how the tune
Of blackbirds took them hunting for a nest.

Where is the boy that looks after the sheep?
Under the oak leaves, fast asleep.
Will you disturb him? No, not I.
If he laughed now, I'd surely die.

He lay as he had lain another day,
In winter, on a rug before the fire,
Warming himself and watching the slow way
Heat crept along a poker of old wire;

And slept; and it grew dark around the floor,
And cold, except where he had stretched his hand.
Then Jonathan came calling at the door,
And Charlie jumped, and answered the command.

Little Boy Blue, his brother's lamb,
Had thoughts as white as snow,
And everywhere the brother went
The lamb was sure to go.

He followed him to war one day,
Which was against the rule.
There never went a whiter lamb
Beside a blacker fool.

They laid him under many leaves, and one uplifted rock;
They laid him in a peaceful place, and walked to war again.
But now the war was over; everywhere a stillness now
Answered to the other stillness, buried with the men.

It was the very end of it, the dark years were done—
Four of them, to count the bitter corners of the land:
One for north and south, and one for east, and one for west;
Four of them as one now, the fingers of a hand.

Four of them as one, yet there was anger in the grasp,
As if the hand would hurt itself, crying with new pain.

But Jonathan was going home, indifferent to the end
Of any life but one now, lying through the rain.

Jonathan had wandered north and west between the hills;
Jonathan had watched the wide unconscious river flow;
Jonathan had crossed and wondered what a man had said,
The other Gentry, floating there, years and years ago.

Jonathan said nothing to himself or to the river;
Jonathan said nothing to the train that took him back.
The soldiers going home with him had noisy, pleasant voices.
He liked them, but he leaned and only listened to the track:

Click, click, clickety click, clickety clickety click, click.
He listened, and it told him of a bullet singing true.
Click, click, click, click, clickety clickety click—
Click, and one was coming home instead of two, of two.

Click, click, clickety click, clickety clickety click, click.
Home, home, and Agatha; he wondered what to say.
Click, click, click, click, clickety clickety click, click.
Kingdom come. Will be done. Death another day.

Click, click, clickety click, clickety clickety click, click.
The rails were not so mournful now, and as he leaned along—
Click, click, click, click, clickety clickety click, click—
He listened, and his lips were open, to the soldier-song.

> Rolling home, rolling home,
> Rolling home across the corn;
> Rolling up, rolling up,
> To the place where I was born.
> Black, black, between the green:
> Plenty, plenty, blow your horn.
>   War, war,
>   Go away

48

And never come
Another day.

Through the gate, through the gate,
Through the gate, and what I see?
Through the gate, through the gate,
They are coming out to me.
Well, well, well, well,
Hello, hello, and how you be?
    War, war,
    Go away
    And never come
    Another day.

III
FORECLOSURE

Jonathan Gentry Fifth, descended long
From him that dreamed a river, and from him
That crossed it and recrossed it in the dark;
Jonathan Gentry Fifth, descended straight
From farmers, and himself the farmer now,
Stared at the April stream. The deeper grove
He stood in had been feathered overnight—
Jonathan could believe it—with high, pale
And singing new green branches; where his boots
Slipped on the stony bank small ferns unfolded;
And here the listless creek, late numb with ice,
Swelled like a serpent, rolling its colors on.
He watched it pouring full between the oaks,
Coming above him smoothly till it fell,
Here at the rocks, and roared; then watched it moving
Busily round the bend that brought the pastures.
He thought of it there, with the sun just risen on it;
He thought of the morning round him; felt the wind
Filling the new-born leaves, filling his eyes
With coolness and the strength of a cast fragrance;

49

Stared; and remembered breakfast. She was waiting.
It warmed him to remember: a dry warmth,
With nothing of awakened woods about it,
A dry and indoor warmth, as good to keep
Inside him as this other one, of ferns.

He walked a few more rods to find the ewe:
And found her, big with lamb, where twisted roots
Had caught her like a rat; so in the flood,
Sometime between an afternoon and dawn,
She drowned. He freed the foot and dragged her up
To lie on last year's leaves—the belly full,
The eyes washed almost empty, a weak blue—
And dropped a word of pity; but turned now,
Hurrying home to the other eyes, the well ones.

Up the white stream he went, and through the green
Black grove that still was young upon the year.
The youth of it rose rankly; Jonathan walked,
Smelling the potent odors, minding the will
That worked in dampness round him, through decay.
Jonathan, in the might of such a morning,
Hastened awhile, then tempered his pace and said:
"Uprising fingers, palms—
The forearms still to come, and the wrapped shoulders—
Upspringing world, you speak,
You sing your power already, and you bring me
News I have needed—I,
Jonathan Gentry Fifth, who love the coming
Of day, and the thrust of spring, and the standing again of stems
        that taper and wave.
I love you now for having what I may not—
What no man may have had, yet there were times
Before my time; I think they had it then—
For having what I may not have, a place
To die into and thence be born again.
Upclimbing vine-tips,

Folded, uncurling ferns,
Buds, ready to burst,
I envy you the womb that cannot wither,
I envy you the jest of a November
That only plays at dying: as he falls,
Pretending all is over, he can drain
Green blood into the April cup beneath him,
The buried cup that sleeps and never spills.
Sometimes, world—deep world—
I think we have your secret, we who walk
On furrows in the fall, that can uncover
Burial-place and seed-bed there together.
Even this moment, maple,
I thought I had it fairly from your fingers,
Gift of the small green gods. But it is going.
Most of the days it goes, and I
Stand rootless, with no future
Underground."

He left the woods and walked into the sun,
That came now like a reaper over the cool,
Flat fields between the last tree and the house:
Reaping the dew, reaping the level shadows.
The longest of the shadows made a lane,
Running an even course beside the high
Black hedge that cut the farm into its halves;
The eastern half was cornfields, but the western
Pastures started here where Jonathan walked,
Spreading unto the grove, whence water tumbled
Quickly, and quickly slowed, and now meandered.
He left the sun and took the lane of shadow,
Watching the light strike over his tall head,
Flooding the right-hand fields until the woods
Stopped it.

Soon the lane ended where the hedge gave way
To posts and woven wire, that followed down

51

As far as the wide pickets bounding the barn lot.
Jonathan, through the gate, stopped in a moment,
Having to see the horses at their breakfast.
They lifted their long faces as he came:
Dolly and Dick the Belgians, plump and mild,
Bob and Mahomet, roans, and Jack the Western,
Daisy the freckled white, and Plug the puller;
All of them smooth and happy, and his friends,
All of them chewing soberly, and blinking;
All of them so but Jack, who rolled a white eye,
Snorted, and jerked his rope; yet soon forgot,
Plunging his nose once more in the nervous hay.
Jonathan smiled and watched them, still as wood,
Then went as suddenly out as he had come.
Breakfast was waiting. He could see the door,
Ample and white, between the pair of maples.
He stamped his boots, approaching, and he thought:
"Laura won't want to hear about her ewe.
Pity it wasn't mine; a special pity."
He mounted the muddy steps, and would have called;
But heard:
At seven in the morning Jonathan heard,
Coming from the horses and the hay,
Coming from a dewy lane of shadows,
Coming from the wet woods and the ferns,
The new song—thump—upon the phonograph;
The brand new words. He loathed them, but he listened:

> It was a band of city boys—
> And girls, we must confess—
> One night along a lonely road,
> A rustic wilderness.
> The picnic walk was ended now
> But they had missed the train.
> The latest bus had left for town,
> And this was their refrain:

Bright lights, bright lights
Shining on the square,
Don't go out, we're coming home;
We're done with country air.
Don't ask us how we'll get to you,
But when we do we'll know
There's nothing sweeter in the world
Than bright lights in a row.

Laura, bending her brown head,
Pouring the coffee smoothly into the white cups,
Looked not up to see what manner of husband
Stood in the doorway.

Jonathan, notwithstanding,
Crossed and lifted her face, and kissed the warm mouth:
Warm with the odorous breakfast she had made him;
Warm with the song.

Laura, quietly smiling,
As if she need not say what thing had pleased her,
Opened her eyes a little wider, and kindly
Suffered his kisses.

Jonathan, hearing the needle
Scrape on the finished record, hurried and stopped it;
Closed the shiny machine that neither mentioned,
Now at their coffee.

Nothing was said between them.
Laura, busy with bread, wove with her brown hands
Figures against the cloth for him to see;
And against her apron.

He cleared his voice reluctantly, beginning:
"I found her in the woods. Along the creek.

53

The mountains folded in upon the full, unconscious river;
The shoremen heard no more, and turned away and said:
"Where is it now, the wailing barge? Only the sun sees;
Only the hill night knows, and a few stars overhead.
Well, let them go and stay forever—and these new ones too."
Was this the shaded river? And these the waiting dead?

More people stood upon the bank to go;
Others had gone before; and thousands came.
But Gentry in his ark,
Proud at the low bow, lifted his forehead high
And watched the waveless water, knowing nothing
Of men before and after. So the shades
Crossed once the final stream. But Gentry faced
Straight downward, shores forgotten.
This was the flowing earth he came to find,
This earth with no men on it; or if men,
They kept an equal pace and a sweet distance:
All going smoothly down against the sun.
The twenty-two companions of the voyage—
He smiled at them indulgently; and smiled
With the same eyes upon the patient pigs,
The heifers, and the ewes. All riding down,
All keeping a dumb distance; though they stared
And whispered who he was; and some of the children
Mimicked his stately walk, with hands behind them.

So thirteen days and nights, and the rough hills
Grew gentler, and the willows
Waved at the edge of meadows whose deep grass
Was walked on by a wind of falling flowers.
Some days the mountains sharpened, and the shadows
Stood with an awful stiffness.
Then the mild slopes again, and opening sky.
Once, where the river widened,
Suddenly dogs barked; cabins smoked in a clearing,

9

The farthest up she ever went, I think.
Up by the big rocks, under the sycamore,
Lying—"
       "Oh, was it twins? Tell me, tell me!"
Suddenly she was straightened in her chair,
And the brown eyes were black with narrow fire.
"Jonathan! Was it twins? And was she sick yet?"
She stopped, for it was plain now.
                     "She was dead.
Jonathan! She was dead. And not a lamb there?
Can there be nothing young of any kind?"
"Listen. It wasn't her time yet. Not for a week.
You knew that, didn't you, lovely? Can't you guess?
The sycamore, remember, is a trap—
Always the roots were coiled as if to catch you.
We said so when we waded up last August.
Well, all this rain had washed them worse—and Laura,
They caught her. She was drowned. But she is dry now.
I pulled her on to the bank, on to the old leaves.
Her eyes—"
       "Don't! I can see them. I have eyes."
But they were closed, and Jonathan beneath them
Guessed the full tears that gathered. So she wept,
Hiding her face with hands too quick, too quiet.
She wept, and Jonathan watched, and heard her saying:
"Nothing has ever grown in me, or will grow.
So my four-footed creatures, when they swell,
Come to the dead end. Drowned!
Nelly, I talked of twins for you. And drowned!"

He waited, watching; then he thought of this:
"Let's see, it's April now, and time for Joe—
Isn't it? Doesn't he always come in the spring?
The last midwinter visit he was snowbound;
But that would hardly hold him off in April;
April, and he's no lawyer any longer;
April, and he comes flying; he remembers

More of our boyhood here than ever I do—
Doesn't he? Don't you think?" But both of her hands
Still were upon her eyes—that heard, perhaps.
"There ought to be a letter."
                        She was quieter,
Suddenly, than the room, and farther off.
"There is a letter, Jonathan. To me.
He's coming Friday morning. I misplaced it;
Burnt it, maybe—careless. But don't bother,
He's coming Friday morning for three days."
"Good. Wednesday, Thursday, Friday. In the morning."

So Jonathan and Laura in the long house,
The house that every Gentry had increased,
Waited upon the brother, and made ready
The room he stooped and entered like a priest.

It was the little low one on the wing,
The last one toward the trees, beside the well.
The first of all the Jonathans had built it,
And hung above the door a silver bell:

The only English thing that he had brought there;
He hung it up to ring his wedding in.
And there they all had left it, under the shingles;
It tinkled in the wind, that wore it thin.

The second of the Jonathans was born there,
But he had builded farther; and the third—
After the war, with Agatha—had finished;
So now there were no hammers to be heard.

The fourth one merely mended what had fallen,
But widened both the porches for the play
Of Jonathan and Joe, his only children:
Two sons, with whom the place had had its day.

They were the last to run from room to room,
Shouting and hiding faces; till the time
They grew afraid of corners in the long house
Where still the spiders drop, the shadows climb.

Their father locked the doors, and filled the wing—
The oldest room of all—with sacks of seed;
And nailed the oldest door; and still the bell
Swung rustily, without a present need.

The boys would come and wipe the dusty windows,
Peering into the first, the little house.
But all they saw was spider webs, and hanging
Bags above the reach of squirrel and mouse.

Jonathan forgot, but Joe remembered.
It was the room he wanted when he came.
They opened it and washed the little windows,
And roped the ancient bed upon its frame.

They brought the table back, and two of the chairs,
And hung old-fashioned curtains on a rod.
It was the room old Jonathan had slept in,
And bred his sons and daughters like a god.

All gone now, and their children's children too.
Jonathan and Laura lived alone.
The upper floors were musty, the grey shadows
Starved at last to skin and silent bone.

The stairways both were darkened at the top,
As if a day had walked up there and died.
They slept below, and ate, and wound their music
Out of a box, and let the shadows bide.

What Laura thought was more than Laura said,
Then, or the next long day, in the dusted room.

56

Invisibly she dreamed; but the dream ended
Brightly on the hither side of doom.

She only was preparing, out of sight,
And out of flying time, a thing to do.
But now it was the hour. The gate was there,
Wide open, and a car was coming through.

Jonathan in front of her was waving;
Joe was slowing proudly to a roar;
Then the stopping engine, and the gift
Of hands, the brown and white ones, at the door.

Jonathan gave all he had to give;
Laura kept the greater part, and laughed.
She told them she was laughing at the new
Brown roadster; it was longer than a raft;

Too much good metal there for single men,
Too much red leather, rounding empty space.
Joe smiled, and if he could have answered further
There was no means to tell it by his face.

He only bid them both climb in the rumble.
"I'll be unselfish instantly," he said,
And took them with him straight across the barn lot,
Into the darkened hollow of the shed.

They left it there, gleaming among the cobwebs,
A bolt of lightning haltered in a stall;
They left it there, each portion of it mocking
The dusty pegs that watched it from the wall.

They watched, and through the quiet of partitions
The horses raised their noses from the hay—
Listening; but the motor's mouth was hooded,
And now the going footsteps died away.

Jonathan, behind the other two,
Could hear the horses listening, or could think,
Swiftly, of all between them: the furred ears,
The softly blowing nostrils, and the clink

Of pistons on the temper of thin steel;
Jonathan could think of this and pause.
But Joe and Laura rose to their own laughter,
Swinging on—while streamers of dark gauze

Moved through her mind and draped it like a garment,
The mantle of the dress the moments wove.
It seemed as if the farm itself were flowing
Up and away, and hiding in the grove.

The day was fair, with breezes coming over
Close to the ground, and cool, yet streaked with warm.
The spring-dam up the world was open, letting
Trickles of life—that promised the full flood—
Run tentatively, gently, over and down,
Nosing the loam, curling along the fences,
Nudging the undulations of parched land.
Joe had come wearily, an endless winter
Laying its load still on him, and his face
Older beyond its time than they remembered;
He had come drooping; but the miracle
Of wind, and last night's water, and deep sky,
Working upon him now as if it only
Saw the one there, the palest of the three,
Straightened him on his stem. "A cellar growth,"
Jonathan looked and said; "something forgotten,
Something almost too late remembered—brought
Suddenly into the sun upstairs. And see?
It darkens, it uncurls, it all but dances."
Joe led them like two older, doubtful children
After him up the hedge row, where the shadows

Shrank to a narrow lane; it was eleven.
"At noon," he said, "we had to crawl clear under;
That was the only shade there was for miles.
Remember, Jon, the big hedge apples dropping,
And almost braining the well hidden boys?
If there is any brain about a boy,
Or such a boy as you were. Laura, look!
We took our hatchets here and trimmed a room.
You still can see the shape of it. An oval.
We lay inside like rats. Oho! the creek!
It's roaring!" So he hauled them suddenly out
Into the blinding light of the west pasture;
And so the morning ended in the woods.
And so the house again, and the slow dinner;
And so all day they followed him, with Laura
Staring between the two at something, nothing.

Jonathan pitched the hay down,
And stopped at each dark manger with a word:
A word for Dick and Dolly, and for Daisy,
A foolish, friendly sentence for the roans;
A slap for Western Jack.

Jonathan in the twilight,
Slowly walking sunward to the house,
Looked. For Laura waited by the low wing,
Lifting both her hands to swing the bell:
Lifting them, and waiting.

Expectant as the evening,
Tilted like a shadow toward the night,
She leaned, as if she wanted to be pulled there,
Drawn against the door, and in, and in.
"Why doesn't Laura call him?"

Then she jerked the bell-cord.
A jangle, cracked and musical, that stopped her—

Standing straight as iron, and coldly flushing.
He told himself he felt the icy warmth,
Flowing within, within.

Joe in the doorway then,
Nodding; but she had warily withdrawn.
A backward step, a waiting, as in terror;
A look; until Joe laughed and came along now,
Taking the path behind her.

He waved, and Jonathan waved—
Jonathan now at the gate, and the three together.
It was the end of twilight, the beginning
Of a cold April darkness, after the sun;
And it was time for supper.

"Well, that was good—as good as ever, Laura.
And I am tired; as tired as we were, Jon,
The night we dragged our legs in—you remember?—
After the day we drove to town, and the team
Broke, and galloped home with a piece of the wagon.
It was the first time father let us go;
And the last time for years. He didn't like it.
But I have always liked it, being tired
Like that, and like tonight. It's a complete
Feeling, to be remembered under your dreams,
A charm put under your pillow when you sleep
Alone, alone, alone. Let's play the song—
Laura, you haven't heard it; it's the latest,
A very good silly song—and then to bed.
All right?"
                    She cried him "Yes!", and Jonathan nodded.
Why not a song—a silly one, a new one?
And so he went and brought it, and it sang:

> Over the traffic, boys,
> Over the red, the green,

Alone, alone, alone, boys,
A bachelor sits unseen.
    Nineteen windows up and never married.
    Elevators, sliding up and down,
    Don't you click and stop, for he's the buried
    Bachelor-mummy-king of all the town.

Over the honk of horns, boys,
Over the taxi lanes,
Over the whistling cops, boys,
He sits and entertains.
    Nineteen windows up and never married.
    Elevators, sliding up and down,
    Don't you click and stop, for he's the buried
    Bachelor-mummy-king of all the town.

Over the velvet rug, boys,
Who's moving, arm in arm?
Why, it's the villain
And his killin'
Pretty, brown, and very willin'
Victim off the farm.
    Nineteen windows up and never married.
    Elevators, sliding up and down,
    Don't you click and stop, for he's the buried
    Bachelor-mummy-king of all the town.

Laura laughed, and Jonathan at last
Laughed too, but why they did so neither said.
"Of course it is the tune; the words, as usual,
Crazy," Joe expostulated, looking
Chiefly at Laura's eyes, that blazed again;
"They come by chance out of bright rattlebrains—
If there is any brain about a song man;
He shakes his head and words come out like those;
The very first he gets go down on paper.

61

And now why not to bed? Good evening, Jon.
See you tomorrow, Laura."
                              But she rose,
Saying she wasn't sure his room was ready.
They disappeared, and Jonathan heard their feet,
Two and two on the gravel, till the door
Opened under the bell; he caught its tinkle,
Down at the other end of the silent house.
He listened, and the silver sound again
Came; and Laura came; and crossed, and kissed him.

Saturday and Sunday yet.
The three of them were children still:
Joe among the woods again,
And they behind him up the hill;
And if they thought of him ahead,
Nothing anyway was said.

Laura spoke to Jonathan,
But not of Joe. Was she afraid?
Was she safer with the tale
Of where the angry hen had laid?
When he spoke it was the garden;
Time for harrow and for spade.

Joe led them down again, and wandered,
Wearily, beside the brook.
He was old again—a chapter
Finished in the fairy book.
"See the ashes in my eyes!"
But neither one of them would look.

Even then she only spoke
Of supper waiting—the last one.
End of Sunday. Milk and bread,
And then the holiday was done.

She turned and led them, faster home
Than either one of them would come.

The brothers called her, but she ran.
They let her go, and picked a way
Across the pastures round the shed.
It was the death bed of a day,
They walked and watched it slowly dying;
Walked, and found a woman crying.

They found her so, but she concealed it swiftly,
Setting the three bowls out and cutting the bread.
They supped in a half silence, until Joe
Spoke of his going soon, and sighed, and said:
"It wasn't long enough—three days, three minutes;
Only as long as one deep breath; but then,
I breathed it; there is that; and it was good."
"Do you remember," Jonathan began,
"The time you talked of staying? Not for days,
Not for another breath or two, but always?
Always! We could talk of that again."
"No."
        "I say we could. This isn't a house
Merely to be brought forth in, learn to walk in,
And then to walk away from and be homesick.
This, with the land it looks on, is a life,
Something to own as utterly as air.
It's yours, it's mine; I love it, and you love it;
I stay, and why not you? Do you remember
The way we two were boys here? How we planned
Those letters on the mail box—J. and J.
Gentry, Incorporated?"
                        "I remember.
I studied my first steps here, slow and well.
This is the place for walking. But the race
Runs swifter where I watch it, and I learned
Too long ago to love it to be changed.

63

I knew it better yesterday than ever.
I know it now so plainly I am sad—
Almost. You see I do remember things,
And it is melancholy, living lives
That overlap, one dead beneath the other.
This one is dead. It breathes a little for me,
Here on the very ground, if I come tramping.
But that one, there, the one you never saw—
Even when you came you didn't see it—
That one is always running, with me on it,
Midway the polished road, midway the stiff
Banners of stone and steel, and the many windows:
Millions of windows, Jon, and I can miss them.
I can be homesick too for all of that."
"For this, too, sometimes?"
                                        "Yes, for both. But listen.
Happy is not the word for that—for the close
Press of an upright universe, a tilted
Brick and glass rectangle of horizon,
A cornered mountain round me of white faces:
All with a love behind them that is my love,
A madness, if you must accuse it so.
The stars above us there, and the smoked sun,
Are never again the same. The roof is nearer,
Studded with neater cunning; and it catches
All of the flying wonder of our talk;
It rings with the deathless din of human voices
Crying across each other and coming back—
All human; we have shut the forests out,
And the dumb fields, and every beast abounding.
It is our place: a carnival, a manhole.
If still we love the country, it is love
Not of the first old Gentry's kind, who came,
Blessing the soil and promising a kingdom.
Those kingdoms are a little rusty now—
For me, for us they are—those backward patches
Lying beyond our empire. Yet we love them.

We love them to go out to, and remember:
We love them to come back from, and be mounted
Proudly again upon the bannered steed,
The iron horse, the animal with rivets.
And so we clatter sweetly, and forget;
And then remember you; and then forget.
I have been happy here, but this is why
I'm going. Do you see? And are you angry?"

Laura, in the half-light of the window,
Silent all the while, but with her eyes
On fire between the two, watched Jonathan now—
Waiting, with his hand upon the table,
Waiting, with his eyes upon his hand.
"No," he said. "Why angry? But I'm glad
You said it all, or something of it all.
There's more, I know.
There's more of it, you Gentrys,
Grandfathers,
Grass-lovers,
Walkers slow and slow across a kingdom yet to come.
It's come; you had it round you all the time;
And gone. It's fading
Sandwise into a desert—I can feel—
A desert where the dry, indifferent winds
Blow, blow, and all the rain of men's regard
Goes round to fall with laughter on the towers
Of towns—the spendid towns! For I have seen
What you will never see, you happy old ones,
Raft-riders,
Sod-breakers,
Steppers upon a garden shore, and singers
Loud of an ancient song,
An over-the-mountain, Eden song.
I've seen the garden wither in the rain;
I've felt the roots unwrapping their strong fingers,
Laying themselves away in a strange

Ground. It's not the ground you walked on, fathers.
Still it is what it is, and I will stay.
Laura and I will stay, loving the least
Vestige and green remainder: loving horses,
Loving a lane of shadows, and the four
Corners of every year. Not angry, Joe,
No; and come and see us when you must."

Soberly then he rose, and Laura, listening,
Wandered into the light, circling a little,
Mothwise in her helplessness; but now
Nothing was left to hear. The brothers smiled,
Soberly to each other, and went out.
She followed them over the grass and through the gate,
Whose posts, in the black of evening, moistened her hand,
Feeling the way. She followed, and they found it
Waiting among the spider-webs—the bright car,
Flooding at once the dusky shed with its silver.
A last goodbye to both of them, and Joe
Backed, and swung the stream of his great lamps
Over the barn, the picket fence, and the house trees,
Over the lane to the road. And now they heard him
Humming between the hedges. So they stood there,
Separate in the darkness, till the sound
Died, and the light was gone.

Separately, slowly,
Each of them familiar with the way,
The two of them walked in without a word.
Separately, slowly,
Each of them possessing a lone thought,
Jonathan and Laura crept to bed.
Jonathan, exhausted,
Stared into the emptiness above him;
Stared, and seeing nothing, fell asleep.
Laura, too awake now
To make a single sound—for she was careful—

Stared, and seeing something, stared again.
Into the void, the ceiling,
Through and into the upper night she gazed,
Narrowing there her eyes, stricken with stars:
Herself, without a name there,
Herself, with light around her like a sea,
Herself alone, waiting upon her day.

The end of April was a dry end, bringing
Never a night of rain, with mornings after
Glittering in the glances of the sun.
Clouds lay, sometimes so low that a tree touched them,
Drenching its budded head; and the rolling sky
Frowned from a little distance; but no rain,
And Jonathan, each evening by the clock,
As if he were the day itself, and the dial,
Spoke of the needed showers.
                              "A dusty April
Never can do the pastures any good;
No matter what the May, we want a spring month
Wetter about our feet than we might like
If we were not a yoke of farmers. Laura,
I am a farmer here because time passed
And put me so; and you because I asked you.
We are a team in harness, though we pull
Unevenly sometimes; which is to say,
You pull as often back as you do forward.
And yet the brutes are matched; I still can think so.
Still, Laura, we can hope for rain together—
Knowing the pleasant pain of being played with.
Weather's a game, and the sky uses us:
Up with the wind and down with the wind—"
                                        "Jonathan,
You're thinking more of what Joe Gentry said
Than what you say yourself. So. Was it true?"

"I am, a little. But I spoke of rain.
At least in the beginning it was rain."

May came with warmer winds, and the sky softer.
Lazier now the scud of white and blue,
Lazier, out of the west and over and down.
It was a gentler month than they remembered;
It was a finer world above them, blowing,
Than either of them could answer to. But rain
Came not through any night, or through the long,
Tired days of Jonathan's labor, that redoubled.

"And that's all right, but where's our summer hand?
I've looked, and asked, and talked all over town.
He doesn't seem to be there any more—
The boy, the man who waited till we came,
Smiled and said he would, and climbed the wagon.
It's work and they don't like it; or it's far
From the red fronts of stores, and from the car line.
Well,"—and he would mutter to the sheep
More than he ever said at home to Laura.
Between the sheep and horses and the corn,
And the new field of oats, and the alfalfa,
He faltered; but went on, and was so late,
Some of these lengthened evenings, that she kept
Supper for him alone in the high oven—
The "waiting oven," Laura learned to call it—
Over the nickeled stove. He came, and stamping
Dust before the door, looked in at Laura;
Cleared his throat and entered, and sat down
Some days without a word. For he was tired,
And his tongue too was tired from its slow moving
Silently by the side of his slow thought;
So weary that it would not trust itself
With words, that might come edged with anger now.
No time for anger, Jonathan believed,
Though inwardly they rubbed him—the raw words,

The other words outside him he could hear,
Often in the twilight, as he stumbled,
Wearier than ever, from the stalls.
He held his tongue and sat, and ate, and rested;
Except that once the legend of the needle,
Scratching around the disc with frantic zeal,
Provoked him past his patience, and at last
He spoke. But he had listened to the end:

> She told him she was lonesome.
> It was in the summer time,
> And the day was long agoing.
> But he only had a dime.
> So he thought until it struck him—
> An idea like a rhyme.
>> "There isn't any better fun
>> (With nothing else to do)
>> Than going arm in arm, hon,
>> Up the avenue."

> She told him he was crazy;
> Better sit at home and talk.
> But he had slipped into his coat,
> And so they took the willing walk;
> And the first new thing they noticed
> Was the children with their chalk.
>> "Sally Jane McArthur
>> Loves Big Bill McGrew."
>> Going arm in arm there
>> Up the avenue.

> They strolled, and now the shadows
> Of the roofs across the way
> Fell upon their quiet faces,
> And the windows in display;
> And she read the printed words
> She never bothered with by day.

69

"Awnings fitted anywhere."
"Cables to Peru."
Going arm in arm there
Up the avenue.

They passed the shuttered banks,
The restaurants along the Row;
Looked, and saw the people dining,
Heard the music playing slow;
And they watched a dirty kitten
Sniff the grating down below.
   "Meow, meow, let me in;
   Open it, and let me through."
Going arm in arm there
Up the avenue.

They almost said "Good evening"
To a tailor by his door.
But it began to rain now,
And it began to pour;
And this is what she said to him
Above the subway roar:
   "There isn't any better fun
   (With nothing else to do)
   Than riding arm in arm, hon,
   Down the avenue."

"Inane, preposterous syllables!"—
Jonathan was saying it at last—
"They are beneath you, Laura, words and tune.
It used to be *Drink Only*, and *Abide*,
And *Aberdeen*, and *She Was Passing Fair*.
It used to be that you could sit and sing
Those old ones, the grave sweet ones, with a something
Solid in them, like a golden wire.
You sang, and it would tremble and commence
Another humming round you; I could feel it,

Even if it was never to be heard.
You were the one I heard. But something happened.
I heard all music too, and heard the heart
Of an old time, a better one than this time,
The strong and pretty worktime of the world."

"Inane," she only said, repeating dumbly;
"Inane"—but then she blazed a sudden moment,
Strangely, and she was more surprised than he was.
"They aren't any more inane than—"
                                        "What?
Maybe I need to know. And I'm already
Sorry for what I said. Than me? Than this?
They keep you well enough reminded, do they,
Of the bright other place you ought to be?"
But she was silent now. And she was sorry,
And kissed him where his hat had left a red,
Straight mark across his forehead. "You are tired.
Here's your supper, Jon, as warm as ever.
There. Oh when, I wonder, will he come—
This necessary fellow we can't find?
When, to save the summer, and save you?
And me? And when is it going to rain again?"

Still the dry days, and still the lonesome labor,
Still the dumb truce between them, and no end.
But then one afternoon as May was going—
Culprit, with the sign of dust upon her—
One afternoon, with not a cloud for comfort,
The gate clicked twice, and Laura, looking out,
Saw a long back unbending from the latch,
Saw the low gate swing open softly; and saw
A tall, straw-colored man glide over the grass.
He came, and she awaited him; and wondered,
Even as he stood capering there and smiling,
Whether it was a man at all, or whether,
Strung so and oddly dangling, he was oatstraw.

71

Or both, she said almost aloud, and asked him
What he had come for; asked, but got no answer.
Only the blue eyes, under the lonely forehead,
Smiled, and the light lids fluttered, and a long
Grimace, as when a slow wind strokes a hay field,
Rippled across the rest of him. The silence
Startled her all at once; he had not answered.
She stared and stepped away from him, and ran.
"Jonathan!"—she traced him to a far field—
"There is a crazy fellow at the house.
Come with me, I'm afraid."

                "What kind of crazy?
Isn't he the kind you can take care of?
I'm busy."

            But he came, and the two found him
Exactly, Laura said, where he had been.
"And been forever. Can't the fellow move?
I saw him move at first—a blinking cat,
Purring and putting his paws out over the grass.
There he is, though. Now what to do with him?"
He heard them coming, and a look of woe
Escaped from him to vanish up the trees:
A curl of mist returning to the sky.
They came, and Jonathan called: "How do you do!"
No answer yet, and Jonathan, amazed:
"Who are you? Where'd you come from? Do you know?"
The long legs bent a little at the knee,
The sideward eyes grew sober, and the lithe feet
Shuffled, as with a sigh the new one sang:

      Way down south in the sycamore timber.
      That's where I come from, that's why I'm limber.
      Went and cut a sapling, threw it in the air.
      Where's it goin' to land, you white man, where?

"Who are you, though, and what's your name? You got one?"

72

Tom, Tom, the son of a gun,
Stole my gal and away he run.
I'm Tom, too.
Stranger, do you chew?

He spat and took tobacco from a bundle
Tied high upon the string about his waist.
Jonathan stepped closer: "Do you work, Tom?"

Never hitch me up, boy,
I'm no mule.
Let me wander free, though,
I'm a workin' fool.

"What did you come away for? Were you tired?"

Pluggin' on a farm, boss,
Never got me weary.
Then I tried the cotton mill—
That'll leave 'em bleary!
Sal ran away with the foreman's brother;
I started round the world, one end t'other.

"I need a man to help me. Will you stay?"

Let me make a hole
In the middle of the straw,
Show me where the well is,
Feed me somethin' raw;
Give me piece of balin' wire—
Pipe won't draw—
And I'm the little man
You been a lookin' for.

It was no use. Laura could hear it coming.
She hummed a cautious sound, and pulled at Jonathan;
But he turned straight away, leading the long legs

73

Up to the empty hand's house in the orchard.
"He had to stoop to get himself inside,"
He told her, coming back almost at once;
"And yet he didn't shorten; he uncurled
And entered like a snake. I left him sleeping,
Coiled like a length of rope—I think a strong one.
Lucky, my Laura. But you don't believe it."
"He's horrible! Not dangerous, I mean—"
"Yes. He is unnatural. No words;
Nothing but jigs and nonsense. But I'll try him.
He'll sleep all day and night—he said he would—
Then wake; and we can see if he's not faithful."

Tom stayed, and was as willing as the wind—
That blew too much that summer, and too warm.
He fed the sheep with singing as he trailed them
Busily back and forth between the pastures:
Nibbled almost to death now, but with resting
They grew a little greener. Then he came,
Swinging his arms behind the puzzled creatures.
They bobbed before him, wondering, yet they liked him.
"Of course. Tom's silly too. So they're at home,"
Laura would frown and say; but Jonathan smiled.
Or he would wrap himself around the corn plow,
Riding a cloud of dust, and sending nonsense
Up to the horses' ears—that never caught it,
There in the wind that wafted all away.
Jonathan was pleased.
                    "But what about him?
Doesn't he ever tell you of himself?
In prose, I mean, and standing halfway straight?"
Laura with her loathing still was curious.
Two months had passed, more terrible and dry
Than either dared complain of, doubting the other—
Doubting his temper, doubting her content.
But she must ask the question, there in the poor
Parched garden, on this side the orchard fence.

"Don't be too loud. His ears are like a fox's,
And though it's been a long day he's awake.
Be careful. No, he doesn't let me know
Anything more than both of us could guess
That day he came, the crazy day. He sings,
And doesn't expect attention. What they mean—
His words, if they are words—I never know.
I don't know what to say of him, or to him.
But then, why talk at all? The substance is,
We're lucky. He was sent us by the gods."
"And like the gods, to send a simpleton!
I hate him. It's as if—"
                              "Well, what?"
"As if—and I can tell it to you now—
As if one thing too much were added here;
One leaf too many, laid upon my back,
Breaks it. I go mad sometimes I think,
Without you ever knowing that I do,
From the hung sky and from the waiting earth
Under it. And now this zany comes,
And sings his death's accompaniment, and grins,
As if my fate had taken the small form
Of a grey, foolish sheep. Oh, I get over it—"
"Do you, Laura, do you? Listen, Laura,
Mustn't go on like this. We'll move away."
"No, we won't. You couldn't. As for me—
I'm sorry, Jon. I'm sorry once again.
I never will say the rest. You know there's more,
But let it be. Let's bury it."
                              "All right."
Yet Jonathan could only look away,
His hands, his feet as moveless as the plum trees
Over the orchard wall, and as the window,
Open to the twilight, of Tom's house.
Jonathan could see it through the leaves—
One window staring at him. Then he listened,
And Laura listened, silently behind him,

75

To the cracked words that floated down around them:
Fragments of a song, Tom's sleeping song.

There was a bird
Of solid gold.
So I've been told.
At least it was yellow.
And it did sing
With a silver sound,
Until it was found
By a foolish fellow.

He carried it home
And builded a cage
Of lettuce and sage,
And slippery ellum.
People came by.
"See here, see here!
But not too near;
It's shy," he would tell 'em.

Some looked in;
But the golden bird
Never was heard
With its song of wonder—
Missing the woods,
Missing the rain,
And the old refrain
Of sweetened thunder.

Sits there still,
Long hour by hour,
And the sky grows sour,
And the wings are folded.
Better let it out,
Take away the wall.

Feathers goin' to fall
And the heart be moulded.

Whatever it meant to Jonathan, he kept it;
Whatever it meant to Laura, she was sad.
But there was not a song that would have given
Comfort in a season going mad.

The fall, without their knowing it, was round them;
They looked, and on a day as dry as ever
Haze upon the grove was trailing signals
Of a lost year, yielding its endeavor.

It died head downward, leisurely converting
Tips of green to umber one by one.
Nothing now to hasten it, and nothing
To check the flowing fall till it was done.

And it was done, and the dead year, suspended
Blue and dusty brown beneath the sky,
Clung, as if the shell of a great locust
Waited upon the wind, itself to die.

The season had grown old beyond departing;
Time was dead, and yet it could not go;
And the turned earth was beautiful; or would be
If any easy mind were there to know.

Laura, like the branches, fixed in fever,
Hanging too, and waiting for an end,
Laura in her silence only wondered
What sudden deed October might intend.

Jon nudged the horses' noses of an evening,
And led them every noon to where a pool

Of water in the creek was growing stagnant—
He himself, or sent the cheerful fool.

Tom went, the drove behind him in their halters,
Seven thirsty faces gazing past.
He went, and he must always sing a mournful
Song, as if it were the very last.

       Rain crow, rain crow,
       Heard the saddest rain crow
       Ever, ever seen
       Since the world was green.

       Rain crow, rain crow,
       Moanin' like a rain crow:
       Never turtle dove
       Lost such a love.

       Rain crow, rain crow,
       Never such a rain crow
       Sobbin' in the hedge
       By the brown field edge.

       Rain crow, rain crow,
       Mortifyin' rain crow,
       Who, who's gone,
       And left you all alone?

       Tall boy, tall boy,
       Leadin'-horses tall boy,
       Look inside and see:
       You're the same as me.

       Tall boy, tall boy,
       Good-for-nothin' tall boy,
       Walkin' there apart,
       Bleedin' though the heart.

Tall boy, tall boy,
God-forsaken tall boy,
What's the time o' year,
And where'll you go from here?

Tall boy, tall boy,
Cotton-headed tall boy,
Home folks gone,
Trampin' all alone.
Tall boy, straw boy,
Pokin' all alone,
All alone.

When the grey corn, more stunted on the stalk
Than any moon remembered, rustled nightlong,
When the shorn lambs grew coats again, and dipped them
Frugally every evening in the dew,
When all the mows were filled with powdery hay,
And Jonathan was weary of old words,
He said once during supper, when the wind,
As impotent as ever round the house,
Whirled the white plaything, dust, above the dark road:
"Laura—Joe. It's been six months, and more,
Since either of us saw him. Overdue.
Didn't he tell us then it would be *three* months?"
"But it has been a busy season for him.
I don't know why, in summer, but he says so;
And says that he is coming—very soon."
"You've heard from him. Well, when is very soon?"
"Tomorrow, late; maybe at midnight; maybe—"
"Good. Oh, that's good news. And so he wrote you.
When?"
         "I don't just know. I can't remember."
"I didn't mean it mattered. Does he say—

79

But then there will be time enough for that.
Three days this time?"
                              "Yes, yes—it has to be!"
He looked at Laura sharply, in surprise,
Then talking for them ended, and the night
Passed over the cool chamber that contained them,
Passing before another day, and dumbly
Joining another night. And now the night.

Eleven, twelve, and half past;
Jonathan was dozing.
Laura at the window still,
With eyes too wide for closing,
Turned and saw him; turned again
And said it softly: "When, and when?"

Not a rattle on the road,
Not a light above the hill,
Spreading forward in a fan,
A narrow dawn, until, until
There it broke—she saw it plain—
And swept the valley like a rain.

There it tilted and descended,
Coming downward swiftly now;
Oh, so swiftly, Laura, swiftly,
As your brow,
Pressing hot against the glass,
Shuddered, fearing it would pass.

It did not pass. The long lights, swinging in,
Startled the barn lot, where the shadows ran,
Awakened and bewildered, all one way—
For safety, Laura said, escaping so
Into the farther darkness of the fields,
The aged darkness, free of these young fears,

This new excitement coming, as it came
Now, this midnight moment, unto her.
She stood, expectant, rigid, her two arms
Risen above her, holding the window frame;
She stood, her beating forehead on the glass,
Longer than death, longer than any world
Would take to turn its silence into sound;
Longer, yet it only was a moment.
When the dark engine died, already Laura
Stood at the shed's high entrance, watching Joe,
Who came; and seeing Jonathan behind her,
Blinking a pair of brotherly, tired eyes,
Laughed; and kissed her quickly, her hands hanging
Straightly beside her; laughed, and said to Jonathan:
"Sorry I wasn't later, so as to let you
Sleep the night out. Now it's badly broken:
Cracked across the middle, like a plate.
I will not say I'm sorry, though, to be here.
It's better than you know to come again.
Six months! And—well, how are you?"
                              "Hello, Joe.
Stranger, you'll excuse this dust before you.
Don't kick it, for it flies and fills the face.
I didn't have time to sweep the farm this morning.
How are you, Joe? Been busy?"
                              "Yes—here, Laura,
Guide me. It's new country, and I'm awkward.
Got a small bite to eat? I took no time out,
Anywhere on the road, for supper. Really?
Good!"
        So while he drank the pleasant coffee,
They talked: three of them there, with none to say
The painful thing that might have lost its pain,
Clear in the lamplight, with three faces round it.

They talked; but not of anything; till Jonathan,
Weary beyond all words, got up for bed.

81

"You take him, dear, and turn him in. Goodnight."
"Goodnight!" and he was gone. They heard him go,
Heavily down the narrow hall, to the end.
They heard him; but he heard them, too; their silence
Followed him and surrounded him, and pressed there
Hurtfully at his ears, as if the walls
Came closer than they ought. He stood a moment,
Staring at all or nothing; then undressed,
Drew the familiar blankets over, and slept.

He woke in the same darkness—in the same
Hour. Was she beside him, and asleep?
Jonathan could answer: No—the silence
Never had been so terrible and deep.
And yet this very stillness gave him doubt,
Till he turned, so, and put his fingers out.

He found her by him, moveless in her place;
Asleep already—long ago, perhaps.
He drew his fingers slowly home, and smiled,
Playing in his mind with harmless scraps
Of hope. But soon her silence, breath and limb,
Stretched beneath the blankets, troubled him.

He rose without a sound and struck a match,
Holding a hand between it and her face.
In the half-darkness she was whole and white;
But the dark eyes, like apertures in lace,
Stared at the ceiling—open as she slept,
Unseeing, though the world went by and wept.

Morning, and Laura waited by the table
Only for Joe; but when he came, his eyes

Never were off of Jonathan, and never
Comforted even there. What word last night,
What sound between them, silent beyond the bell,
What thing was he afraid of, Jonathan wondered?
"Well, have you seen our Tom?"
                              "I have."
                                        "And did he—"
"Yes, he did. A song and dance. 'The Rain Crow.'
Afterwards I tried to make him talk.
Doesn't he talk?"
                  "Oh, no, he doesn't need to.
Jon can understand him as he is.
Songs, you know. And real ones—maybe old ones.
Not the silly stuff you like, and I like."
Jonathan grew patient. "He is silly.
I never said he wasn't, or have praised
His songs, although I like them secretly.
They're silly too—and make a perfect match
For these that come on rubber."
                              "I'll agree.
Laura, Jon, there isn't much to choose.
But now I have to know one thing about him.
Where did he come from? Did he happen here?
I asked him, and I gave him time to answer—
Vainly. Does he understand a question?
What does he understand?"
                          But even then
A shuffle in the pantry made them listen,
Startled, till it ceased, and Tom began:

> Over the mountains, boys,
> Come long lonesome way.
> Over the mountains, boys,
> This many a day.
>   Didn't like them goin's-on
>   A little bit, a little bit.

Tied my yellow handkerchief
And out I lit, and out I lit.

Over the river, boys—
Big one runnin' west—
Over the river, boys;
Thought that the best.
    Didn't like them goin's on
    A little bit, a little bit.
    Tied my yellow handkerchief
    And out I lit, and out I lit.

Over the open country,
Good roads runnin' north.
Look for better people;
See what these are worth.
    Didn't like them goin's-on
    A little bit, a little bit.
    Tied my yellow handkerchief
    And out I lit, and out I lit.

Over the open country,
People about the same.
Everybody ornery.
Don't know who to blame.
    I don't like this goin's-on
    A little bit, a little bit.
    Tie my yellow handkerchief
    And lickety-split, and lickety-split.

Over the lakes and yonder,
Injuns may be good—
Whittlin' red new babies
Out of cedar wood.
    I don't like this goin's-on
    A little bit, a little bit.

Tie my yellow handkerchief
And lickety-split, and lickety-split.

"A sample!" Laura cried, and looked at Joe,
Who only looked at Jonathan and said:
"Bring him in here. I want to see his eyes."
But Tom had ceased as simply as the song.
No sound of going, yet the pantry, searched,
And afterwards the kitchen and the barn lot,
Brought no tom cat prowling. "He's a tom cat—
Slippery, and long," said Laura shrilly;
"I for one don't like his meowing much.
Do you? Do you?" But neither had attended.

Afternoon, and what was now to say?
Four o'clock, and where to send themselves?
"I'll tell you. Don't we need to go to town?
Jump in. I'll take you. Jonathan, come on.
There's room for you up here."
                                        So off they sped,
The three of them, with Laura in the middle,
Fingering at the gears and crying "Fast!
Eight miles, eight minutes—can you make it, Joe?"
"No hurry," Jonathan said; but up the long hill,
Over and down, and round the Johnson curve,
Round, and then straight on they roared, till the town,
Lying upon the left, lay there to see.
At the cross-roads they slowed. "Too sharp for speeders.
We're speeders," Joe was saying. "Now, tomorrow,
I'll go to the right here, won't I, driving back?"
For a quick moment, turning, Laura swept
The way they had not taken. "Yes, you will.
You will. But there's this half a mile, remember.
I think you'll never make it"; though they did;
And bought their few unnecessary things;

85

And turned for home. "Now slower," Jonathan said.
So all the way in silence, in the last light.

The sun had lingered long above the house,
Yet not too long for Jonathan, who watched it
Going, red, by the grove, and when he lost it,
Shivered a little, suddenly. "It's nothing.
Nothing but a fear of nights," he said:
"These nights, when things can happen. But they won't."

It was the night of all his nights if Jonathan had known;
A true alarm; but now he sighed and laid it well away:
Down among his oldest fears, forgotten with his hope.
But that would be remembered, too, upon a certain day.

He only felt the night around him, dark, without a star,
Heavy, like a fur; and then he felt a drop of rain.
Another, and another; but they stopped, and while he waited,
Nothing came at all, and nothing came that night again.

"I couldn't have expected it; the drouth is not to break
Till something else has broken here—what? and who? and how?
Nothing will declare it." Yet the weight about to fall
Hung above his head and snapped a cable even now.

He walked indoors and found them wildly opposite each other;
A table's width between them, but a world between their eyes;
Space that Laura looked across and trembled, leaning toward it;
Something though that frightened him, as when a shadow flies.

Something there had frightened Joe, staring at it still.
Something there had fascinated Laura. Yet she turned:
"Jonathan, be careful. We were walking on the edge—"
"Of what?" But she had caught her hands, as if the fingers
     burned.

"What I was saying, Jonathan, was nonsense.
I meant to tell you simply of an errand
One of us has to run, and that is me.
I left the most important of our packages—
Spice for Sunday dinner—at the store.
How could I be so foolish? But I was,
And it is there; and since it's Saturday night
I'll have Joe take me in and get it. So?
You're tired. You stay."
               "All right. Go on along."

When Laura, coming slowly forth at last,
Murmured that she was ready, Joe had gone.
There at the gate, his lights along the road now,
He idled. She could see him through the glass;
Or see the lights, enough of him to know;
And here could see her husband, tall and friendly,
Coming to button more of her brown sweater.
She met him as he came with both her hands
Upward, as if to hold him there, and kissed him.
"Goodbye," she said, and ran;
And that was all.
But the hung weight was hurrying to its fall.

Jonathan, alone among the shadows of the room,
Heard the minutes pass, but heeded not their starting back;
Heeded not the panic that was on them as they ceased—
Stiffened there with something seen, trembling on the track.

For Jonathan the time was dull; for them the time was dead.
The hour had come, the weight was down, and still it would not
    rise.
A desert space before them with no river going round;
The stop, the awful end; but none of this was in his eyes.

He closed them, and the circle of the silence was complete.
He opened them, bewildered. Joe and Laura. Were they here?
The car had stopped. Or had it stopped? Why the humming
    still?
And why those deeper voices coming near, and near, and near?

Jonathan, awake upon the instant, filled the door—
Shutting in the light, but soon his shadow leaned and spread,
Enclosing her at last, embracing all of her together;
Possessing her forever, beautiful and dead.

"I loved her, Jon; she was my brother's wife;
I loved her therefore only, and that much.
It was not little, either, as you know.
So I have been unhappy this dry while,
Watching her love go out of her and wander
Like a lost star that would return its heat
To some familiar cluster in the sky—
Familiar if she found it; but she didn't.
Not me, Jon, at all, and you must see it—
Nothing but cities; she had fallen in love
With cities, and though broken on the spires,
Dashed like a windward bird, she still must cling there,
Loving the very edges of the stone.
I did my best to pet the panic out.
She did not hear me, so I talked to you—
I talked as I was going, there in April,
Of cities and the love of cities—thinking,
After I left, how Laura would defend you.
In her own mind at first. And then with words.
Therefore I was silent these six months,
Coming at last in hope. But it was worse then,
After the drouth, after your tuneful bumpkin.
So! And tonight. There wasn't any package.
I knew there wasn't any, yet I took her—

I—to the fearful end. For at the cross-roads,
Even as she had threatened, it was 'Right!
Right! And away forever! Or I'll jump!'
I faltered then, but not the wheel, that followed
Left, and left—and pulled us on so swiftly,
Who would have thought a woman could stand up!
It was as if the wind had wanted Laura.
Maybe it had; or one mistaken star.
At least—well, there's no more. You want me, Jon,
How long? For I can stay or I can go.
How long? Or are you done with me, as she was?"
"Done? Nothing of that. Yet I'll not beg you.
There never was enough of Laura stayed;
So go. My word to her was always 'Longer,
Longer, Laura, longer.' If she went,
Maybe it was a word too much that moved her.
So go. But you are welcome, Joe, till Doomsday."

"What if you went with me? This is finished."

"No, nothing is finished. Nothing fails
But fails before its time. It's not my time yet.
When that has come I shall have more than failed—
My kind and I then perished altogether.
To cease is not to fail, and may be honorable.
At least I see some honor in an end
Not hastened, not escaped: an end accepted.
The first old Gentry would have had me stay.
I think he must have been the kingly kind
Who dies with what is left of a long staff:
A stick, a piece of nothing, but his hand
Holds it, and his voice goes through the kingdom,
Bigger than ever, bidding the dust come down.
The first old Gentry—Jonathan his name—
He would have told me stay. And I shall stay.

It is the only word that has a meaning,
Now in our death of names."

                              "It is a good word.
Listen."

        For the night was marching off,
And the slow feet were awful till they ceased.

"Listen."

        For the morning, come again,
Moving the trees apart, was there to calm them.

"Listen."

        For the semblance of a song,
Meeting the day, meeting the dawn and falling,
Quickened the separate brothers; and it sang:

                    Over the mountains, boys,
                    And down the river middle,
                    Took long lonesome way
                    To solve old riddle.
                      Adam and Eve,
                      They dug and spun
                      Till the Lord got tired.
                      Then where'd they run?

                    Over the mountains, boys,
                    And down the river middle,
                    Ask that fellow there
                    With the broken fiddle.
                      Adam and Eve,
                      They dug and spun.
                      And so must every
                      Other one.

                    Over the mountains, boys,
                    And down the river middle,

Won't learn nothin' new,
Hey diddle diddle.
　　Adam and Eve,
　　They dig and spin
　　Till the Lord he's tired
　　And turns 'em in.

A WINTER DIARY
(1935)

A Winter Diary

This was not written then, when measuring time
Ran smoothly to unalterable rhyme;
When even song—but still it is unsounded—
Kept the pure tally that has been confounded.
This was not written then, when sudden spring
Not yet had threatened winter, and no thing
Stood colder than the skin of apple trees.
Now every top is bursting into bees;
Now all of them, solidified to light,
Reflect a cloudy fire, as high, as white
As any sky in summer; and at last
Sharp edges of a shadow have been cast.
Thus sudden spring, with sudden summer near,
Has made a certain winter disappear:
The winter of all winters I would keep
Had I the power to put this warmth asleep
And make the world remember what I saw.
But who has power against a season's law?
Who lives a winter over, who is proof
Against the rain of months upon his roof?
A certain winter fades that I had thought
Forever in live colors to have caught.
A certain moveless winter more than moves:
Runs backward, and oblivion's great grooves

Lie deeper in the distance, and tomorrow
Nothing will be there save mist and sorrow.
Therefore must I fix it while I may:
Feign records, and upon this single day
Tie months of time together, in pretended
Sequence till they once again are ended.

. . . So it is autumn, when the city reaches,
Pulling us home from mountains and from beaches;
Down the curved roads and from the crescent sands
To oblong streets among divided lands.
Yet not us four. It is the year we stay
And watch the town-returners pour away.
Now the last stragglers of the stream have gone;
Here now we stand upon a thinning lawn—
The shade wind-shattered, and the cut grass sleeping—
Here then we stand and to the country's keeping
Tender four faces. Not a leaf that falls
But flutters through a memory of walls;
Flutters, with more to follow, till they weave
This solitude we shall at last believe.

. . . October sunshine, and a summer's day!
Yet not the heaviness long wont to lay
Slow skies upon our heads and bind us round
With the full growth of a too fruitful ground.
The morning sun was southerly, and noon
Came swiftly, and the day was over soon:
An airy thing time tossed us for our pleasure,
Blue, and wide-blown, and rich with gold leaf-treasure.
The solid green is gone, the trees are fire:
Cool fire, and top-contained, without desire;
Not caring if it lives, for lo, all day
Wind bullied it and bore the sparks away.
October sunshine and red-ember drifts;
So the long burden of a summer lifts.

. . . November rain all night, the last of three
Dark nights and mornings. We have been to see
The brook that piles grey water down the meadows.
Grey water, and there is no sun for shadows;
No wind for bare tree-talk, no thing but spreading
Rain; no thing but rain, wherein the treading
Crow-feet leave thin tracks, and grass is drowned
With a contented and a final sound.
Safely indoors now, with a fire to dry us,
We hear a whole long year go slipping by us—
Backward to die, with nothing left ahead
Save solitude and silence, and a thread
Of days that will conduct us through the cold.
The window-panes are waterfalls that fold
Small misty visions of our valley's end.
The rain is sewing curtains that will rend
And rise another day; but shut us now
In such a world as mice have up the mow.
Thus do we know ourselves at last alone;
And laugh at both the kittens, who have grown
Till there they lie, prim figures by the fire,
Paws folded, aping age and undesire.
The boys would have them up again to play.
But they are sudden-old; it is the day
For dreaming of enclosure, and of being
All of the world time missed as he was fleeing.
They think, the furry fools, to live forever.
So then do we, the curtains lifted never.

. . . It is December, and the setting sun
Drops altogether leftward of the one
Long mountain-back we used to measure by.
The maple limbs swing upward, grey and dry,
And print the lawn, now naked for the snow,
With lines that might be nothing. But we know.
We see them there across the bitten ground,
Dark lace upon the iron, and catch the sound

97

Of half a world contracting under cold.
Slowly it shrinks, for it is wise and old,
And waits; and in its wisdom will be spared.
So is the frosted garden-plot prepared.
The withered tops, arustle row by row,
Fear nothing still to come; for all must go.
That is their wisdom, as it is the horse's,
Whose coat the wind already reinforces,
There in the blowing paddock past the gate.
The four of us a long day, working late,
Confined her where she grazes, building the fence
She leans on; yet she would not wander hence.
She drops her head and nibbles the brown grass,
Unmindful of a season that will pass;
Long-coated, with a rump the wind can ruffle;
Shoeless, and free; but soon the snow will muffle
All of her four black feet, that study a line
Down to the ponies' corner under the pine.
So have the field-mice, folding their startled ears,
Burrowed away from owls and flying fears.
So have the hunters ceased upon the hills;
The last shot echoes and the woodland stills;
And here, along the house, the final flower
Lets fall its rusty petals hour by hour.

. . . So, in December, we ourselves stand ready.
The season we have dared is strong and heady,
But there is many a weapon we can trust.
Five cellar shelves that were but layered dust
Are wiped to kitchen neatness, and confine
Clear jellies that will soothe us when we dine:
Crab-apple, quince, and hardly-ripened grape,
With jam from every berry, and the shape
Of cherries showing pressed against the jar;
Whole pears; and where the tall half-gallons are,
Tomatoes with their golden seeds; and blunt
Cucumbers that the early ground-worms hunt.

98

The highest shelf, beneath the spidery floor,
Holds pumpkins in a row, with squash before:
Dark, horny Hubbards that will slice in half
And come with pools of butter as we laugh,
Remembering the frost that laid the vines
Like blackened string: September's valentines.
Firm corn, and tapering carrots, and the blood
Of beets complete the tally of saved food;
Yet over in a corner, white and square,
Is the big bin with our potato-share.
Then seven barrels of apples standing by.
We brought them down the ladder when a high
Stiff wind was there to whip us, hand and cheek;
And wheeled them to the barn, where many a week
They filled the tightest chamber; but they found
More certain safety here below the ground:
The Baldwins to be eaten, and the Spies;
But Greenings are for betty and for pies.
A dusty cellar window, old as stone,
Lets in grey light, a slowly spreading cone
Sharp-ended here, and shining, at the shelves.
All of the other spaces wrapped themselves
In darkness long ago; and there the wood
Remembers a great sky wherein they stood:
The twenty trees I walked with Louis, marking,
Once in a mist of rain; then axes barking
Through the wet, chilly weeks, with ring of wedges
Under the blows of iron alternate sledges,
Louis's and Laurier's, of equal skill.
These were the two woodchoppers whom the still
Small faces of the boys watched day by day.
They sat among brown leaves, so far away
We barely could hear their shouting as the saw
Paused, and the great trunk trembled, and a raw
Circle of odorous wood gaped suddenly there.
Now maple and oak and cherry, and a rare
Hard chestnut piece, with hickory and birch,

Piled here in shortened lengths, await my search:
Coming with lantern and with leather gloves
To choose what provender the furnace loves.
From wall to wall a dozen resting rows:
We shall be warm, whatever winter blows.
So for the range upstairs a mound uprises,
By the back fence, of birch in sapling sizes.
Old Bailey cut them through a lonely fall—
He and his axe together, that was all:
They in a thicket, and the white poles gleaming;
Now a high frozen pile the sun is steaming.
We shall be warm, whatever north wind catches
Any of us outside the rattling latches;
Down the sloped road, or where the yard descends
To the barn's angle with its gusty ends,
Or higher, beyond the garden and the orchard—
We shall not be snow-worried or wind-tortured.
The armor we have sent for has arrived.
The great book spread its pages, and we dived
Like cormorants for prey among the rocks;
And chose, and duly ordered; and the box
Came yesterday. A winter's woolen wraps:
Thick-wristed mittens and two stocking caps;
Three fleece-lined jackets that will turn all weather,
And one cut neat for ladies out of leather;
Red sweaters, nut-brown shirts, and rubber-soled
Great workman's shoes for wading in the cold.
We shall be warm; or we can stamp indoors,
Wool failing, till the supper and the chores.

. . . So quietly it came that we could doubt it.
There was no wind from anywhere to shout it.
Simply it came, the inescapable cold,
Sliding along some world already old
And stretched already there had we perceived it.
Now by this hour the least one has believed it.
Snippy, the lesser kitten, lies entangled

Deep in the fur of Snappy, where a dangled
Feed-sack drapes a box inside the shed.
I found them with the lantern, playing dead:
Those very creatures, Snippy and her brother,
Who in the orange sunset tumbled each other,
Lithe by the stepping-stone. Through such a night
How often have they put the frost to flight;
How often, when the blackness made them bolder,
Have they confounded time, that grew no colder.
Yet not this night; they recognize the god,
As in the barn the black mare, left to nod,
Stands in her blanket, dozing. I have come
From tending her, and heard the ominous hum
Of branches that no wind moved overhead;
Only a tightness and a stealth instead.
The stiffened world turns hard upon its axis,
Laboring; but these yellow lamps relax us,
Here in the living-room at either end.
She by the south one, I by the north pretend
Forgetfulness of pavements; or remark
How very dead the sky is, and how dark—
In passing, with the air of two that pore
On things familiar, having been before.
It is our way of knowing what is near.
This is the time, this is the holy year
We planned for, casting every cable off.
That was a board-creak; that was the horse's cough;
That was no wind, we say; and looking down,
Smile at the wolf-dog, Sam, who dreams of brown
Clipped fields that he will lope in when he wakes.
He dreams, and draws his ankles up, and slakes
Imaginary thirsts at frozen pools.
He is the wolf-dog, he is the one that fools
New comers up the yard; for gentler beast
Prowled never to the pantry for a feast.
He is the boys' companion, who at dusk
Ran rings with them tonight, and worried the husk

Of daylight in his teeth, and stood his hair
Wind-upright. Now he sleeps unthinking there,
Companion of the boys, who long ago
Climbed the dark stairs to bed. So we below
Should come there too, we say; and say it again,
And laugh to hear the clock tick out the ten.
We are not sleepy; this is the holy year.
Let it tick on to midnight, and for cheer
Start coffee in the kitchen, while I spread
Bright jam upon the goodness of cut bread.

. . . We were awakened by a double shout:
"Get up, you lazy people, and look out!"
There was a weight of stillness on my eyes;
But in my ears innumerable sighs
Of snowflakes settling groundward past the glass.
I stood and stared, saying for jest "Alas!
My sight fails, I can see the merest dim
Milk-whiteness!" "We must bring it up to him!"
Cried one; and both were going, when I told them:
"Dress!" So now, as breakfast waits, behold them
Marching through a mist of falling specks.
They stop and raise their faces, and it flecks
Their foreheads till they laugh; then treading on,
Leave tracks across the swiftly thickening lawn.
I let them go this morning for the milk—
The car wheels turning softly in a silk
New coverlet as wide as eyes could see.
The chimney smoke was rising, round and free,
From every ridge of shingles: even there
Where Grandmother waved and pointed at the air.
The wolf-dog running with us need not pause,
Tasting the untamed whiteness; for his jaws
Dipped as he loped along, and fiercely entered
Now the far past wherein his mind was centered.
Back at the barn the Shetland ponies wheeled,
Biting each other's manes, their little field

Grown boundless by some fantasy, and fenceless.
They romped like shaggy dogs, and were as senseless,
Fluttering at the gate, as moths, and small.
They waited for the big one in the stall.
She whinnied as we came, and only stopped
When I rose up the ladder and hay dropped.
She will have finished breakfast in an hour.
So we, and through a sudden whirling shower
Shall bring her to the ponies. Then our talk
Will come once more to sleds, and up the walk
I shall again make promises; and keep them,
Thinking of flakes and how a wind can heap them.
This wind is gentle, and the grey sheet sways.
I am no prophet if it falls and stays.

. . . All yesterday it melted, and at night
Was nothing, and the prophecy was right.
But in a play-house corner stand the sleds,
Almost as high as the excited heads
Of two that will be on them when the slopes
Glisten once more. And so the boys have hopes
While I have present pleasure; for the ground
Grows musical wherever I am bound.
The mud was gone as quickly as the snow:
An afternoon of thaw, but then a low
Crisp sunset sound of shrinking, and the crack
Of coldness like a panther coming back.
Tonight the snowless evening and the moon
Kept my late feet contented with a tune
More ancient than the meadows, where the stones
Rise ever up: unburiable bones.
The bareness of the world was like a bell
My feet, accustomed, struck; and striking well,
Let the rung sound be mingled with the dry
Primeval winter moonlight flowing by.
Alone outdoors and late, the resonant lawn
Moved with me as I lagged, and moving on

103

Bore all my senses fieldward to those bones
Of permanence, the unalterable stones.
There is no such intensity of lasting
Anywhere out of meadows, where the fasting
Grasses worship something in December
Older than any moist root can remember;
Older than age, drier than any drouth;
Something not to be praised by word of mouth.
I did not praise them then, nor shall henceforth;
But shall remind me, so, what change is worth:
Timothy round a rock, and daisies hiding
Something that will be there again—abiding
Longer than hope and stronger than old despair;
Something not to be dated under the air.
I looked at stones; and faces looked at me:
Sidewise, always sidewise, past a tree
Or slanting down some corner, or obliquely
Squinting where the moon fell, and as weakly.
I saw them not but knew them: the tired faces
Of those who may not leave their acred places:
Those of a time long gone that never dies.
You know it by the darkness of their eyes,
And by the way they work to comprehend
Who lives here now beyond a century's end.
Who lives and does not labor, and makes light
Of the grim gods that once were day, were night;
That carved a cheek, bent breasts, and knotted hands.
Not one of them withdraws or understands.
Not one of them but looked at me; and I,
Intruder here, seemed helpless to reply.
Not by their older choosing are we here,
Not by their doom made free of gods and fear.
Was then the better time? I said; and thought
How excellently winter moonshine taught
The shapes of winter trees. That maple there,
How shadeless, how upflowing, and how fair!
Even without their leaves the elm-limbs drooped;

The alders leaned; and birches interlooped
Their lacy, blackened fingers past the pines.
The great dead chestnut where the loud crow dines
Writhed on, its mighty arms unskilled to fall.
The evergreens were solid over all,
And hickories and tulips, few of limb,
Held what they had straight out for time to trim.
Was then the better world, I wondered—daring
Suddenly now an answer from the staring
People of old days, the accusing faces.
But none of us, tree-watching on these places,
Ever will hear a sentence from the source.
Gone is their blood, and spent their bitter force;
They only live to chafe us down the wind
And leave us ever afterward thin-skinned:
Wondering on them, the only-good,
On whom these lighter feet too long intrude.

. . . We have had company of Friday nights.
We have looked out of windows till the lights
Of cars too long in coming dipped and streamed;
Then ended by the door as time had dreamed.
Two late ones from the city, blinking here
In the warm lamplight, with the kittens near—
These have been shown their room, the spare northeast one;
Have laughed and begged a bite: even the least one,
Even a crust to pay them for the ride.
Already coffee bubbled, fit to glide,
As quickly as cups were ready, from the spout.
Already there were cookies placed about;
And soon the supper entered that would keep us
Longer awake than wise, with talk to steep us
In every winter's moment we had missed.
So we unrolled our pleasures, till the list
Grew endless, and the meaning of it fled.
So, as the boys before us, up to bed.
For all of us a lazy breakfast waited,

With coffee and tobacco, brownly mated,
Warming the day to come. We tilted chairs,
Lit pipes, and fingered forks; till unawares
Time bore us half to noon; and looking out,
We argued what the weather was about.
Some said it would be overcast till night,
Settling themselves forever; but the right
Was mostly with the walkers and the curious.
First then the barn, where the black mare was furious,
Tossing as I excused our long delay.
No answer, but the eyes among the hay
Dived languorously and said I was forgiven.
The cutter by the car could not be driven.
I found it years ago and dragged it here
To a dry floor and braced it; but the clear
Curved figure will be never swift again.
Snow or no snow, it is for living men
Another last reminder of the old
Dim people who are dead. A crimson fold
Of lining flaps and braves the window frost.
But all the rest is poor and language-lost:
No bells to shake, no orders to be going
Down a long hill where only time is snowing—
Flake by flake forgotten, till the white
Far past of it is shadowy with night.
We took the road and turned, and crossed the bridge;
Then, needing not to beg the privilege,
Crossed neighbor Allyn's meadow to his row
Of sandknolls; then, as all the cattle go,
Between the roundest couple home to tea.
So Saturday, and night, when we agree
What games shall silence evening, and what talk
Shall bring the ghost whose breast is brittle chalk.
So Sunday, with a visit to the great
Grandfather pine that guards the burial gate.
Neglected there, the town's first graveyard lies
Where once the Hurlburt roadway took the rise,

Bringing a country mourner up to pray.
But year by year the woodchucks have their way,
And higher mounds are there than used to reckon
The small well-buried length of smith or deacon.
So all the week-end over, and the pair
Departed; and a blizzard in the air.

. . . That second snow fulfilled us while it lasted.
But now for two brown weeks the fields have fasted
Under a windless, under a lukewarm sun.
Christmas Eve and New Year's Day are done,
And here we stand expectant, straining dumbly
Toward a long stretch that will not lie so comely:
Three dark, inclement months before the spring.
Or such the hope; we want no softer thing,
No disappointment deepened day by day.
That second snow, dissolving, drained away
Too much of sudden glory, and too much
Of the towered god whose mantle we must touch.
There was no blizzard in it after all.
Only a thickening sky, so slow to fall
That Monday passed, and Tuesday. Then a hush;
Then a faint flick, as if a fox's brush
Had gained the woods in safety, and the hole;
Then steadily, steadily down the winter stole.
All afternoon it hissed among some clump
Of shrubbery, and deepened round the pump;
All afternoon, till time put out the light.
Then the black rustling through the soundless night:
Dark flake on flake colliding where no gaze
Of beast or person followed. Dim the ways
Of snow in great high darkness; strange the sound
Of whiteness come invisible to ground.
And yet the lamps awhile allowed the glance
Of a stray whirl of moth wings blown to dance,
Confused, beyond the four and twenty panes.
Here once we sat and watched the autumn rains

107

Stitching a wall of water. Now the snow—
A frailer fall, and gentler—came to sew
New raiment for the sun-accustomed sashes.
The upstairs window that a north wind lashes,
Beating the maple on it gust by gust,
Hung silent, like a picture; but it thrust
Pure light on brilliant branches, layered well
With silver that as slowly rose and fell,
No visible lawn beneath it, and no thing,
Round or above, save blackness in a ring:
A prone, suspended skeleton creeping hither,
All knuckle joints and bare bones twigged together.
Next morning then, with Christmas five days off,
What wonder if we called this well enough?
What wonder if the two boys prematurely
Counted upon continuance, and surely
Bragged of a snowy hill for him, the guest:
The expected boy, of all their friends the best,
Due now from deep Virginia on a night;
Their own, to play a week with out of sight?
So off they hurried, pulling the sleds behind them,
To cross the nearest meadow-stretch and find them
Somewhere a perfect slope that they could pack:
The runners for the hundredth time and back
Deep-sinking through the softness, with dragged feet
To finish a rough design and leave it neat.
I watched them for a little from the road,
Then called, and she came with me to the snowed
White forest edge, and over the wall inspected
The prints of birds; or how a deer directed
Leap after leap to gain his inland thicket.
A pine branch sagged to the earth, but I could flick it,
Filling my neck with flakes as up it reared,
Snow-loosened of its many-pointed beard.
Meanwhile the cry of coasters over the hill,
With moment interruptions, clear and still,
That said the feet were staggering up again.

108

We came, and Sam the wolf-dog joined them then
In a loud, urgent welcome, bark and word.
For he had crossed the field to make a third,
And close-pursued them, snapping at their feet
Now up the slope, now down; then off to meet
Plump Snappy, most companionable cat,
Who, plowing the snow alone, arrived and sat
Like something stone of Egypt, not for play.
He watched us, two by two, slide swift away,
Then turned his head, encouraging the weak one,
Snippy, the little sister, the grey meek one,
Who half from home had squatted in a track;
And wailed until we saved her, walking back.
That was the day, with four days still to come,
We prophesied long whiteness; hearing the hum
Of trees contracted slowly in no wind;
Or watching the clouds a clear sun dipped and thinned.
That was the night the low moon, all but waned,
Came to me once—upstarting at the strained
Hurt sound of something strangled in the woods—
Came to me at the window, over floods
Of waveless shining silence, and I said:
There is a month of coldness dead ahead.
But Thursday of a sudden thawed it all,
And Friday, like a silly thing of fall,
An innocent late-summer thing, declared
Calm days, with every melting meadow bared.
So when they blew their horn and gained the gate—
Those weary three Virginians—only a late
Cool breath of proper evening blew to greet them.
Sam leapt out ahead of us to meet them.
Then the old rejoicing, four and three;
With talk of the north till bedtime, and the tree
We all must bring tomorrow: a picked pine
To anchor in a room with block and twine.
We found it, best of several by a swamp,
And sawed and bore it hither amid the romp

Of boys and tumbling cats, that on warm haunches
Settled to watch us trim the bristling branches;
Looping the ends with silver-studded cord
And lo, with more than patience could afford
Of cranberries and popcorn needled through:
Now red, now white, now one and one, and two.
From every room, when darkness well was down,
Came packages of mystery, in brown
Creased paper if a boy or man were giver;
But if a lady, candle-light would quiver
On multicolored tissue, gold and green.
Then silence, with a glow behind the screen
To point our way to bed, the lamps unlighted.
Then dawn, and stairs acreak, and something sighted
Even beyond the door that we had closed;
Then breakfast, and the mysteries deposed.
No more the ache of waiting; shed the power
Preeminent of any future hour.
That was the height; the rest was going down,
With random walks, or driving into town,
Or sitting after sunfall over tea.
We tidied rooms and set the spangled tree
Midway the snowless lawn, and spiked it there—
Popcorn and berries on it, and a square
Of suet tied with string to tempt the flying
Birds. But there were kittens always spying,
Ready to pounce and punish; and at last
A brief wind laid it over like a mast.
The rest was milder pleasure, suiting well
Our seven tongues that had so much to tell.
We talked. And then the final day was come.
Farewell, you three! And if the end was dumb,
Remember this: there was no charm to say
As down the hill your fenders sloped away.
So Christmas Eve and New Year's Day are done;
And still the lukewarm, still the windless sun
Possesses what it watches: hidden here,

A barn and painted house, from which appear
Four little figures scanning a clear sky.
It doubtless will be clouded by and by,
And doubtless yield each one his small desire.
Now only tracks, minute upon the mire.

. . . O welcome night-wind, crazily arriving,
You had not warned us till we heard you striving,
Here and at every corner of the house—
Now a great beast and now a nibbling mouse—
Striving in every stature to undo us;
There was no rumor of your marching to us,
No swift annunciation; or eight hands
Loud, loud had hailed you, giving you our lands,
Ourselves, and all this valley to unsettle.
We only lay and heard you; heard the rattle
Of shutters, and caught the groan as you went on
Of nails from weather-boarding all but drawn.
We only lay, pulling the covers higher,
Until at dayrise, grouping about the fire,
We greeted a hundred frost-hills on the panes;
Looked through, and saw the still wind-worried lanes
Thrash heavily; and walking out a little,
Said the snapped, hanging branches were wind-spittle.
Nor was the blowing over; still at twelve
High limbs were double-curving, like a helve,
And through the day, beneath white clouds and round ones,
All was a sea, with us the happy drowned ones—
Drifting among the layers of thin cold,
Self-separated. Some, the slow and old,
Slid lazily, floating beyond a world;
But some were childish-violent, and curled
And slapped our willing foreheads as they raced.
Layer upon clear layer built a waste
Of space for minds to work in, high and low.
Then the loud night that bade the softness go,
With iron for morning ground, and every print

Of dog or man foot stamped as in a mint:
All metal, all eternal, if this cold,
High, many-shelving universe could hold.
It held; and laid a film across the pond;
Laid more, and laying others, brought the fond
Brown wolf-dog there to slide beside the boys—
Bewildered, but enchanted by the noise
Of brittle alder-sticks and clapping hands.
So now the ice in hourly thickened bands
Is pressing tight around us, pond and lawn.
One moment, and the mighty gale was gone,
Far-whistling. Then a silence, and the fall
To nothing. Then the crisp iron over all.

. . . Slap, slap, the sound of car chains going by,
With elsewhere only stillness, under dry
Fantastic heaps of white the wind renews.
It reached us evenly, as snowfalls use;
But there were days of fury when the air,
Whirled white as flour, was powdery everywhere;
Till now the finest grains, like desert sand,
Wait upon eddies they will not withstand.
The snow-plows on the highway come and go:
Not vainly, but a devil takes the snow
Some windy times, and then the car lanes fill
Along the leeward side of fence or hill.
The boys are in the snow house we had made
Before this blowing weather overlaid
The first wet fall with something crisp as salt.
Four walls we packed without a single fault
Between a pair of solid shutter forms.
A roof, an eastern door away from storms,
Two windows at the ends—a bread knife cut them,
Neatly, but there was then no way to shut them—
A piece of crate for cushion, and a bag:
This is their windy fortress that a flag
Flies every day in front of, and that Sam

Lies guarding, less the dragon than the lamb.
There was a man with anthracite for eyes,
And pennies for his buttons; but he lies,
Forgotten, uncreated, where he fell.
There was a castle wall beyond the well
With store of snowballs piled against a siege,
And apples for the starving, lord or liege;
But now it too is levelled, and delight
Dwells only in this hovel at the right.
Below the sheds and halfway to the wall
Stands a lean ice house, windowless and tall,
Whose ancient door hung open day by day
Till the last shining cake was stowed away.
When ice was fourteen inches teams were hitched;
Saws buzzed; and like a waterland bewitched
The silver floor divided, line and angle.
Then loaded trucks, with pairs of tongs to dangle,
Teasing the helpful boys until they tried—
Slipped, fell, and were convinced. And so inside
Sleep twice a hundred pieces of the pond,
Preserved against the dog days and beyond.

. . . These are the undistinguishable days.
This is the calm dead center of the maze
Whereinto we have wandered, and in time
Shall wander forth again, and slowly climb
A wall the other side of which is change.
Now everything is like, with nothing strange
To keep our hands aware of what they do.
This is the winter's heart, that must renew
Its steady, steady beating when an embered
Joy is all we have, and thoughts remembered.
Therefore do I listen while I may,
Monotony, to what your whispers say
Of systole, diastole, and the ribbed
Sweet rituals wherein our wills are cribbed.
Therefore shall I count the doings here

Of one full day, and represent the year.
We rise at eight, but I an hour before
Have put the pipeless furnace in a roar;
Descending slow in slippers, robe, and socks
To where, as in some Southern ship that rocks,
Dry cargo-wood inhabits all the hold.
Our destination only the days unfold:
Tier on tier down-sloping to warm weather.
But many a hundred chunks lie yet together,
Snug in their odorous rows. So I inspire
Last evening's spent and barely-breathing fire;
Pull off my gloves; ascend the under-stair;
And smoke a chilly moment in a chair.
Then up again. But they are coming down,
Each head of hair in tangles at the crown;
And suddenly we smell a breakfast waiting:
Bacon and yellow eggs; or, alternating,
Buckwheat cakes with butter for anointing;
Or third-day porridge, grey and disappointing.
Prepared with steaming water and the comb,
We gather about the range—the morning home
Of kittens, too, and Sam the wolf-dog, stretched
Full length behind it while our plates are fetched.
The Irish hands that laid our dining table
Were up in early darkness, whence a fable
Of ghost or saint, night-walking, has its rise.
We listen, masked amusement in our eyes,
And finishing our fare, proceed to measure
Whether this day is planned for work or pleasure.
There is a woodshed faucet where I fill
Two water pails, and through the winter-still
Bound morning beat the music that she loves:
The restless mare whose foretop, smoothed with gloves,
Will hang with hay-stalk in it while she drinks.
She knows my coming footfall, and she thinks
To speed her slave's arrival with a neigh.
I am too proud to hurry; yet the hay

Seems due her, and the water, none the less.
So up to where last summer's grasses press
Their rustling weight on weight; and casting down
High pitchforkfuls, I stuff the slats with brown,
Stiff breakfast which the clever ponies hear.
I listen to their trotting, small and clear,
Round the curved path to where the western door
Stands open night or day, whatever roar
Of winds or pelt of snow drives ruthless in.
They are from northern islands where the din
Of winter never daunts them. Unconfined,
They wander about the paddock till the mined
Mute hayfall wakes their wisdom. Then they race,
Two blown and hairy creatures, into place.
I leave them there, slow-nibbling, eyes astare,
And go to prod the motor in his lair:
Four thousand pounds inert, and chilled so well
Some mornings I can barely solve the spell.
I have been baffled when a weakened spark
Has failed to fire the monster, and the dark
Webbed shadows of the room have missed his roar.
I have discovered drifts against the door,
And shovelled; I have watched a winter's rains
Turn ice, and been in misery with chains:
Now on, now off, now broken and now mended;
I have as often wished a year were ended.
But now the long thing moves, and backing out
Brings Sam, who disobeys my daily shout
And lopes to where the open meadows tempt him.
I could be angry, but his ears exempt him,
Waiting erect and friendly when I come.
My way was longer round; but now the strum
Of pistons will be answered by his feet,
That guide me to the milkhouse, dark, unneat,
Where the day's pail awaits me. Then the mile
Retravelled, past the cemetery stile
That leads among the six-foot frozen mounds.

115

There have been mornings when I heard the sounds
Of pick and frozen shovel at a grave;
But mostly snow and timeless silence—save
That cries of farmer children ring in the wood,
Where the white Hollow school long years has stood.
Some of them wave and call my distant name;
Then bells, and marching in to serious game;
While I at my own corner mount the hill
Past Bailey's house, and hers, where now a still
White shaft of smoke that bends above the brook
Declares Grandmother up. A pause; a look;
Good morning to her, cheerful at the door;
Then on to where the barn receives the roar
Of cylinders again until they cease.
Now to the restless mare, whom I release—
High stepping, in perpetual surprise—
To where the ponies shake their shaggy eyes.
All day will they be three beyond a gate,
Ground-musical, and free of their estate;
While we that own them, in and out of doors
Must labor at our self-appointed chores.
Now the grey tool house where the chisels hang,
And hammers lie, and saws with sharpened fang
Rest nightly on their nails, invites my skill.
I am no maker, but a floor can fill
With shavings from the least instructed plane.
Or there is wood to split, come snow or rain,
When the black stove grows hungry, and the dry
Deep kitchen box demands a fresh supply.
Ten times the barrow, loaded, piles its pieces
High at the woodshed end, till all the creases
Fold a fair week of darkness, and the dented
Chopping block is with cold wounds contented.
There is one root the garden still can give.
Under the snow, under the stubble, live
Our golden parsnips, planted and forgotten.
Nothing of them is altered or frost-rotten.

116

The blunt pick thuds in the ground, and up they heave:
A miracle for winter to believe.
I bring them in for dinner on this day;
And while the kettle, boiling their ice away,
Fills half a room with steam I take the road
Once more, to curiosity's abode:
That box where now the mail man will have been.
Arriving slow, I thrust my fingers in;
Draw letters forth, a bundle, or a card;
And out of time abstracted pace the hard
White ground again to where three wait for me.
No ancient courier with a king's decree
Rode ever up a hill and brought so much
As these chilled messages the mind can touch,
Restoring warmth, reviving every word
That yesterday with its own motion stirred.
Meanwhile the boys have had their little school:
Two pupils and a mother, mild of rule,
Who after beds were made and dinner planned,
Called them to where the home-built easels stand
And where the primer waits that one can read.
The younger mind admits a younger need:
Long blocks that tilt together till a boat
Sits sailing; or a castle with a moat;
Or dungeon towers to keep a kitten in—
The almond-eyed four-footed Saracen.
To painting then: tongues out and foreheads glowing,
With bannerets of bright vermilion flowing
Over and up and down; or blues, or blacks,
Full to the very corners past the tacks.
One thing remains: a paragraph to trace
On paper from the blackboard's printed face.
The boy leans long upon the table leaf,
Procrastinating; for the task was brief,
And both of them had still an hour to play.
But there he leans, unwilling, till the day
Brings twelve; and half-past twelve; and brings the white

Sealed letters that are now the noon's delight.
So dinner, and a nap for everyone
Where neither snow may enter nor the sun.
So then the afternoon, that still is short—
Midwinter lags behind the sky's report:
Each day a little longer, but the dark
Comes down before a coaster may remark.
While there is light we seek the genial store,
Off by the covered bridge; or wanting more,
Ride over two east ranges to the town
Of brass that bore the body of John Brown.
Here pavements like a puzzle run and spread;
And here a shop front, gold by gaudy red,
Demands immediate entrance; for a dime
Buys anything, land-born or maritime:
A ball, a wooden car, a masted boat,
An outboard motor that will never float;
A magnet's curve, completed by a bar;
A leaden blue policeman with his star.
So home across the ranges, past the edge
Of evening, till the last high-drifted hedge
Declares the clear necessity of chains.
So out to frosty spokes and windy lanes
Where the snow, blowing, whips the wrist and scatters;
Then upward, while a broken chain-link clatters;
Upward into the barn, the engine dying
Soundless; but the ponies are replying,
Huddled before the big one at the gate.
Scarcely we listen, for we estimate
Two hours this side of supper. Time for tea.
We light the lamps and sip the mystery,
Cup after shadowy cup, with toasted cheese.
There are no country moments like to these;
When afternoon is night, and night belongs
Like a dark heirloom of descended songs
To four that sit in solitude and hear them
Through the fond nothingness that nestles near them.

From the warm circle of the shaded lamp
At last I walk to where the ponies stamp
And the tall guardian mare is loud with thirst.
A boy with lighted lantern sheds the first
Long pair of scantling shadows on the snow;
While I, the water-bearer, dimly go
Through the great backward crescent drawn behind us.
There have been evenings when she would not mind us—
The lurking mare, complacent down the meadow.
But now a clear low whistle cleaves her shadow,
Precipitately arriving. So we lead her,
Plunging, past the corner post; and heed her
Sighing as she nuzzles in the pail.
The lantern from a high and rusty nail
Swings gently, casting circles on the hay.
The kittens somewhere, noiselessly at play,
Keep watch of us, and scan the waiting door.
They love a barn, but love the kitchen more;
And lessons still may linger in each mind
Of the long milkless night they sat confined.
We leave the ponies munching in their room
And blow our lantern black, resolved to come
By starlight home—Orion and the Bears
Low-shining; but aloft upon the stairs,
Bright Castor holding Pollux by the hand.
Now endless evening, like a painted band,
Starts moving, moving past us, and we seize,
Soft-reaching, all that momently can please.
There is an hour for singing, when the book
Lies open, and a rolling eye may look
For prompting at the words of Nelly Gray,
Darby and Joan, The Miller, Old Dog Tray;
Malbrouck that went to war, and Hoosen Johnny;
Or over the ocean, over the sea my bonnie.
The dominoes that once amused us well
Lie in their box and envy bagatelle,
Whose twenty balls, thrust up the tilted board,

Pause and return—click, click—a thousand scored!
With game or song the clock goes round to eight:
Past time for two to sleep, whose laggard gait
We must not hope to hurry up the landing.
Each elder then knows where a book is standing,
Tall on the crowded table; and begins
What may go on until the darkness thins:
Page after page upturned against the light.
For so it was, on such a nipping night,
That Holmes, or Doctor Thorndyke, heard the bell
And raced with lawless death to Camberwell;
Or Watson, in an alley with his master,
Felt the steel fingers as a crutch came faster:
Tapping, tapping, tapping, till the court
Blazed with a sudden pistol's blind report.
This is the hour, and this the placeless room
For smooth concocted tales of lust and doom;
This the remote, the sanctuary year
When the safe soul must fabricate a fear.
Many a milder evening passes, too,
With Royal Casino, Rummy, and a few
Swift-changing hands of High-Low-Jack-and-the-Game.
But then three weeks ago the chess men came;
Since when, no night so busy that it misses
The march of angry Queens, whose scalloped tresses,
Stiffly erected, fly to guard a King.
We are two novices, and rashly fling
Pawns, bishops, knights, and rooks into the fray;
Yet time and blood have taught us wiser play.
There was a gift at Christmas time of Tarot—
Untaught, but we can shuffle them and harrow
A loreless mind with him, the Hanging Man;
So all those numbered mysteries that plan
What future folds the player, and what past
Is carved upon the great Tower overcast,
So every wand and pentacle and sword
Lies curious, unfathomed, on the board.

We have been known, as never back in town,
To idle till the clock weights settled down,
And till the sound of ticking ceased unheard.
We have rejoiced some evenings at the word
Of neighbors driving over; when the names,
Smith, Prentice, Landeck, interrupted games
With something else of equal clear delight.
For there was talking now into the night,
With news of health, and trips away from home,
And how the kitchen beer went all to foam.
Gossip of Hautboy, Dibble, and Great Hill,
Gossip and jest and argument, until:
Goodbye, Smith, Landeck, Prentice; come again;
Goodnight. And so a day is ended then.
Each four and twenty hours, until we rise,
Go thus. And thus the holy winter flies.

. . . February flies, with little summers
Hidden in its beard: unlicensed mummers
Performing April antics for a day.
The sun from the horizon swings away;
The sky melts upward, and a windless hand
Scatters the seeds of warmth along the land.
They will not grow, for ice is underneath,
And every creature tastes it. But a wreath
Lies thrown by playful chance upon the smiling
Meadows that a season is beguiling.
Today was so, but we were not deceived;
Though what the wolf-dog and the cats believed
There is no art of knowing. They pursued
Our every venturing step and found it good:
Down the crisp meadows to the aspen grove;
Over the highway, where a salesman drove
Dry wheels on dry macadam; then the neck
Of Harrison's pasture to the Hollenbeck.
We stood, the seven walkers, on a stone
And watched the river, waveless and alone,

121

Go slipping, slipping under, gravelly clear.
Snippy, a mile from nowhere, crouched to peer
At nothing in the sand; then bolder sat.
Three weeks, we said, and she would be a cat
With fearsome crying kittens of her own.
Ten months with us, no more, and nearly grown!
So Snappy, arriving plump and solemn there,
Good-natured sat, the guardian of the pair.
There was a barn foundation to explore,
Ancient of fields beyond. The rotting floor
Forewarned us, and we did not enter in;
But strolled, and where tall timothy had been
Lay half an hour on stubble under the sun;
While Sam, excited by a scent, must run
Low-whining up the fences; till a voice
Recalled him, and we made the hapless choice
Of eastward marshy meadows for return.
The hummocks mired us, but a cat could learn
The causeway's secret truth; and what we lost
Came back to us at home with tea and toast.

. . . Since yesterday a hundred years have gone.
The fore-and-after season, living on,
Rouses itself and finds its bitter breath.
This wind holds on to winter as to death.
There is no end, we say, and sauntering out,
Northwestward lean till we are whirled about,
Mute neck and shoulders stinging with the snow;
Or on this Sunday morning think to go,
Foot-heavy, where the giant maples spread
Their smooth enormous branches, long since dead.
Still in this waste of wind they do not fall;
But stiffen, like old serpents sent to crawl
On dense, on layered air; until the charm
Is lifted, and descending out of harm,
They lie leaf-covered, rigid in decay
Until the last small worm has turned away.

Here in the woodland clearings they patrol,
The wind drives steadily upon its goal.
But yonder where the hemlocks lace together
There is a sudden calm, a death of weather.
The shade is black, as once in late July
When here we walked escaping yellow sky.
The shade is black and even, and the snow
Comes filtered to the open cones below:
Slowly, slowly, slowly; strange the hush,
Here in this darkened desert of the thrush.
No hermits now; yet bands of chickadees
Tread fearless of us, chirping in the trees.
The ferns of June are withered on the rocks
Midway the icy stream that bends and locks
This needled promontory where we stand.
Oh, happy time! when nothing makes demand;
When all the earth, surrendering its strength,
Regains a taller potency at length;
Sleeps on in purest might of nothing done
Till summer heaves on high the exacting sun.

. . . Ice everywhere, a comic inch of it.
Four veteran walks of a sudden sit
Wide-sprawling; but the cat that went so sure
Waits in the shed, distrustful and demure.
On this one day the dark mare, left inside,
Stands munching while the startled ponies slide—
Their path a river, and the river frozen—
Until a barn's captivity is chosen.
Ice everywhere; but over Goshen way
Ice on the mountains: murderous display.
Down the wild road to where the lanes were dry
We crept on crunching chains; then letting fly,
Passed houses till we gained the known plateau.
Yet now no more familiar, for the glow
Of crystals, like an ocean, blinded eyes
Untutored in the way a forest dies:

123

Slim birch and maple, sycamore and larch
Bent low before the mysteries of March;
Bent glassy-low, or splintered to a heap
Of glittering fragments that the sunrays sweep—
The sun, ironic, heartless, come to glance
At death and beauty shivering in a dance.

. . . I have been absent through the ending days
Of March beyond the mountains, where the ways
Of all the world drive onward as before.
I have been absent from the windy door;
Have gazed on travel-mornings out of flying
Windows at a distant winter dying.
But not our own, I said; and still believe
There will be news at home of its reprieve.
Nothing of that can change. And yet the doubt
Creeps into me as I look homesick out
On farms that are reminding me of one
Not distant now, beneath the selfsame sun.
A further valley, and a further range,
And I shall see if anything be strange.
Another dozen stations, and the three
I have been absent from will run to me,
And tell me if they know. At which the tears
Come premature, and stillness stops my ears.

. . . That very Wednesday, going to Great Hill,
The ruts all melted and the road was swill;
The hub caps foundered, and a number plate
Rose out of mire to recognize the spate.
All underground was overflowing for us,
Helpless until a wakened workhorse bore us,
Backward, absurd, to dry macadam land.
So April, with a wild unwelcome hand,
Showers proof upon us here of winter gone.
Our visitors on Friday night are wan:
Town-tired, and do not know it till we tell them.

The stripling cats, until we thought to bell them,
Havocked among the juncos, dropped to feed
On what the lawn still held of husk or seed.
A hundred misty bellies and blue backs
Move unmolested northward, leaving tracks
On certain darker mornings when a flurry
Satins the ground—not deep enough to worry
Those busy bills that, helped by hopping feet,
Find out the fruit of barberries and eat.
The apple barrels, picked over, have revealed
How many Baldwins never will be peeled;
The fungus spreads, and spots of deathly white
Show where the teeth of time have been to bite.
The wolf-dog has abandoned us by day;
He is in love across the scented way.
Nothing can keep him when the wind arrives;
He chews his chain, or alternately strives
Till the round collar slips and he goes running.
The ponies' noses have as old a cunning.
There is no forage yet, but they can smell
Green tropics creeping hither, and will fell
Each night a length of fence for dumb escape;
Then stumble back at breakfast time and gape,
Wit-withered, at the breach they cannot solve.
So, as the weeks implacably revolve
Of early, windy April, come the sprays
Of wood viburnum in the pathless ways
Where rocks and bent witch-hazel boughs declare
Once more their truce, awakening to air.
So, as the world turned sunward, Snippy died.
In the dim middle of a night she cried,
Desperate upon the steps; and lived a day.
But we have laid her slenderly away.
Her young within her she was not to bear;
So Snappy sits disconsolately there,
Under the branching crabtree; faced about,
Fixed on the clods, as if to stare her out.

. . . Spring is not yet; though how can this be long:
This crush of silence, this untimely-wrong,
Wide, cruel weight of whiteness, wing-descended
Even as we declared the winter ended?
Last night it happened. Everything, unwarned,
Suffered the soundless swoop of him the Horned,
The Universal Owl, whose ruthless plumes
Settled like death, distributing our dooms;
No feather heavy, but the sum of all
Seemed ultimate: earth's sepulchre and pall.
Not a flake settled on the flimsiest twig
But stayed; until this morning all were big
With monstrous moveless worms, that in the sun
Drip swiftly; but the evil has been done.
How fair it was last evening, when our lamp
Shone out on fleecy lilacs; yet the damp,
The clammy hand of this last dying snow—
How terrible to touch, and inly know:
This is the breaking end. So now at noon,
Divided, we behold the orchard strewn
With murdered buds and down-demolished branches.
So, by the graveyard, death upon its haunches
Sits in the form of great-grandfather-pine's
Chiefest of giant limbs, whose blackened lines
Trace there a new design of death across
Bare stones for whom no novelty of loss,
No morning news of woe can tell them more
Than that another winter shuts the door.
Divided thus—admiring, yet appalled—
We watch the season, poor, unfuneralled,
Pass with no mourners on; and recognize
What most we loved here impotent to rise.
If any sight could soften us to spring,
It is this melted, this emaciate thing.

. . . So April's plumefall was the last one, leaving
Nothing behind save midmonth warmth, and heaving

126

Roots, rain-drenched on many a sodden day.
Now even the rain is gone, that kept us grey;
Even the rain, preserving darkness too.
After the flood dry weather, hot and blue,
Washed every stain of winter off, and brightly
Gave us this world, so changeable and sightly:
Grass upon the mountains; smokeless-green
May fire that will not languish till the lean,
Brown, bitten earth, monotonous with stone,
Hides under hotness, leafy and alone;
Shade everywhere—as here beneath the crab,
Where Snippy lies, and rumors of Queen Mab
Bring bees to set the blossoms in a roar
While marvelling children pace the petalled floor;
Shade then for her, the borrowed Tabby, lying
With three new kittens, curious and crying:
The summer's offspring, not to be confused
With those somehow more brave that March misused.
Now the sleek mare is shod again, and trots
Each day beneath her mistress, over lots
Green-rising, or along a sandy road:
Each of them glad, the bearer and the load;
But I that walk to meet them down the lawn
Remember lazy mornings lost and gone:
Remember the cold, remember the lantern, hanging
There by her nose at night, and blizzards banging
Somewhere a shabby door; and my decision
Goes to the old, the February vision.
How old it is now, only a rake and spade;
Only a wolf-dog, panting in the shade;
Only a coatless, an oblivious pair
Of boys for whom all days to come are fair;
Only her warm hand, patting down the seed
Where sunlight lingers and the frost is freed;
Only the hay-land, live again with snakes;
Only these things can say what memory aches—

127

Oh, vainly—to recapture; only such
Can tell of the holy time our blood will touch—
Oh, never again, and never; only June,
That sings of something over deathly soon.
Already the mind's forgetfulness has blended
Music with music; and the months are ended.

THE EYES
(1935)

The Eyes

Turn where he would that autumn, when the time
Was evening, and there was no wind at all;
Turn where he would he saw them, and he said:
"I am grown old, it is my ending fall;
These are my visitation." Then he smiled.
"They do not see that I am reconciled."

As lightly then as this he bore the eyes
That out of every evening stared at him.
Turn where he would they found him; past the door,
Past trees and down the lawn, or through the dim
Road light that bound him in, a noiseless river.
So lightly could he look, so little shiver.

So little did he fear them at the start,
He missed how much the person in them changed.
It never was the same tall body there,
Nor the same hair, so carefully arranged:
So perfect and so parted, with a white
Down-line that was indelible by night.

It seemed a woman's hair, and then a man's;
But always it was drawn upon with fire:
Cold fire; and cold the eyes, whatever bones

Held the spare flesh as on a frame of wire—
Dangled, inconstant; but the staring three,
The eyes and that one line, would always be.

Would always be, he said. It was October,
And the last leaf had settled to the lawn.
So the last night was there that he would turn,
Expecting them in silence to have gone.
Would always be. He said it, half aloud,
And trembled; for the rigid one had bowed.

Only an instant, but it seemed enough:
The eyes gone swiftly out, the line erect.
Then the head vanished, and the shoulders flowed
Like a mist backward, till the dusk was specked
With lingerings of terror. So they faded;
And there he stood, knowing himself invaded.

Turn where he would the face must follow now;
Sleep as he might, his lids come cool together,
Something more cold than peace would enter, slowly,
Like a mist inward, till the mind's calm weather
Ceased, and a shouldered figure gathered form
Out of pressed distance and the soundless storm.

Nor would the eyes that watched him, and the hair—
Unblown, for all was windless there and wild,
Unblinking, for there was no rain to fall
Though the fog drifted and the sky was piled—
Nor would the triple watcher then unfold
Merely the tale of time and growing old.

Something more terrible, for him alone,
Something without a name until he said it.
Yet so far he was tongueless—asking now
What old forgotten guilt had lain and bred it.

Ruthless on the couch of what lost deed.
What wound, that so long afterward could bleed.

What evil? But he ever had been blameless;
He had been praised too sweetly not to know.
There was no saint more mannerly of conscience;
He had stopped short and let the others go:
Stumbling into errors he could see
Too clearly not to shun them. He was free,

And knew it—could remember, could remember
Multitudes of gentlenesses done:
Angers turned away until they withered,
Challenges unpampered, and the one
Deep lust that is the darkener of eyes—
Oh, love had been the better thing, and wise!

With this for past he could outstare the present.
Whatever face it was, he would come smiling,
Tomorrow, after sunset, and implore it
Fiercely to speak. He would himself—beguiling,
With memory at his back—demand the charge;
Then, listening, explain; and be at large.

He was not waited for. The room he lay in—
Stiffened there, with lids too dry to close—
Tilted at some moment after midnight,
Standing him halfway up; so he arose;
Took step; and like a walker in his sleep
Found the whole firmament with eyes acreep.

They moved as if at random, round and round,
And slowly, till he tried to look away;
When, suddenly assembling, they transfixed him
With a cold, single stare, that he must stay
Forever now beneath; as if his life
Lay victim to some never falling knife.

"It will not fall," he said, "it will not fall.
This face will never utter what it knows.
The words I have awaited will deny me
Even a malediction at the close.
The final and the sacrificial jest
Is silence and those eyes along the west.

"Two eyes, and only two, with parted hair
On high to make their mockery more sleek;
More sure my cold confusion, lest I breed
Some courage from that gaze, and stand and speak.
If now I should address that shining sneer,
It will not hear," he said; "it will not hear.

"This mind will never open to my words.
I was convicted easily and well.
Too late for pleading now." And yet he started;
And the black sky became a listening shell,
Contracted in an instant to the size
Of a thin voice beseeching. "Awful eyes—

"More awful that you never yet have closed,
More terrible than any sightless end—
Let down your weight of malice, slowly, swiftly;
Make it in thunder, make it in ice descend,
Make it in mist befoul me, cry me lost;
Spend, spend yourself, although I be the cost!

"I will go under gladly, so I know
One moment of my enemy's close breath.
I can be parted happily from night—
This night—if I but catch the look of death.
Be hideous and torture me, be slow;
Only begin, and let the levers go.

"What engine are you, stealthily devised?
What hand is there, what purpose past the dark?

134

I beg an instant's vision of the power
So hidden that a world may not remark
How strangely I am visited, how long
I linger in suspension for no wrong.

"No wrong unless you name it, for I say
That I have loathed the bright way and the cruel.
I have seen bodies burning, but the match
Never was mine, and never was I the fuel.
Never have I been thievish after pleasure.
I have kept home, I have respected measure.

"I have not been that plunderer of joy
Who drinks our brother's blood and creeps away;
Letting it dry within him till the rust,
Like a fine crafty poison, spreads decay:
At first a potent hatred, but grey time
Enfeebles it and whitens it to lime.

"I have been bravely diffident, like love;
I have been lawful, keeping our sister's peace.
No lamb has ever huddled to its mother,
Fearing my steps; inviolate the fleece.
Lust ages, but love steadily is younger;
I have been patient, I have not hurried hunger.

"I have not sped the day, oh, terrible eyes.
Nor shall I now boast longer. I have ended.
Nor was it boasting, Gazer; it was truth,
With pride and with a little anger blended.
If you have heard me, even the anger goes.
I was exhausted, waiting." He arose,

Still like a walking sleeper, and still waiting;
But no word came for answer from the eyes.
Only they glittered lazily, and gathered
Fragments of mist, gathered them magnet wise,

And wreathed them into smiles, and slowly slept;
While in his weak astonishment he wept.

They would not even trouble to undo him.
Time was long, with evenings still to come.
He looked again; they dozed and were complacent.
He tried to call again, but he was dumb.
It was no world for words, his feet were saying,
Leading him in at last; nor one for praying.

"I will outmock them then," he lay and whispered.
"Tomorrow must I seem indifferent too.
Tomorrow when they waken they must find me
Difficult, unreachable, and new.
I shall not even wonder if they still
Keep station there, wishing me endless ill."

But never has there been the strength in man
To move all heaven, putting it out of thought.
And so he must remember and look upward—
At nothingness all day; but evening brought
Dead stillness like a cannon at his heart:
The stillness of a battle timed to start.

Strain as he would to flee it, when the hour
Came suddenly with trumpets, he was waiting.
He looked, and they were there, and they were ready.
The toying time was over, and the baiting.
At last they were full weaponed, shaft and pike.
They were too cold and close now not to strike.

It seemed a woman's face and then a man's,
Swift-altering, swift-clearing; but the eyes
Changed never; they were fixed upon his trembling;
They stared beyond all pity and despise;
They waited without feeling, like the hands
Of judges when the nameless prisoner stands.

They waited, and he waited; then a voice
Broke heavily through stillness like a wave;
Far off, but heaving inland, and pursued
Uncountably by others, till the brave
High shore of his new courage shook and crumbled;
Then he was ready, then for all time was humbled.

"You will not be destroyed," he heard them saying;
Thickly rolled the waters, deep the waves;
"Nor comforted"—oh, hoarsely came their laughter;
"The final word is not the word that saves.
It is the merest verity, and men
Never may lose the sound of it again.

"This night will bring the end of us—the eyes—
And soon the hair you hated will be clouds
Parted with summer lightning; so our words,
Remembered, will resume their ancient shrouds,
Deep in the pit of time." But now they reared—
Armed waves of unrelenting war—and speared.

"We are the host of persons you denied.
We are the men and women you have slain.
Escaping after death, we wandered hither—
Home—and shall remain; and shall remain.
There is no such eternity for you.
The whole of you must perish as it grew:

"Quietly and palely, out of hearing,
With every dreadful gentleness confessed;
Nothing into nothing will go swiftly,
Passing us then whom you have not possessed.
We shall not know the moment, or inquire;
Forgetting you forever by this fire.

"The death of you is nothing, for you never
In all of time were implement to anguish.

137

We waited for the terror and the iron;
You softened them to love and let us languish.
Love? But it was feebleness and fear.
Pity? It was judgment and a sneer.

"We should have been invaded, as the sun
Drops suddenly, a serpent, into shade.
We needed to be threatened, as the knife
Flies, and there is blood along the blade.
There should have been an ambush and a foe,
With after-wounds, remembering that woe.

"There should have come against us in the dark
Hard hands, with sharp desire upon a cheek.
The eagle does no honor to the lamb
By kindness and the folding of his beak.
Our food was never danger: not a taste
Of fury, not a tempest hot with haste.

"These, these you must refuse us like a god.
You condescended to us, and we died:
Witnesses that you had been the savior:
Meek, meek! but swollen inwardly with pride.
Safe, safe—it was not worth the dying for.
We should have perished otherwise, by war.

"Or should, surviving battles all the way,
Have ripened to the center, and been warmed
By love that is the after-core of pain,
By pity that wounded wisdom has informed.
We should have lived or died—for it is one—
Full in the wind, full in the burning sun.

"For too much shadow, pale one, and excess
Of caring, we condemn you now to know:
The end of you, the all of you, is nothing.
Cold, cold the coming daylight and the snow.

Cold, cold! And so farewell, uncruel-kind,
Unborn, existless monster of the mind!"

When he could lift his face the sky was empty:
Soundless, like eternity, and white.
Dead white the falling dome; but where the ground was,
Greyness, as of ashes fresh and light.
But round his feet a darkness; and no day
Ever would burn the least of it away.

Tomorrow, and then always, it was round him,
A field of perfect darkness that he paced.
Not stumbling, for that wilderness is stoneless,
And over it hangs still the whitened waste.
No dawn or evening now beyond his eyes.
No alteration ever till he dies.

THE MAYFIELD DEER

(1941, 1959)

NOTE

The preface to the first edition (1941) said in part:

"For the incident from which *The Mayfield Deer* takes its start I am indebted to two or three pages of an Illinois county history which I came upon several years ago in my brother Frank's office at Tuscola.

"The particulars were these, as remembered by a doctor who in his youth had been present at the scene. In 1841 an old hunter, straying in search of a doe he had lost, was asked by certain settlers whether she might not have been shot; and answered that she wore a red flannel neckband and a brass bell to show that she was tame, adding in anger that if anybody had shot her he would 'put a bullet through him if it was seven years afterwards.' He kept a turkey bone in his belt to call her by if she still lived. But the settlers feared only for the safety of a neighbor boy who to their knowledge had recently brought in the carcass of a deer with a red band and a bell about its neck, and who even now had these tokens hidden in his house.

"There the narrative stopped, for the old man did not return and the boy was never exposed. But *The Mayfield Deer* goes on, after a beginning which borrows these details and several more, including the anachronism of the stranger's eighteenth-century hunting clothes. That is to say, the story as I found it was even more interesting for the action it suggested than for the situation it provided.

"But I was still not done with my source, which in the summer of 1940 revealed itself to be not so much history, perhaps, as legend. For so I interpret the circumstance that, sitting on Armin Landeck's lawn in Cornwall, Connecticut, a few days after I had finished the poem, I became aware that his grandfather, Mr. Charles Maulick, was telling me the story of the old hunter and his deer, of the red band and the bell, in the full belief that it had happened within his hearing when he was a boy on the Wisconsin frontier. I do not say I doubt that it happened then and there. But if it did, could it have happened at about the same time in Illinois? Or did it ever happen save as legends happen, everywhere and necessarily? It is a fine question, the very existence of which, far from weakening my faith in the tale, doubles it at least. I now assume that my debt is not to an incident but to an arch-incident, not to a single leaf of history but to a bound volume which many imaginations have inscribed."

In this edition *The Mayfield Deer* has undergone many minor alterations and has been shortened by a third, largely through the elimination of some celestial machinery for which I could no longer discover any function.

M.V.D.

1959

The Mayfield Deer

I

Old Richman took his turkey bone and blew
Three piping notes. "Hi, Nelly!" But no deer
Came ambling. Not a hair of his lost doe.
Somewhere, his eyes believed, she nibbled oak buds:
Jack oak, and cold; burr oak, November's breakfast.
Not here, though. So he angled to the bluffs
And let the river guide him where it moved,
More slow than his own moccasins, more brown
Than his blown walnut fringes, into Mayfield.

Five cabins there: one where the ox trails crossed,
And four that scattered partway into prairie.
Four for the sky's directions, but a fifth one
Centered in simplest man, with goods to serve him:
Coffee and wagon tires, barrels, whiskey, combs,
Salt, muslin, sugar, sickles, and axle grease.
Old Richman stooped and peered; but when the echo
Of his thin voice was all that moved in the store,
Vacant of men this morning, he slipped on
To where smoke rose the highest: west and south
To the last cabin. There they were. And there,
By an outdoor fire of oak logs, children rubbed
Red hands, and when they saw him stared astounded.

There was no man like him in Mayfield: none
Drifted as he was, pure, from antique time.
Long rifle; knitted cap, green, white, and red,
With a tassel; powder horn; clean walnut clothes,
Leggins, and pouch, and knife, and tomahawk:
They stared at him, the tall one, while he stood,
Himself a starer, counting their hands and eyes.
But most his speaking hushed them; for the sale
Of settlers' gear was languishing, and men
Strolled toward him past the fire, and he said suddenly:
"Hello. I'm here from fifteen miles up Ambraw,
Looking for my lost deer. A little doe,
Tame as a wren. You'd know if you had spied her."
The sentences flowed softly, from so far,
So strange a source.
                              Seth Golliday the younger,
More than a child and yet unknown for man,
Measured him through the smoke and said: He is steel,
Blue steel, and angry strong; he came up slowly,
And hung there like an old brown hunting picture,
Quiet, as in a dream; but even then
I saw the straightness in him, and the stiffness,
The ramrod wrapped away. And the still eyes;
And the lean throat, that purrs. He is a stranger,
Someone almost to fear; yet he brings with him
News of the world that never is to stop,
Never to be run down. Except for strangers,
Who but could say the spring had lost its curl?
Seth glanced a moment sideways at his father,
Slouching among the settlers. Did he know
This huntsman? Or did any of them guess
How, godlike, he had spread all space between them?
The Buells today were auctioning their trumpery,
Lugged from Ohio two poor years ago.
Tomorrow they would crawl and some day cross
The river, and some other day descend
On acres in Missouri which in time

Would hold a house like this one, blown and empty.
The wanderer before them was not homeless:
Strange, but he more belonged here than most men;
More, it might be, than Nancy. Seth looked slyly,
Leftward across the fire, to where she listened,
The flushes beneath her eyes not meant for him.
For an old man, a stranger. Seth could see it:
Nancy had felt his own eyes and refused them.
Nancy was staring too. Not like his brothers,
David and Ben behind her, the two huskies:
Not doubtfully, half sneering. She believed
Something too much, he said. And now his ears
Opened to take the talk of elders in.
Thus far he had not listened. His old failing:
All eyes and understanding, without sound.
His vanity, almost: this feeling out
The fair deep cold in strangers; lusterless
Himself, yet first to love another's light.

"John Richman, ain't you?" Mr. Buell stepped forward.
"Heard of you; but never I thought to see
That hunter in the flesh. We're selling out;
Making tracks tomorrow for the Purchase.
Been there?" But when Old Richman only nodded:
"What's this you're after? Deer meat? Not much of it.
Mayfield's lived on deer meat for six winters."
"No." The voice was leveller still. "A live one.
And tame, as you'd have seen by what she wore.
Even a fool would see. A flannel neckband,
Red, to spy her by, and a brass bell,
Not big, that she can't budge without it jingles."

It was not fear at first. There would be time
For terror, and a time for tears, for death.
First it was naked shame. Seth felt it rising,
Suddenly, out of the silence round his heart,
Like a wide outward flood: wider than he was,

Wider than him and Nancy. Now he knew.
And was she sorry, at last, that she had begged him
For the two trinkets; begged him for the bell,
The neckband; shamed him till he shot—Oh, Nancy!
The noise of it, remembered, sent new waves
Wide upward till they reddened all of Mayfield.
The grey November town turned deep and trembled.
Nor could his ears shut out the sound, resuming,
Of elders at their talk.
                    "And will she know you?"
"She comes when I say Nelly. That's her name.
Nelly. And she will let me lead her home.
A mystery why she went. I've had her since
No size at all. Hi, Nelly!" And his voice,
Thinned suddenly, sang past their startled ears.
"That's how I call. Or this way, if I need to.
It carries half a mile in the right wind."
He held the bone for Mr. Buell to see,
Then blew "Hi, Nelly!" twice. The same three tones
But longer, and more loud upon the cold.
They tore the smoky morning, then kept on,
Piercing the prairie air high over Mayfield;
Then out and on, slow dying.
                    David grinned,
Nudging at Ben and whispering: "Old ninny!
Him and his lady deer! Come back to the sale."
But no one else went with them, for Old Richman
Still was there, was statue.
                    "I'll look further.
Yet it won't be much use beyond the Barrens.
The next east bend of the Ambraw, and I'm done.
A deer won't stray past twenty miles from home,
No matter what she went for."
                    "Are you sure—?"
Seth's father had begun, but then a silence.
"I see how you were minded. Am I sure
She's anywhere? Well, no. But till I've tramped

148

The limit I ain't sure she can't be, neither."
"That's not it. Or quite. I mean—" "Go on."

Seth cried without a sound in the black air:
Father! Don't! And desperate, he faced
Full round as Nancy did. Her eyes were on him,
Frantic with fear.
    Not his.
       Or else it was,
And that was why his shoulders and his feet
Moved after Ben and David. For already
The listeners were behind him; far away
His father was explaining. "Have you figgered—
Could anyone, not noticing, and maybe
Bushes had ripped the band off—could a fool
Have shot her?" So the answer, when it followed,
Muffled itself for Seth, as distance wraps
A gun's report in silence.
      But not safety.
He had no hope; he knew it and confessed it,
Once there were the cabin logs to lean on,
Safe on the other side where Ben and David
Rummaged among the barrels. The sale would soon
Be over, David grumbled, if the crowd
Could leave the old bone-tooter and come back
To business. Till they did so he would rummage.
Something might be worth a plugged half dollar.
Seth nodded lest they notice him too closely;
Took up a worn axe-handle; tried the grain;
Counted a pile of crockery; and then,
When neither of them heeded, ran to the road,
The rutted trail southwestward into silence.

Yet there was sound; for even in the slow wind
Corn leaves right and left of him made music,
Rubbing upon each other. Buells had shucked
Both patches for the auction, and gold ears

149

Lay in his father's wagon: a fair bargain.
Only the leaves were left, and the bare tassels,
Angled awry by frost before gloves came,
Stripping the stalks to this. He listened, running,
Then slowed his pace to the wind and the husky tune.
It was a private music, unperformed,
Unburdened. Yet it said to him: Go back;
Ahead is only ruts and more such music;
Beyond the corn the wild grass rustles too,
And the brown flower stalks, stubborn in the wind,
Break a thin voice. Go back. And yet his ankles,
Aching, would not let him turn and find
The smoke still slanting blue above the Buells;
The squat store further on; his father's cabin;
Nancy's, where she might be now, to leftward;
Then, rightward, Thorsten's house. But the old fellow
Long ago had darted to his counter,
And a horned thumb already tapped the scales.
Mayfield was there complete if Seth could turn:
Complete and more, for settlers come at dawn
Still lingered at the auction, and a stranger—
Seth, as if his own name had been whispered,
Wheeled. And there it had.
                              Nancy was crying
"Seth!" There, in the corn, in the cold, she was waving
And calling "Seth! Come here! Come out of the road!
Quick! Where I am! Quick, so he won't see you!"
Between two rows arustle she was standing,
A little crouched, as if for his example:
Crouched, and with her scarlet muffler dangling,
Wind-long, from her throat. "Come here, Seth, please!
Come!" And then she quieted, for his feet,
Alive at last, were flying to obey.
But as he came she whisked and fled; till stumbling,
Both of them, through bent stalks all the way,
They reached a place where nothing was but corn:
No road, no Mayfield, nothing but dry music

Saying its mind around them, and black clods
Cold at their feet, and greyness overhead.

They had not touched each other often; never
Dared beyond the warm blood's delicate doubt.
So when she fastened fingers on his sleeve,
Straightening him to her; and when the red
Raced up to reach her eyes, till the dark lashes
Kindled, and the blue between was fire—
"Nancy! Why!" But Nancy only shook him,
Fiercely, and cupped her mitten at his mouth.
"Seth, don't say it, over and over and over.
This is no time for scolding." "But I never—"
"Yes, you did. I knew it at the Buells;
Weren't you saying 'Now! Nancy is sorry'?
Seth, you ran away." "I couldn't stand there."
"So I saw. And he saw, and he's coming:
Now, on the road. Be still!" She pushed at him
And leaned away, and listened through the corn.
"To follow me?" Seth put the monstrous question
Not as believing words or his own voice.
She answered faintly: "No. To follow her.
He's going nine miles down. Then, Seth, tomorrow,
If she's not anywhere—no tinkle sounding,
No flicker of red in the Barrens—he'll be back.
He says he won't try farther. He's to stay
At Thorsten's house tomorrow night. Not ours;
Not yours, although your father asked him."
                                        "Nancy!
Father asked him something else. I know.
Nancy! What will he do if someone, someone—"
"Shot her? In the breast? When she was facing—"
Her voice at last, collapsing with her shoulders,
Shook, and he reached to touch her as she turned:
"Seth! She might have come to you and given—
Seth, you could have stood there and untied—
She never would begrudge them—here!" And Nancy,

Tearing her cloak away as if it burned her,
Plucked at a crimson string until it loosened,
Flashed, and fell in sparks to the chilly ground.
He watched it fall; and heard her hands unwrapping
The bell from its white paper; till the brass
Gleamed free, and as she trembled cleared the air
Of everything save music's one dark note
Of danger. Then she dropped it, and a final
Clink was all he heard except for his heart.
"Nancy," from a throat he strained to steady,
"Nancy, yes, I could have. But he asked,
My father asked Old Richman—tell me now."
She did not lift her face from the spent bell,
Which he too leaned and studied while she said:
"First you ought to know the way he sounded,
And how his eyes grew shallow with a high,
Wild stare, as if the lids had burned away.
The sound, though: that was first, and that was why
I followed you. The meaning, Seth, was there:
In the quick rise, the sudden crazy change
To someone else's voice, some animal's,
Some devil's—now! I've told you everything."
He hesitated. "No. I want the words
Themselves, as Nancy Emerson would say them."
"Well then he swore," and secretly she watched him,
"He swore that he would put a pointed bullet
Straight through the head, the head—please, Seth!"
        "Go on!"
"Of anyone that killed her. Just as soon
As such a thing was certain he would fire.
Even if it should cost him seven years
Of searching, he would do it then; and dare
All living souls to blame him afterwards."

The minutes blew between them and swept on
Like snowflakes under night, till Seth announced:
"We'll soon be cold here, standing like two stumps.

Come." And he hurried past her, stepping high
To miss the lovelorn trinkets where they lay,
Paired in their brightness. But she stooped and took
The flannel by an end, as snakes are taken,
And fearfully, as she followed, wrapped it tight,
Ten times, about the hollow brass, the ball
Wherein a pebble sang. He heard it once,
For over his shoulder came: "I meant to leave them."
"But he might strike across the field tomorrow.
He's coming back tomorrow, Seth. I told you."
Only the stalks replied where Seth's feet scuffled,
Parting the tangled rows. So strong, so straight,
The young back there before her; and so still.
"Go easy, Seth, we're nearly at the road."
But he marched on, and she could only falter:
"I am so wicked. Never did I dream
When you came in from hunting, that gone day,
And told me of the marked one, and I teased
Till back you went, for me—you didn't want to—
And I walked partway, meeting you at sunset
With something in your pocket, two things, prizes—
Never did I dream—"
                    "We're at the trail now.
Watch," was all he answered, gazing home
Toward Mayfield; and she cast a hopeful glance
Southwestward. There an old man with a gun,
Turning his back on morning, still diminished
As the two ruts ran single into haze.
"See, Seth. The other way. Old Richman's passed us,
Safely, and long ago; and now he's gone
Forever, maybe. Look with me and see."
"Then home," he said; for he already picked
His way across the margin of wet weeds.
"Come home. But I'll go first, to keep them there
From thinking things. Even at that I'd rather
They thought some things than others." "Such as—Seth!"

And Nancy ran beside him, pulling soft
At his stiff sleeve. "All right, but till we're nearer,
Talk to me, Seth, as if I were a person:
Your fastest friend; the one that dreams of you
Most often, night and day; your sweetheart, Seth;
For that is what I was, and what I will be."
Suddenly, in the sunstream of her words,
He melted, and the still head tumbled over,
Captive once again, for her to kiss:
With a young quickness, then the hands away.
"Nancy, you are! I know it! And I'll never
Blame you more than me. Or half as much."
"Yes, more." "Not even half. When he comes back,
Tomorrow, and when I tell him—" "Seth, you won't!"
"I won't so much as mention—" "Seth, be still!
You didn't see, you didn't hear what I did."
"Now you come after, Nancy." "When you promise.
Say it, Seth. You'll wait till I am with you,
And you'll not speak till I do; and if then,
Not till you see me twist my hands like this."
But the worn red, unwinding, stippled her sight,
Releasing the held tears. And thus he left her.

II

To Thorsten first. But the counter, when Seth came,
Dozed vacant of the bent hands, the familiar,
And the dim eyes that peered, disdaining glasses,
Were absent from the shadows. Then by magic
Thorsten was there. "My boy!" The peaked face,
Pointed a little upward from old need,
All mankind being taller, took him in.
"Two bachelors this morning, at a bargain."
"I saw you at the Buells, but—" "Then you ducked us.
Didn't you want to hear your father answered?
Fabulous, the answer. Richman, now,

He swore—" "I know, I heard it. Someone told."
"Yes. Emersons have ears."
                              Seth waited, wondering.
"Need me, Seth? Or just knocked in to find
What Thorsten knows? That's nothing. Thorsten thinks;
Come morning or come midnight, Thorsten thinks
A little, though his wisdom is to One's
As brass to gold, as little bells to thunder
Death himself will fear on Judgment Day."
"You think, then—" Seth was certain, but he asked.
"I think Old Richman's rifle, cold tomorrow,
Will warm itself in my house by the fire,
Like his old legs. They will be stiff by then.
But not his tongue; the hunter keeps it oiled.
He isn't ready yet for the last quiet,
With burr oak branches laced across his throat."
Seth backed away. "My boy, it was but fancy.
Death is disguise enough, and maybe no one
Covered her where she fell. He wouldn't find her.
Meanwhile, Seth, the best thing for some people
Is silence, utter silence. For example—"
And the sharp nose, new tilted, shot a line
High over Seth's head, far as to the rafters,
Where the eyes travelled, confident, and where
They lingered a wise moment on the smoke
Of beams and blackened webs before they fell,
Searching for Seth again. "Silence is best."
"You know, then." "Thorsten thinks. A form of knowing
Inferior to most. Yet none is better,
Here in these latter days when no god burns
In bushes, and the angels, fed on air,
Are just about as useless." For his eyes,
Dimming among the beams, had come back empty.
"You think, then, you believe, someone is safe,
Someone who is sorry?" "Two that are.
Emersons have ears, and were this Babylon,
One pair of them would dangle with red gold

Purloined from a gazelle. The mighty hunter!
Nimrod's youngest brother, safe and sound
In Mayfield, Illinois, if he can think
With Thorsten and be silent." "Nancy, though—
I wasn't there to hear you, but his words—
She told me. They were terrible. His eyes—"
"Seth! Beginning now!"
                For boot feet stamped,
And the latch rose slowly, letting his father in.
"Morning, Seth. Your son and I were—" "Thought so.
Wife's been hunting for him. She can't burn
The bedsteads, and I won't do kitchen work.
Woodpile, Sethie. Double time, now. Git!
Thorsten, there's some settlers here from Bush Creek.
Outside now. I told them—Sethie, git!"
Then, when the door had boomed: "I told them both
Your whiskey was the hottest west of the mountains.
Thorsten, if I bring them in—that is,
Will you mark up three tumblerfuls on time?
Credit's healthier soon. That corn of Buell's."
Seth ran, and barely heard two strangers hail him,
"Hi, there," as he leaned northeast for home.

The wagon ruts were thawing in the sun.
Four ways they wandered, shining: back to Buells;
Right to Thorsten's cabin; on to home;
And left as far as Emersons; or farther,
There where the north trail needled the horizon.
The low sky overlaid worlds beyond Mayfield:
Hundreds of them, he said, and all like ours;
Like ours, that is, except for one thing, danger.
He slowed then to a walk, letting his mind
Slip northward into safety and snow silence:
Northward past imaginable towns
Where no one stirred and only coming winter
Circled the sleepy windows with white hills.
But northward, fifteen miles, was where Old Richman,

Only this morning, blowing upon a bone—
So now for sanctuary his tired thought
Rested in Nancy's house. Under the eaves,
Under the quilted spread, under the square
White pillow she was putting them away.
That was where she kept them: in the loft's
Warmest and darkest corner. That was where
Nancy in the nighttime dreamed of him.
That was where, once, his own ghost, climbing
Carefully out of the covers and huddling low
Through Mayfield darkness, shunning all minds aprowl:
That was where a copy of him hovered,
Once, and warmed itself in the lit scent
Of cheeks that burned to lie against his own;
Till the flame found him, flying to its cause,
And wrapped him close; and his two moving hands
Melted into honey at her waist.
His pity almost spoke itself aloud.
Not anger now, accusing; not the need
To know if Nancy trembled. For he knew.
Her heart was his: sweet beating in them both,
A sound for either's ears and nothing said.
He knew as if she told him how the bell
Sang in her bed, and how the band embraced it,
Remembering a dear neck that oak leaves now
Had blown six nights to cover. Thorsten said
Oak branches, but—how much had Thorsten guessed,
And how could he have guessed it? Did he know?
Did Thorsten more than think?
                              Then Seth was home,
And as the wooden hinges creaked and swung,
Thorsten at his back still seemed to whisper:
"Silence is best."
                    But there his mother waited,
Little and bright, her black eyes feeding birdlike
Instantly over all of his set face.
"Why, Seth, you're not yourself this morning. Father

Scolded too much, perhaps. I wasn't mad;
Not really. But I must have wood. Come here!"
And Seth walked over slowly to the arms
Whose favorite work he was; whose only pleasure
Came when they pleased him too. As not this day,
She felt; so Clara folded them behind her.
"What's the matter, Seth? I see it isn't
Me, or a little kindling. Or your father.
Not even Nancy, maybe, for a change.
Then you can tell me." "Mother, it is nothing."
"Or you can let me guess. But that takes time,
And then it may be over, and I'll miss—"
"Mother, if it were anything you'd have it.
If it were mine to give. Tomorrow, maybe;
No, the next day; no, not even then;
Sometime, though, I'll tell you. For there's something."
"Dearest boy, I didn't mean you had to.
I mustn't be a beggar. Sometime, then.
But only if you want to. I can wait
Forever. Meanwhile, though, the fire must burn
And dinner must get ready. Off with you!"

She laughed and let him pass her, sober-sided,
To the back entry, where the odorous chunks
Waited to fall in quarters or thin eighths
As iron decided. It was rest to think
Of nothing now but numbers, it was bliss,
Letting the blade be deputy to act.
The axe's weight, directive, and the helve
That must be balanced thus or not at all—
The right hand slipping upward on the swing,
Then down, and oak divided—on and on
Seth labored at his game, the wooden circles
Daring another stroke, and then another,
Till the four parts that fell became four persons,
Separate in their truth. Nancy was there
Untroubled, all the blue strength of her eyes

Conspiring with black tresses, tossed to tease.
And Thorsten with his talk of oldest Norway,
The icy land he left so long ago
That fairy tales were facts, for he remembered
Trolls upon a bedstead, and his mother's
Charms to send them cackling, and the giant
Warriors braiding silver in their hair.
Seth's own mother, third, who made no secret
Of how she favored Seth among her men:
Half hero now, half slave, unfree to form,
Untaught to fix his matter in the mold
Of coming age and coldness; better so
For one so birdlike by him, who could peck
At bits of him forever, and sing low,
Sing high the soothing notes of her near love.
Then fourth, and no less separate, no less safe,
The figure of a huntsman strange with fringes,
A sudden alien, old and brown among them,
Risen out of story books; but standing
Tall in the flesh, nor ever to be tamed.
So long as there was silence past the door
Seth held him thus, a purposeless thin stranger,
Miles on miles away, as if through crystal
Mountains that the wind heaped toward the sun.
Only the fourth he was, a thing the axe-edge
Built in a neat pile opposite to Nancy,
With Thorsten and his mother spaced asquare:
All angled from each other, and all noiseless.
But the first whisper changed it. For he heard:
"Seth! You have enough now. Come along!"
And instantly but one of them was there:
The last, the different one, who left his station,
Moved as if by other hands, and hither,
Inexorably, his feet not ever lifting,
Shuffled until he stood, his gun-barrel lowered,
A woodpile's length away. Seth found his voice
Too soon for sanity, too thin for sound.

159

"You've come!" he cried. "You know it!" But the words
Were bodiless, and Richman only stared,
The gun-barrel still descending to its aim.
"Seth! Whatever nonsense are you up to!
Seth!" And the specter vanished. "Seth! Come here!"
The door behind him, not with its own anxiety,
Shrilled on its hinges. "Seth!" But as he turned
Impatience in her ended. "Here, I'm helping.
Aren't you well, Seth? Leave the rest for David.
I'll carry what we need now." "No," he said.
"I'm well." "But Seth!" And instantly her hands
Pressed at his cheeks, pulling them down to feel.
"Malaria, it may be." "Mother! No!
I tell you it is nothing. Run back now,
And I'll bring this right after, in four trips."

She raked the ashes forward and pretended,
Now with her wrists, her back, that count was lost
Of Seth's incomings: one, two, three, and four,
Till the full heap was there. So only when
Flames crackled, and the brown smoke turned to blue,
Did either of them venture. "Little mother,
Look!" And Seth was merry; or he thought,
Managing a poor grin: This is merry.
She could not be deceived, yet she responded
Skippingly in kind. "Dear me, that's better.
You aren't a ghost now, opening my grave,
My long forgotten grave, by scary moonlight,
To show me all the horrors that can walk.
That's better, Seth." "Now do you say it's nothing?"
He must believe her lie. "Yes, lamb, I say
It's nothing. Something, maybe, but not now."
"No, not now."
                    But then there was the noise
Of Ben and David coming, with their father:
Three famished giants, prompt upon the noon.
"Sethie, you didn't get here when I told you!

160

And like I told you: lightning up your shins,
With mountain panther grease to slicken that.
Clara, did you boil him when he come
And pull out half his feathers? You're that mean
To Sethie: always stomping on the colt
Like some long-legged mare in pesky flytime.
That's why he ain't half growed. You raised up Ben,
Dave too, a far sight better: soft and sweet.
That's how to do for boys." He grinned and staggered,
Stumbling among the four feet of his sons,
Spread stationary, listless, from the wall.
They had not seemed to hear, though David drooped
One corner of his mouth and winked at Seth.
"You'll make it yet," he prophesied. "You're coming,
Meanness or no meanness in your ma.
Our little Ma!" For suddenly he caught her,
Passing with the plates, and held her clear
Of table or clean floor until she gasped,
"Now, David!" and he set her safe again.
"Why, you're not even feathers! Throw you out,
And you'd come back like smoke. Or like the pair
Of river wrastlers Ben and me took care of
Down by the slough that day. They ground so thin,
With being throwed and whirling back for more,
They whetted down so pitiful, we rubbed them
And packed them in our pipes, and whiffed them out—
Why, six or eight good puffs was all they made.
A piece of button sucked up in my stem, though;
Ain't been drawing since. I should have thrashed him
Till nothing but a hole was left to burn."
Ben's testimony tallied: a slow nod.
But then he scowled and mumbled: "Mine's a drawing."
"By Golliday!" The father at the wash-stand,
Honoring their fiction with a doleful
Countenance cold water had not sobered,
Sighed heavily. "By Golliday and God!
I won't be safe from now on anywhere.

Blizzards, chilblains, ague out of doors,
And then you ringtails, riding high for Sunday,
Ramping up and down our home and hearth.
My pappy was the better man at that.
He tied us good and hung us, head and hair,
Like seed corn to the rafters while he et.
We swung, but couldn't reach him; and he roared
Till Bashan was a deaf-mute sucking dove,
Laughing at the sight. My little brother,
Simon: now he changed one night to corn.
Real corn. Both ears was red. Real Indian red.
I know, for I remember how the fire
Showed through, and how old Pappy jerked him down
And roasted him and buttered him, and—well,
That's why there ain't no Uncle Si for Sethie.
Godamighty, Ma, when's dinner coming?
Auctions be the coldest times on earth.
My appetite's from working to keep warm."

"How was it, Seth?" His wife, alert to lead him
Safely away from something, swung the crane
And lifted as she talked a fragrant lid.
"How was the auction? Buells all satisfied?
Clear? And are they setting off tomorrow?
Dinner I guess is ready. Are you washed,
David and Ben? Go on now," as they growled.
"No food for bears unless they shine like babies.
And wet your hair to comb it. Who all came?
Many out of Mayfield?" "Some. But say!
Ever hear of Richman, old John Richman?
First white man ever settled in this county.
Farmed it in the brush, up north a piece,
Maybe a dozen years. Or his boys have.
He's not a natural farmer. He's the old
Deer-shooting kind. Big Indian killer too.
They say he was in wars back east, and scouted
Once for a British lord, a redcoat captain.

162

That would a been his father, though; for John
Ain't lived forever, rusty as he looks.
However, when the mountains of Virginny
Boarded too many people, and the deer,
Them bobbing white-tail roebucks, thinned a bit,
He dandered up and lit: built him a raft,
A pair of poplar logs, with planks across,
And then on top a tent. They all got in;
He had a wife by then, and standing boys;
And I do hear she held him down the best
Of any female woman ever chose
To sit on fire; for Richman was a roaring
Bonfire once a Monday; they got on
His catamaran and floated; down the Kanawha,
Down the Ohio, far as to the Wabash;
And then, by God, by Golliday, they poled—
Just thinking of it tuckers a man out—
Upstream to Ambraw, little poky Ambraw;
And last up that to somewheres in our county.
Years it took, I reckon, what with floods
And rapids and low water and five mouths
To fill with squirrel meat. Deer, too, when he sighted—
Say, though, that's my story. He popped in
To the auction." "So? I wondered if he hadn't.
How does he look? What is he here to tell?"

She drove the questions at him, happy now
For one who wanted nothing down the table,
Nothing but rest, and eyes turned well away.
But when she looked, torture was there again,
Working to make of Seth a twofold stranger.
Then she must labor more, and urge the tale
Even till Seth should listen. "What is he here—"
"He isn't here. He's gone already, hunting
For a pet doe that didn't like his dander.
Or maybe she was green-sick; though I won't
Spread yarns against a lady. He said lady.

163

She even had a name." "What was it?" "Nelly.
Nelly Richman. Haw!" And he blew out
A sudden breath of laughter, blended soon
With Dave's and silent Ben's. But not with Seth's,
That rose upon a high note, strained and queer,
And startled his still mother, who could whisper:
At least it helped him, trying; who could say:
I'll keep it going now; who never dreamed—
"Well! And will he punish her, poor thing?"
"Her! Oh, no! Not Nelly! There's a rag
Tied around her neck, to tell the pretty by,
And bells to ring the answer when he toots
That turkey bone; he's got a toothpick fife
People could dance to: Turkey in the Straw!
She'll come to him, he says; and then he'll swing her
You know where: his corner lady home.
No! The bullet's waiting in his gun
For boy or man that dropped her, if one did.
If any fool—I asked him, and he blazed
Like feather grass, and spit me full of sparks.
Come seven years, he'd let the daylight in
With lead, and dare a flea to shake a finger."
"Well! And did he dance a wicked reel
Through Mayfield? Did he threaten one of ours?"
The owl's eyes might have told her: the spread stare,
The feet that gripped the chair rung, perching tight.
But all they meant was misery, to the tune
Of a broad mouth replying: "No one here,
None leastwise that peeped. So he went on,
And won't be back till sundown time tomorrow.
Go see him then; he's turning in at Thorsten's,
And you can slip and tattle if you know
Some gun that's cooling. Even if you don't,
Go see; for he's a sight to cure the blindest.
Sethie!" For the boy was edging off,
Pale with an unknown purpose. "Don't forget
That corn I bought this morning. Feed them curls.

The wagon's full outside, but there's as much
At Buells, and when this load is in the crib
I want the other top it. Ben and Dave's
Got business with their pappy till it's dark;
So you'll be scooping corn, and I advise
That Sethie, our best boy, scoop dinner first.
Or so his little motherkin, and so
The ladykins—they all say Sethie's best."
"Don't tease him. You're his father, and God's will
Is not that any little one be scorned."

"Who's little?" David pushed his plate away.
"Goliah, that's his name, the rate he grows.
He'll soon be sassing me to sling a rock
And slug the baby giant. Like I slugged
That roaming doe of Richman's." Seth, uplifting
A foot, was suddenly moveless, tongue and spine.
"I mean," said David, "like as if I did.
Don't worry, anybody. He'll be back,
But not for me or Ben, or for Goliah.
Or even little Ma, that maybe craved
A ribbon and a bell, and set her boy
To hunting for them one night down the river."
"Now, David!" And his mother gasped again.
"Funny! You would think old Turkey Tune,
Come back already, called us up for judgment.
Nothing to be afraid of, tiny Mam.
If you'd a seen his fringes, and his frills,
And heard the way he piped, you wouldn't shiver."
"David! Do I shiver? What's got in
Your goosehead?" But he only grinned and stared
At Seth's returning ankles. "Pap was right.
Fall to, spindle shoulders. I'll scoop too."
"Dave!" But he ignored his father's roar,
And checked his mother's whisper: "Seth's not fit."
"Ben is all the help, Pa, you can use,
And Seth can hold his end up on the corn.

Now both of you forget. And little Ma,
You mind me even more. So Seth ain't well!
I s'pose you aim to bundle him up good
And fix him a rock candy sugar tit.
Peppermint Ma!" And bouncing down the room,
He made as if to catch her; yet knew well
The ways she could elude him. "Come on, Seth!
She's halter-shy and head-proud; but she'll follow.
She'll watch us by the wagon. Won't you, Ginger?
Laugh, that's good."
                For suddenly her eyes,
Freeing themselves from Seth, remembered mornings
Longer ago than Mayfield; and believed
Her eldest once again. And so her youngest
Had eyes for only David as the door
Swung light for them to let November in.

And so Old Richman even then was whistling,
Miles away. "Hi, Nelly!" But no deer
Came ambling. Not a hair of his lost doe.

III

The turkey voice, November's monotone,
Preceded him southwestward, pouring three
Small notes that only birds came by to hear,
Or, sitting still, cocked heads against the cold
As bobbing rabbits paused and naked trees
Caught ravellings of music blown to thread.
It was eventless country for a tall
Rememberer of mountains, for an old
Light-stepping hunter, homesick for his prime.
Yet this was Richman's country too; his eyes
Lived lazily at home, familiar long
With infinites of grass: green world or brown
As earth absorbed the season, and west winds
Sent ever on and on their waves of change:

Horizons always flowing, and the few
Far groves a fleet of islands sailing past
Yet never disappearing: time aswim.
The muddy river, leftward of his way,
Had sycamores for listeners, and low
Black bluffs that sometimes melted into swamp:
The water waving cattails as it widened,
Glistening underneath the ragged nests
Of birds that but a month ago were loud.
The sycamores, the saw grass, and the rushes:
It was a place for Nelly if she knew;
If nature still was in her, and if breath.
Home-suckled, paddock-winded, she might well
Have been no match for wildernesses spreading
West and south from Mayfield, or for bends
Like bowknots in this Ambraw, or—he stamped—
For shooting fools, for boys with idiot guns,
For girls with blood-red mufflers. Instinct, squinting
His vision and slowing his footsteps into stealth,
Darkened the road till nothing but those two,
That blazing girl, that lad with the goose look,
Shone visible: the river sponged away.

The crimson girl, the goose lad: were they one
In love, in secret knowing? Were they his
To stalk and take tomorrow should the world
Be blank ahead, with no bell tame to this?
He blew again, restoring the whole scene
To sight. And yet to silence. For no sound
Proved even his own presence; even he,
Shrunk to a pipe, was helpless. And a rage
Possessed him. If those two it was that—
                                        "John!
Madman!" Susan, whispering from her grave,
Labored in the cold to quiet him:
And time had been when crystal in her voice
Could wake him out of passion. But not now.

Susan was six years dead, and he had honored,
Slave as an old man is to a slow-found wife,
Many a day the hummed, the plucked rebuke.
But not this trip, he shouted, driving his wrath
Like prey, like stubborn prey, before the beater,
Forcing the laggard animal's last speed;
Not here and now, if Nelly had been tricked:
If his one living pleasure—if the boy,
The girl—but then he ceased. It was not certain.
Children will blanch at nothing; and if love—
Well, who had business blaming puppy blushes?
Here was the Ambraw still for him to trace
As far as Bush Creek Barrens, where, with night
Soon falling, and the tavern being warm,
He could await tomorrow. Then once more
The bone call; and if Nelly still was truant,
If no ear pointed suddenly and pulled
Four delicate, curious feet to where he wandered,
Mayfield again; and those.
                  So he went on,
Frowning because of three late sons that Susan,
Thrifty, had left him with. They sagely plowed
His prairie with no mercy on its green,
No memory of the waves that once he counted,
Washed from the springs of west. They were at home,
Dandy and Paul and George, and he could hear them:
Yes, that's wise; be certain beyond doubt;
And even then be doubtful; nothing done,
Nothing regretted, Father. They were Susan's;
They would approve. His, too; but sober strangers,
Homes for a heart that otherwise went ranging
Companionless, unchilded, after flesh
Of no man's making blindfold in a bed.
Dandy the least of all, yet he was rarest,
Reckoned the price of Nelly; it was he,
That morning, who had followed to the road,
Praying to him, even, and protesting:

168

Ant's eyes are to acres as your pet,
Your daughter doe, your mite, is to this prairie.
Yes, Dandy would applaud him in his doubt.
Whereat Old Richman, racing his lean mind,
Arrived again at anger, where he heard:
This way, master, this way to the kill.

He leaned and travelled swifter, his long feet
Trailing a perfect line to where the sun,
Now lowered into haze, hung over night.
There was an hour between him and the Barrens,
A funnel of diminishing dark time
Whereinto deer might stray, and even the strongest
Founder. So he lifted song: "Hi, Nelly!"
And listened as three tones converged in dusk.
Then silence, as of suns already ended.
This one, though, was stubborn about dying;
Round and farther round it cast its curves
Of tawny breath on cloudbanks, on the tips
Of sycamores, on weed heads, and the feet
Of waterfowl that, trying a last flight,
Bore under them their bent legs lately gilded.
And now the Barrens, blackened out of view,
Evaded Richman's question, and a tavern
Twinkled in the gloom, inviting sleep.

The sun that set on Mayfield gilded gold.
Seth's second load of bright ears, brought to crib,
Shone yellower in last light than the backs
Of Buck and Thad the oxen, who beyond
A log barn's eastern corner drooped in shade,
Ruminant of supper. Rusty gold,
These pullers, yet they missed the glory now
Of double color: amber-lighted corn.
David, upon the end-gate like a god
Of winter harvest, flushing in the sunstream,
Heaved another scoopful into darkness,

Grunted, and stood straight. "The last one's there,
At your end of the wagon. Throw it in:
That's right. You weren't behind me very much.
Something will make a man of you yet, Curly."
His wind returning, Seth upstraightened too,
And leaning on the buckboard grinned his thanks:
For praise, and for the feast of David's tales.
There was the fable, rubbed again to shining,
Of Crockett's dive through January water
Till the hot springs were round him, and he rose
And thawed four counties, spewing; and the history
Of Wabash Betsy's husbands, nine tired men
But true; and then the chronicle of Fink,
Who fought all day with gelded alligators—
Ignorant, for there was no outward sign;
Except that females, coming up at dusk,
Devoured the fat hindquarters and sang hymns
So doleful that he bellowed, adding bass.
For these, and for the brother whose best love
Declared itself in roaring, and for hours
On end with no third pair of eyes between them—
Richman's! He remembered. So, for more:
"What of the river rats, the Yadkin bullies—
You know, the ones you wrestled with and threw?"

But David was already vaulted down
And headed toward the oxen. "No time now
For nannigan. Let's see what's hot for supper.
Hi there, Thad, you thief, you carrot hog;
Hi there, Buck, you buzzard!" And he thumped
Both rumps until they drummed a hollow laughter.
Forward, though, their mirthlessness remained:
His everlasting wonder. Whited eyes,
Bland foreheads, and the irony of horns
That curved away from danger, tipped and sleek;
The patient dewlaps, deaf to any scolding;

The split hooves, and the long mud-sluggish tails—
He thumped again, but louder, calling back:
"Sethie, how's the horses working out?
Emerson's, I mean. You know I mean
Doc Emerson's. You ail so often, Sethie,
Going for extra pints of rotgut rhubarb,
You're like his own big boy to little Doc.
How's his horses doing, now that mud's
The password?" "Dave, I never have been sick."
"Lung sick, no. But heart sick. Now don't say
You never got girl fever in the nighttime,
Or broke out in the spring with Nancy rash.
But let's get back to horseflesh. I tell Pa
It's coming fast, no matter how he figgers.
Sight for sore eyes, too, if you could look
Past girlflesh. Hocks a splashing, heads a shaking,
Tails all rippled out behind like water:
Sethie, that's a sight. But Pa won't trade
These here he-women over, these milk barrels
With nothing but brown vinegar inside them.
Hi there, titless wonder," thumping Thad,
"Here's your forkful; chew it up and gum it,
Goosey." Both of them, beyond the stallboards,
Rolled their eyes at David, unconvinced,
Unblinking, while he talked their virtue down.
"Now take Old Richman." There it is, said Seth;
Sooner or later, Richman; but he swore
He wouldn't be the tongue-tied ninny now
He had been. "Take the Tooter. Can you fancy
Someone like old Tommyhawk, old Laceleg,
Grieving for a lost ox? Making mournful
Music till it waddled up, the high-hip,
And soaped its nose, and bawled, and followed home?
Don't guess you can. I can't. A filly, though:
That's more the way. 'Murder!' Till she jumps
And nuzzles him: 'Dear me, nobody did it!' "

171

Seth, his eyes on David, said aloud:
"You think nobody did it?" David yawned.
"And what if Ben or me, or little Ma,
Or Pap, or you, or Thorsten, or the Doc,
Or Mrs. Doc, or Nancy, or some Buell—
They're lighting out tomorrow, they'd be safe—
Or Thorsten's dog, to round the business out,
Done it? What's the chances he'll find out?
Who'll blab? Besides, the county's got four corners,
And Mayfield's only flyspecks on the longest:
The wagging southwest bobtail, the panhandle.
Who's dunce enough to tattle? You know me.
I don't shy at cyclones. But I'd shut
This mouth of mine tomorrow. Reason why?
Partly because I'd be ashamed to shame him:
Him and his dear old musket, that a moth
Flew out of when he tapped her. Did you notice?
Partly, though, because a hoot owl told me—
Yes it did, don't tinker with the gospel—
Richman, being a real fire eater once,
Might gorge himself again: just for a minute,
Maybe, just for a tick a bitty time;
But what's the difference then? No, there'd be risk,
And who'd I be to hang my heart up high
For Nelly's Uncle John to polkadot?
No, Big Sethie. Mum's the Mayfield password.
Just you listen. There won't be a peep."

But Sethie only stared, firming his lips,
And followed David out to where the mudlot
Glistened in the kitchen candle's beams.
The stare was still upon him as he paused,
Then crossed the floor and took his mother's kiss
Half absently, half eagerly, pretending
Nothing was left of noontime but her cries.
And she believed him. Most of it was gone:
The harried brows, the panic. Only this,

172

The set lips, and the too-wide-opened eyes,
Only this much lingered. And she laughed
For David's sake: tall doctor to her son,
Himself a son whose goodness had branched up
Till shade from him was feverfew, was quinine.
"Hungry?" But she answered her own question,
Bustling from the coals with pans of corn.
"Tired?" But she was certain of Seth's aim.
At half past seven something in the barn
Would need him; then, two minutes after that,
A whistle would be whirling Nancy's cape
Like wind about her shoulders, and her hands,
Quick at the latch, would let the evening in;
Then both outdoors, and dark. Here Clara ended,
Sightless, nor imagined more of time
Then Seth would take returning; at which hour
Candles would puff again, and her beloved,
Shining with smiles, would shoo her off to bed.
Contented so, she watched him with his brothers:
Three of them, as different in their silence
As three starved strangers meeting at an inn;
With him the tippled landlord husbanding
His tattle till the moment they were full.
He nodded now, benevolent in the one
Deep armchair they had never left behind them,
Lugging here so little save themselves.
He nodded: but the sons ignored the father,
And only Seth among them met the eyes
Of her the fifth one, searching if he smiled.
He smiled; and though she wondered how the lips,
Their freedom gone, still dallied with delight,
How eyes like that, unaltering, unmerry,
Still could be faithful sons to her sore bidding,
She would not ask too much; nor would she mind,
This once, if Nancy added her few simples
To David's horehound draught, and summed the cure.
Go, Seth, she inly prayed, and come back shining.

I shall not be the cause, but come back banging
Doors, and guttering candles, and badgering me,
Sleep's poorest subject, home to contentment's kingdom.
Go! And as he went she waved, unseen,
And tracked him with her fancy; Seth the older
Bawling: "Where's he gone, that flowery boy?"
And David never winking if he knew,
And Ben as deep as ever in warm doze.

Seth, his shoulders hunched, his palms acurve,
Whistled: and found his wrists pulled suddenly down
By Nancy: "Didn't you see me? I was waiting.
It wasn't time, but Mother drove me mad,
Bending about and wondering if fever—
Seth! Where are your hands now? Come and find—
There! Now, Seth, you tell me—" But he took
The mittens from her cold, confessing fingers
And rubbed in silence, hushing the hungry voice.
"Nancy," at last, "you hid them? They are lying—"
"Yes, of course. Up under. But the thing
I couldn't wait to hear, Seth, was your promise.
You kept it back this morning, and I won't—"
"Listen, Nancy. Maybe I'll say yes,
But listen. They all know it: everyone
In Mayfield, Nancy, knows who killed the deer."
"I won't believe it." "Thorsten does." "Oh, Thorsten!
And Thorsten's dog: the pair of them go poking
Midnights, don't they, round among our thoughts?"
"I can't say how, but Thorston said it plain—
As plain as he says anything. His dog:
I wonder. That would be another tongue
To wag at me and tease me into telling."
"Seth! You haven't said; you haven't—" "No.
But Nancy, it was hard. Always in corners
Hearing the others say it. David sees."
"He can't." "He does, though. Or so nearly does—"
"There! I thought so. You imagine this."

"My mother, too." "Seth, look at me. You're mad."
"Remember, it's black dark. But I am sure
They've guessed it, every one of them. I'm sure,
I tell you. Dave keeps saying it is nothing:
Richman won't be dangerous; doesn't mean it.
But once he warned me. Thorsten, too. And Mother—
No, she didn't, either. All she saw
Was sickness in me. Not tonight. At noon.
They warned me, saying silence was the best."
"It is, it is!"
            "But Nancy, there's the truth."
"Why, truth's a silent thing. Whatever it is,
Wherever it is, it simply is. It doesn't
Sound like anything, it doesn't rattle."
"Or ring, like little bells?" She caught at his sleeve,
Lifeline to her, anchored in the darkness.
"No, not even ringing." "Not for you.
But something like a noise inside my head
Won't stop until I tell it to: aloud,
With others listening." "Others? But how many?
All the world? Most of them wouldn't hear.
They couldn't. So the truth is just the same,
No matter how we miss it. What's to gain
By howling it in the ear of an old stranger?"
"Maybe. But I don't mean him alone:
Richman. It's the noise inside my head.
Even if no one's near it keeps on humming:
'Better than being sorry is saying so;
Better than holding truth is handing it over;
Better than guarding secrets—' " "Seth, I said
I'd only be five minutes. Let me go
By giving me that promise!"
                        But he held her.
"Sweetheart—you remember how we said it,
There in the corn, in the cold?—I'm not afraid.
But truth is what I hear: this noise is truth,
Begging to be once more a silent thing.

175

You say it's one already, but it's bound
Like music to a bone inside my head,
That trembles. So it trembles too. Oh, Nancy,
Nancy, we can stop the bone with four
Short words: 'I killed the deer.' Is it a promise?"
"No, you haven't made it yet; we haven't;
For, Seth, you said it: 'We.' The two of us
Must promise, and I won't. Or haven't yet.
Quick, for I must hurry: give me word
You'll think of it all night; but only think;
And let me see tomorrow what the sun,
That helps you so, will say. For I can't help.
Nothing I say is good enough, is wise—"
"Nancy! You're the best one!" "Next to your mother."
"No. And I don't blame you more than me."
"Not now. But if I let you break our silence—"
"Break it! It is broken! Don't you hear?"
"Nothing. Not a whimper, not a hum.
Listen, Seth. Silence is so sweet.
Listen!" And her hands were at his head,
Holding danger out. "But it's inside,
I tell you. Soft it is, like something coming;
Loud, like something nearer." Yet the night
Said nothing, and her hands fell; nor did his
Give comfort to them, chilling at her side.

"There is one thing," she said. "Truth wants it quiet.
Both of us say that. Well, what of anger:
Richman's, that would sleep if no one stamped
And woke it? Should it wake? Would that be truth?
Or would it be truth's nightmare? What of a gun:
Richman's, that will dream in darkened corners
All of the days to come unless insanity
Jogs it, and it jumps with its own thunder?
Should it? And would that be truth? Would silence
Ever again come down on him, on us,
If you—Oh, sweetheart Seth, think long of this,

Think all night long with me. I won't be far;
Each word that's safe inside you I will hear.
You'll keep it so till morning? Till the sun
Looks in on you, on me? You promise that?
Do! It's nothing. Hurry and say it, Seth.
She's watching at the door. I know the sign:
The crack, the little light." "Yes, Nancy, yes.
It's nothing. I can promise. Not to speak
Of Nelly till the sun does. After that—"
"Hush!" And she was off, her footfalls sounding
Steadily back across the darkened iron
Of earth's November; till the crack she knew
Spread to a bright rectangle, framing her,
Then narrowed into nothing; while he stood,
Studious of silences, and heard,
Echoing still within him, anger's guns
That jumped with their own thunder. What of them?
And how was he to think of them all night
With Nancy thus away?
                          For now he missed her,
Doubly in the chill void, and he moved,
Invisibly, as if to follow home.
But home was not with Nancy. It was where
Another face, unsleeping, fondled his:
One mask that wooed its likeness in a dream.
Even across the distance it disturbed him,
The likeness, and he rubbed his cheeks for knowledge
Of the true flesh that night came on to cool.

Not homeward, though, but leftward: down a path
To the ox trails' silent crossing; to the store;
Then south and a little east to where a candle
Flickered in Thorsten's window: the one star
Open upon the world, for wide Orion
Hunted his dogs by dark, nor had the Scorpion
Lashed his own tail tonight and reared to see.
Seth paused. He was not coming for confession;

If Thorsten had guessed his secret he could keep it,
He and his elk dog—careful! There they squatted,
Side by side, compact and hunched and grey,
Watching the embers. Quiet now, he said,
Or the crunched ground will bring them sniffing out;
Then "Hello, Seth! Come, boy, come toast your boots
By Thorsten's magic fire!" He must be careful,
Standing where he did, with the high window
Flooding his face behind them, not to stir.
Better to have them thus, Gard's pointed ears,
That Seth could see, a match for what was hidden:
Cheeks and nose and chin all pointed too,
All needle-sharpened, stiching upon the flame
Some tale of woods in snow, some lichen web
Of far-off people dwarfed by seas and time
Till here they swarmed, live motes upon a lens
At the small end of memory.
                                        Seth could smile,
Remembering himself the little smiths
Who found a pair of orphans in the pines
And rubbed them with their beards till the frost, going,
Left them with scarlet thumbs. And east by Sweden
There were the sisters, simple in their love,
Who never went to market save as three.
Uncuttables, the word was, for a legend
Bound them as one, with cords as light as lamb's wool
Holding their hands together as they swung
Down rocks upon the mountain, and skipped then,
A triple wind, like April into town.
But witches owned the rocks; or were the rocks;
And one of them could change from hard to soft
And vanish, or be sitting there and peering
As the three maids climbed home: the leftward one,
White Elsa, dancing always up its back;
Then balancing; then over. Till the day
The cord snapped, if there was one, and White Elsa
Dropped to the valley floor. Yet when they got there,

Spiralling down the mountain, she was gone.
White Elsa had not fallen, Thorsten said.
She balanced, then was air; and now is granite.
For the one rock was double from that moment.
Elsa had entered witchdom; and a warmth
Will prove her still inside, as cotton sleeps.
There was the black woodcutter whose black wife,
At sunrise of the day that opened spring,
Bore him a babe as white as cream or goosedown.
He raged, and called it bastard, and ran howling
After the landlord's son whom she had pleased.
He heard him at the border of the forest,
Chanting a lover's lay; and hurled his bear-knife.
It missed the happy throat a fernleaf width;
But that was not the end, for all the March winds,
Gathering breath at once, blew under the blade,
Upheld it while it turned, and sent it flashing
Back to the thrower's forehead, which it pierced
As needles do a hen's egg. So the end
Was spring song and a wedding, white with black:
Whence all the grey birch folk that wander in thickets,
Threading the darkest month with slivers of light.
For the landlord's son was guiltless. Spring himself
Was the father: Spring, defending his only child.
There was the crooked foal, and the sleek mare,
Its mother, who must hide it from her stallion
Lest the high hooves, contemptuous, come down.
There was the moon that once, when not a cloud
Was shining, slipped to oblivion past itself.
There was the groaning hemlock, and the pine
With lightning for its parasite: a curl
Of incandescence, hissing a hundred years.
Yet all of these were staled ones. Something new?
Or nearer? These were long ago, and Thorsten
Lived in the live world too. He might be thinking.
Thorsten only thinks: so Thorsten said,
And put his wisdom lower than the One's.

Who was the One? And where? And did he sit
In silence now, and know? Then did he see
Things still to come? And was it simple seeing,
Or was it wishing someone might choose well?
But if he saw beforehand, why the hope,
And how could he, Seth Golliday, not feel,
First and last and midway, what to do?
Maybe the One was truth: so loving silence
That he not even broke it with commands;
Though were he thus to speak all space would fill
With order, and a final stillness reign.
Yet he had never sounded; as if truth
Were not a thing that should be but that is:
Whatever and wherever, haply is.
But that would prove the many, not the one.
There might be armies of them, disagreeing
Night on night forever, day on day
Till doom blew down and buried them like coal.
Or did they care at all? And did the One,
Their watcher if he lived, their far-off king,
Care any more for stillness here than howling?
Where he must be, what news of war, arriving,
More than as birds could wail? Or last as long
As fly-whine in an instant of hot sun?
Yet there was something here that wanted quiet:
Here, in his very head; and he must think
All night, so Nancy told him, of her way.
Of hers and Thorsten's too: the way of dumbness.
That way, safety. This way, that he dreamed of,
Peace. A day of peace. Oh, that it come!

But Seth looked only in at Thorsten's shoulders,
Motionless between him and the flame;
And at the pointed ears erect beside him,
Partners in brown study. Once they quivered,
Twitching to lie back, with no least noise
To cause it; and the feet of their beholder

Shifted of a sudden, answering this.
Then nothing; till a log's end, settling softly,
Brightened the room with sparks, and Seth, retreating,
Knew it was time to run.
                    So he remembered
Nancy. Was she sleeping where the bell,
Atinkle as she tossed, reminded truth
Of a deep sleep betrayed? Or would her eyes
Stare watchfully until the ghosts of his,
Stealing over Mayfield, floated in,
And smiled, and said a promise had been given?
Nancy had his promise for the night.
Not afterward. But now, and his pace quickened,
Duty was determined. Slipping home,
And putting the candle out, and climbing off
To the cold bed by David's, he would lie
Till sunup, thinking long and long of this:
"Should it? And would that be truth? Would silence
Ever again come down on him, on us,
If you—" Oh, sweetheart Nancy, he would try.
And there, in the darkness, in the stillness, stood the door.

The candle that he saw moved in his mother's
Hand, and a whisper clove him to the heart.
"The man your father told about, that old—
Seth! Is he the danger? Somehow, Seth,
Are you the one he—Seth! Is it a fear
Of Richman? Tell me!" "Mother, I'm not afraid."
"But be afraid! It's wiser. Let me hear,
And then let no one else forever and ever.
Let me have it all, Seth, where it's safe.
Then silence. That's the best. Don't be afraid
This minute. Tell it quickly. Then be still."
Wisdom again. And Thorsten's way of silence.
Nancy's way of begging for a promise.
David's way of laughing danger down.
No, he said. I'm glad I haven't told it.

For that would seal it in, and a shut noise
Will shake all earth to pieces, let alone
One head, one person. No, never to her.
Never to anybody till he comes.
But the rude certainty of that, uprearing,
Struck at him straight again, and the wild blow
Staggered him, so that he almost needed her hand,
The free one, frantic now upon his coat.
"Here, I'll take this off. While you sit down
And tell. Or shall I do it for you, Seth?"
She tugged at a breast button, slipping her fingers
In at last to press them over his heart.
"Now! Shall I be deputy, and swear,
By this white candle and this beating blood,
That you, Seth Golliday the Second, shot—"

"No!" His strength went all into the word,
Shocking her with its shrillness. Both her hands
Steadied the candlestick as Seth got up
And rushed like fury past her. "No!" he said.
"You'll never understand. You think you know.
Thorsten thinks he knows. And Nancy." "Nancy!"
"Yes, and why not Nancy? You'd be last
To take her side on weekdays. Now on Sunday
Woman and child are one. Her mother, too,
No doubt, and Thorsten's dog, and all the Buells."
"Seth!" And he was sorry for her face,
That none but he had whitened, none but he
Had shrunk till it was pitted with small fears.
Yet he could no more touch her than his tongue,
Chill in his throat, could change. "I tell you, Mother,"
And his own ears, unhappy, heard the cold,
"I tell you I won't talk. And I can't listen.
The same tomorrow, too. And after that,
Always! So—" "But Seth! Just for tonight!
Just so I can sleep." "And so truth can't."
"Truth!" "Someone else's mother. Goodnight now,"

Swinging up the ladder, "goodnight, dear."
The gentle word, saying itself despite him,
Softened his hold on the rung, and he almost fell;
But clung, and added: "Mother dear, not always.
Sleep. I didn't mean—" But she was holding
The candle high and crying, and the red,
Lit in her face again, was answer enough.
Now for the night of thinking. But his knees,
Drawing themselves up sluggishly under the quilt,
Ached, and his cheek on the pillow never had known
Such comfort, such caresses. Until slumber
Smoothed him. And smoothed Richman, in a room
Nine miles southwestward, parallel to this:
To longitudes of darkness, and to this.

IV

They woke at the same instant, having dreamed
At sunrise of each other: Seth of one
Half man, half panther, Richman of a boy
With buck's eyes that high terror had made ugly.
Himself the terror, Richman only frowned
With shame at oversleeping; and as soon
As day was wide around him, with the river
Running once again and prairie hens
Whirring above the great grass no one plowed,
He scoured the level region west and south
In semicircle glances. Nothing there,
No Nelly. It was more than twenty miles
Back now to home and Dandy, and the park
Where nothing like a wall had kept her close
Save loving it and listening for him.
The limit for a deer's foot lay behind;
Yesterday he crossed it, and today,
This morning, he would mark it with his gun,
His tomahawk, his turkey pipe; then Mayfield.

He slipped the narrow call bone from his belt,
Fingering both its ends, and tempted oddly
To ripple a whole horizon with its sound.
Then, if she had mind, and she had motion,
Who but herself would hear him, at dead center,
Saying her name like this? He said it, low,
And listened. But he scowled almost as soon.
He was a child to think it. So in scorn
Of the white sun that faced him—a fair sky—
He set his course northeast again, by the river,
And by the land that heaved due north for home.
Impatiently, but then more slow at last,
With sanguine zigzags left and right when groves
Peopled the skyline, and his hope appeared
Like houses over marsh waste, over worlds
Of weed top, roof of rabbits, floor of birds,
He tramped the shining ruts, that once the sun
Lengthened till they blinded him: a track
More bright than water, sliding into Mayfield.

But the last day could hesitate, be long;
Be loving in its slowness; for the store-man,
Grizzled midget, host to him tonight,
Expected him at darkfall, not before;
And Nelly, being nowhere else, was here,
Between Bush Creek and Mayfield, or was nowhere.
He scowled; and the boy's eyes were focused there,
And the girl's eyes, where Nelly's last had been.
He took a swifter step, and his long fingers
Tightened upon the stock; but then relaxed
As suddenly. There would be time for this,
And meanwhile there was music; which he blew
In three high mournful measures, letting them go
Reluctantly, uneager for the test.
They failed, and he went on; detouring farther
And farther as the low sun licked the iron

Of morning ground and slimed it under heel;
Impatient for the end, yet slow to come
Where even he must say, This is the end.

Seth's dream, that went with darkness, was no worse,
Remembered, than the light of yesterday,
Which, flowing into shape, mingled at once
With knowledge of this morning, whole and kind
In its new brightness. Nothing in his dream
Had been of truth or Nancy—why was that?
But down the ladder, busy at the fire,
Was someone else who waited. "Mother," he called,
"What time is it?" A pause, then: "Sun's up, Seth."
"How long?" "Oh, half an hour. The rest have gone,
I said you needed sleep, to bid the Buells—"
"Mother!" And he thundered on the floor
Like horse hooves. "But I've got to wave them off
As much as anybody! Lester, Bob—
I wouldn't miss goodbye to them for millions."
Then he was down and hugging her, unmindful
Of the small lines, like bird prints, everywhere
On the flushed face. "Breakfast will be ready.
Hurry," she pulled and said. But still he held her.
"Goodbye, my lady Golliday. No breakfast.
Thank you if you waited. But the Buells
Won't wait. They may be hunting Lester now,
And finding him at Thorsten's, where I'd be.
Mother, let me go. You're holding on
For dear life, like as if—" "You're holding me."
She lifted her best face and tried to smile.
"Why, so I am! Well! There!" And he kissed her
Nimbly. "Now it's your turn. Let me go."
"Seth, you're just pretending. I must hear—
How wrong was I last night?" He stared away,
Shielding his strength against returning shafts
Of memory, of pity. "You were wrong."

185

She groaned as if a great weight, having lifted,
Only were now impossible. "You mean,
You never did? Nothing's to be afraid of?
Richman—that's not it, not it at all?"
He kissed her many times, quietly, carefully.
Why could he not say something, why could his lips
Not lie? For she was rigid once again,
Despairing of this comfort that must go
More brutely, more abruptly, than it came.
"Look at me!" she begged him.
                                        But the most
She got from him was radiance that, remembered,
After the door stopped echoing, filled the room
Like double sunlight, dizzying her eyes.
She ran to call him, but the outward day
Was poor by her comparison, and dimmed
A brightness in the young back swinging off.
"Seth! I'll see you when?" But her small voice
Was smaller than she knew, and she must nod,
Pretending that he answered: "Home at noon,
High noon, my tiny weeper, yet don't wait."
The memory of these words she said for him,
Proving a presence here, was all she had
Of pleasure in the morning, all she saved,
Improvident, against the after blank.

Seth, swinging past the store, glanced in and thought:
They all will be at Buells; and glancing on,
Good! I'm not too late, they still are there:
Thorsten, and the Emersons, and three
More Gollidays than me and my lost mother.
I could have brought her too, but then her cheeks
Are ruined past the chance of any right
Farewell and God be with you. His own cheeks:
He rubbed them for assurance they might give
Of quiet in him elsewhere; for the sound
Of indecision, suddenly come back,

Whirred in his head and tricked him into pausing
Here where he must go farther. And go swiftly.
The sun behind him, lifting a little higher,
Shot to the topmost arcs of the wagon tires
And shone like four split diamonds, while the brass
Tips of the ox-horns mimicked ruddy gold.
Lester would be climbing to the seat,
And Bob beside his sister would be squirming.
Swifter, if at all! Seth forced his feet
Till there the Buells before him waved as clear
As clock hands, and he barely knew that Nancy,
Lifting the baby round for Mrs. Buell
To bundle with last blankets, turned and stared
And trembled; or that David at her shoulder,
Buzzing above the infant till it laughed
And blinked among its foldings, rolled an eye
Like Thad's in his direction; or that Thorsten,
Small in the crowd, so busily ignored
His coming that the fact was loud as ice.
These three: they were his vagueness. Having these
All here was what had misted his fine morning.
And still they were to face.
                                        But now "Hello!"
From Lester, heaving bags up two by two.
"Thought you had forgotten." As if wind
And blizzard snow together on that day
They lost themselves in the slough, dividing death
Between them like good partners; or as if
The coming home half frozen when the bobsled
Found them, and their mothers rubbed them whole:
This, or the Mayday baskets they had trimmed,
Each one of them for Nancy, though unknown
To the other till she told, and bound the boys
Like Jonathans together in shy faith;
Yet Nancy had preferred—he waved a slow
Arm, and so acknowledged Bob's salute:
The little brother, solemn by Samantha,

Holding fast to her for something safe:
His twin, but they were different. Here were more
Than half of Mayfield's young ones blurring out
Like candles, and the elder night, returning,
Cast even deeper shade on him and Nancy.
He looked at Doctor Emerson, whose glasses
Glistened under the visor of his cap;
Next at Nancy's mother, high beside him;
And so at his own father, who with Ben
As witness shook the hand of Mr. Buell
For the last time, insisting loud again:
"It's a bad month, I warn you, to be bounden
Overland for nowhere. But good luck,
And don't drop any children in the river.
Mississippi's big, and whirls them down
Like beanstraw. Like the time I took a raft—"
"God bless you, neighbor Golliday; and Ben,
And David. Little Seth—but that's no longer
Quite the proper label—Bob and Lester
Say they're going to miss you. And Samantha.
You miss them. They count upon it. Doctor,
Thank you for the times we had you in.
Better pay from heaven. Goodbye all!"
For now he had his whip in hand, and the oxen
Knew, and the axles gritted as their cold
Grease permitted motion. "Goodbye, friends.
There won't be grander people in Missouri."
"Lester!" And Seth mounted the near hub
For one more private meeting. "I'll remember.
Write me how the winter is out there.
And Bob. And big Samantha. Goodbye now."
Then he must jump and watch them, with the others
Hidden behind him, waving as he waved,
And as the cumbrous vessel, half reluctant,
Half dauntless, plied the earthways, pulling west
Like something not with sails yet helmed and blown.

"They'll meet Old Richman, won't they?" broke the spell.
"Won't they now?" his father rumbled on,
Responsible for sound again in seas
Of silence over which a death had flown.
"Sometime today he'll pass them; and he'll peer
At baby like he wondered if she wore
Deer ornaments. They might be luck at that:
Bounden overland of a November!"
When the rest kept their silence Seth could feel
How the big face bent up, addressing air:
"There won't be godlier settlers where they go
Than they are. Bet a yoke of bulls on that."
The wager had no takers in the sky,
Or if it did they lost. "Who'll come here now
And settle like these did, and raise up four
Spry dandies? One a spring? The man to come—
I hope he won't be old. We wouldn't want
A Richman stumping round, his breeding time
All past except for trouble."
                                    Seth, at a silence,
Turned; and only three still faces found him.
Golliday the eldest, with his Ben
For bodyguard, was going; and the doctor,
Almost home, was leading his tall wife
By ten short steps or more. Only the three
Still faces met him, startled, as he turned
And saw how Nancy, stiffened in the middle,
Hunted his gaze. She had it. But those two
Beside her, why were they so faithful close:
David, never gone from the girl's shoulder,
And Thorsten, who had crept until he seemed
More Thorsten's dog, with slave ears, than himself?
All three of them at once there, facing Seth,
And by no planning either. Or if so—
Why! Nancy had told them. In her terror
Nancy had talked. And the sun, whitening down,
Poured him full of purpose not to do

189

Save what his own day ordered, not to hide
In any other's darkness; even Nancy's,
Thrusting at him thus.
                           But Seth, his eyes
On hers, and on the sweet throat working there,
Melted into a dream that the sun lighted,
Of them together all of this fair day:
No matter where, but one in their slow wandering,
And one in their sly discourse, half content
With hinting and half miserably mute.
Yet it would be love's misery; and the tears
Tore at his eyes, remembering all the days
When dreams like this were beautiful in their sadness,
As of a thing impossible. For now,
When there she hung so ready, and a word
Might bring her, he must put the dream away.
At last there was but one bold thing to do:
Simply to turn and go. Yet even then,
Mysteriously, as if the most he heard
Were meaning under a vision, Nancy slipped
Two words into the stillness: "Seth. Remember?"
Thorsten, if he listened, only proved it
As Gard would, quivering; and David said:
"Sethie boy, you coming home with me?
Buells is gone, and we got work." But Seth,
Shaking his head, delivered it forever
Of David's ancient hold on him, and Thorsten's,
And doubled sharp away. "Seth! Remember?"
"When you coming then?" "The best thing, boy,
Is silence." These he heard, and then was off.

Northerly he went, past Nancy's house,
Past Mayfield, with the six eyes on his back
Like bees that will not loosen; yet he lost them,
Running, and was never now to learn
How Thorsten hooked a thumb in David's elbow,
Halting him; how David laid his hand,

Heavily, on Nancy's farther shoulder;
And how she dipped to follow; but then was still.

As, fasting, many a youth has left his kin
And fed on hunger's distance till it dwindled,
Darkening, and let one only light
Shine inward; as a Chippewa man-child,
The bark lodge lost behind him, strayed by lakes
Unrumored and through forests of no fame
Till wilderness was all, and with the wind's
Hush he caught a far wet sound of singing,
And marked the otter's voice, and heard it call
The name that he must go by while he lived;
As desert boys, with butterflies for wing-mates,
And pollen in a pouch to charm them, fled
The hogans of their fathers, flying on
Till, centered in the four skies, something fell
And dusted them with knowledge; so the son
Of Clara, and the charge of three that gazed,
Sped northward out of Mayfield, slowing his feet
To ox steps when the stubble left and right
Was all the world to note him, and another
Town was there, but miles beyond his mind.
Colebridge. Then more settlements. And then—
But that was Richman's country. When this day
Turned on its high noon hinges he would turn.
Only for peace he went, away from fire
And breakfast, and the voices raised to pour
That other song of silence, that rejected
Burden in his ears; which only listened
Now for what the emptiness before him
Uttered; or would utter if he moved
Serenely, holding on to his true self;
Silently, as moves the winter moon
On windless evenings, slipping up the east;
Or now, as out of season, out of sight,

Moons beyond the daydream might be drifting:
Circles of no color, sun-described.

Only for peace and silence, his own silence,
Here on the road, with regular slow steps,
He wandered: his own silence, and the song
Of truth that he would measure, note by note,
If the sky held, and skill were in his brain
To bring it closer, closer; when, arriving,
Nothing about its structure would be strange;
For even now he heard it past the bars
Of his still bashful purpose. When the sound
Of his own voice declaring unto Richman:
"I was the one," should reach him, tired and clear,
Giving the lie to safety, he would know
All music, and the gladness of his feet,
Turning him swift about, would stamp the time.
No need of random voices veering down
From a divine high darkness, ordering him.
His order, known already, only waited,
Like love, upon the one, the tuning word:
Self-spoken, or it would not sound at all.
Meanwhile the sun lay friendly at his side
Like a warm frost on everything: on fields,
On weed rows round their edges—poor men's fences,
Thorsten once had said—on rutted lanes,
On barns, on houses, lonely in their fewness,
Each among its hope of starting trees;
On levelness forever, and no end.

Nancy, David, Thorsten—three names threaded
His memory, and his thought returned with guilt
To the half-gods he harshly had abandoned:
To three he heard, and to a fourth one, home:
All human, and all helpless, lacking him.
The whole one he had left them for, the still one,
The far one who would never show his face,

Lacked nothing; was indifferent to steps
Turned toward him, whether stealthily or loud.
Arrival there was everything, was joy
In a known end, a truth at last recovered;
And yet the whole one's joy could not increase
Past its completeness now, in the clear quiet
That pulled Seth swifter, swifter, as center pulls
Circumference, as magnets little men.
The swiftness was the thing, and now this wish
To be with one, the person past all persons,
Who never paid with pleasure. Only joy
Unspoken, and the mind come there to rest.

Then it was noon above him, and his open
Ears were of a sudden filled with words
Unshaped except by silence: "This is he,
Seth Golliday, who, willing to be seen
By no one or by all, says: It was I;
Who, willing to be heard by all or no one,
Turns here with the sun, and when it sets
Will speak the same truth elsewhere: It was I.
And if the hearer proper to the words
Be wrathful, or if mercy listen too,
If death or life pursue him, all is peace
Henceforward, since his courage has been found."
Seth heard it, wide as wind, and heard himself
At the hushed center saying what tonight,
At Thorsten's, would be easy after all.
Easy. And the tightness at his heart,
Like a long cord uncurling, trailed away
Forgotten, trimming the prairie as he turned
With a pure line of grace that rippled endless
Over those humps of grass to the horizon.
Seth heard himself as clearly as a far
Small bell might ring reminders; and it did,
With nothing in him now to hate the brass
Or fear it, and with nothing in his eyes

To wish away the band of burning red
That circled the sharp sound. While Richman stamped
And stalked the northeast way to Mayfield, choking
His mercy with more thoughts of Nelly dead.

V

Thorsten, locking in upon his shelves
The last light that had shone there when the sun
Played still on twine and package, circled the dusk
With brisk eyes, for the whole of it was round him.
Seth had not come home; his mother, slipping
At four o'clock to find him, cried it out
Like death news; which was why this ancient face,
Sharp in the window webs, had scoured the roads
Both ways, and only left them when a customer
Coughed, or once when David rumbled in;
Or, minutes after that, when Nancy rattled
The doorlatch, clattering in and clinging there
Like bittersweet on blown walls. "Mr. Thorsten!
Nothing has been said. But then you know.
I saw it. Sir, I did. Tell me if Seth—"
But all at once she went again, ashamed
And helpless, and no wisdom from his throat
Went with her, for there was none. And he swallowed
Modestly, as deprecating guesses:
His or Gard's beside him, for the beast
Pointed his ears at something dead ahead,
Something in the dark there past his house—
No! Something in the window; where a faint
Coming of redness warned him, and he looked
Swift up to where a column, starting out,
Bore sparks awhile then dropped them, spent with cold.
Someone, and he said the soft name, Seth,
Someone—but he knew, and Gard's hair, standing,
Settled it wasn't Seth—had come and poked
The fire up, nor had wanted any light

Save that until the master came, and someone—
Someone! Thorsten frowned at the evasion.
Richman, only Richman. And his hand
On Gard's insistent hackles felt the fear.
Yet with his other hand he pushed the door
Wide open, wanting all of it at once.
And there he had it: Richman crouching low
At the green oaklogs, watching how they smoked.
Then it came, the flame, and up he reared,
Facing with no surprise the one behind him.

His knitted cap was off, and the long hair
Went every way in wildness. "Well, I took
Your word for it, and made myself to home.
Saw the store light going, but presumed
You wouldn't mind some help here. That's my way.
Never knocked on door-wood since the time
I thumped and old Fitzwilliam thought it thunder.
That was in Virginia, where I—" "Welcome,
Mr. Richman." "Let the Mister go.
I'm Richman or I'm John. And you'll be Thorsten
All the while I'm here. That name enough?"
"Yes," and Thorsten grinned an open blessing.
He let Gard go, his bristles having fallen,
To nose the hunter's moccasins for dog-names
No wind had yet erased, and then, when Richman
Patted his high ears, to saunter and nudge
The gun that propped itself in a far corner:
Tall, and with the parti-colored cap
Hung carelessly atop it for a muzzle.
Back to the fire then, pleased with what he knew,
He travelled yawning, and so quickly slept
That both the old men saw it for a sign,
And nodded.
              "You'll be hungry," Thorsten said,
Sidling to a cupboard. "And your coat.
Or shirt, if that's more proper. Hang it here,

Now that the room is heating, and I'll bring
A candle you can tidy yourself by."
"Thank you. And you're right, I had no breakfast.
Overslept at the Barrens. I'm no sluggard,
But feather beds are poppy fields to me,
And I outsnored the night." "My mother's beds
Were famous." "Where was that?" "In Norway." "Oh,
Foreigner." "And from a cold place, too.
A valley full of ice until May melted
Even the rocks, we said. And then the flood
Came wonderful. We slept, though, on our shelves,
Hugging the stove, and laughed at ice and water."
"Knew a Swede once, back in Delaware."
"I'm Norwegian." "Never felt the winters
More than horsemeat does. He grew a coat
Of body hair an inch thick, so he swore.
I never saw him shirtless." Richman yawned,
And crossed the quiet floor to where a candle,
Curled upon its gilt stem by the mirror,
Showed him his fool's tousle. "I'm a sight.
Especially for you, a fancy liver:
Bachelor, and Swedish." "No, Norwegian."
"Knew another Swede, but he was plain.
No ornaments except a reddish wife."
Richman, hunching low to comb his hair
By a dwarf's glass, looked tolerantly down
At Thorsten and his painted cupboard doors.
Another candle lit them, blue and red,
And played inside on bowls resembling beasts;
On striped mugs, and where partitions ran,
On bands of silver, deckled at the edge
With gold nails. Thorsten hummed, not noticing;
Or feigning so, for he must practice calm;
And contemplated supper. "Sir," he said,
"There's bacon, not too lean, and with our bread
There's honey. My own neighbors were the bees.
Or sorghum if you say. It pours like winter,

And only warms you afterwards, inside.
The bread would be of corn, and this year's yellow."
"Thank you, Thorsten. Anything would do,
And self-invited fellows can't be choosy.
But these are best of all; and you're the best
Man cook, they tell me, crosswise of the county;
Or cook, a little bird just hopped and said.
You didn't hear. It was the hunger tit."

Thorsten thought of Seth and dared a smile.
What danger? Richman fitted his poor house
Like furniture, homemade and humbly lived with.
This could be an evening between cronies,
Chittering like to like, if Seth had not—
And looking round, and noting the smoothed hair,
He saw that nothing still had smoothed the eyes,
That in their old way bristled, as the white
Stubble of three-day beard beneath them glared:
The chin sharp up and forward, yielding none
Of its first animal purpose. So he prayed
That Seth had lost his way, and that some northern
Cabin where he sought it took him in
Two hours ago, and had him, safe and fed,
In a charmed ring of chairs; till Richman laughed.
"A shilling for your fancy. Let me help.
I've tossed a heap of hoecakes in my time";
Whereat his host, chiding himself, remembered
Supper, and bustled off.
                        While in another
Cabin, by another starting fire,
Clara stiffened up at every crackle
And kept her eyes on David, who by the door
Paced giantwise, his shoulders in a shape
Of dread, his face a drawing by strange hands.

And while the doctor, dipping his grey head
To have his daughter clearer, studied the flush,

The poison rose red flaming up and up
Till the moist lids were all that saved her, staring.
The bishop's pawn, competing in his mind
With Nancy, brought him alternately back
To the lone board before him; both were problems,
And not a soul in Mayfield could assist.
But who now was the kindler of this red,
This all but final red? For the youngest cheek
Can whiten after too much chills and burning.
He took a pawn in passing, while his wife,
Worn to the quick, sighed also; but the maid,
Bride to a silence, stained it with no sound.
In her own thought another silence grew:
The one that would be round her when Seth's whistle
Failed. It would not be there, like the wind's
Dear voice. She only knew this, slowly now,
As in the meadow of her thought a thistle
Planted itself and spread, and thorns insisted:
Where is he walking now, what is he waiting
To hurry somewhere and do? Hurry yourself
And say it. Beat him there, the foolish boy,
And say it with your own tongue, that can tell
An old man of a young man, and remind him,
Why, of a sweetheart too—even to laughing,
Even to arms, denying the cold grave.
The danger of it shook her, not the shame:
The chance that somewhere, safe in so much darkness,
Seth was keeping silence, hers at last,
And loving the sun's prospect when tomorrow
Both of them would meet in it and smile
Good morning, lucky morning, and God's day.
If this were so, what madness in her then
Said: Hurry along and shout it; break the bond
Of stillness that you begged himself to swear?
That was it. For Seth had never sworn.
That was it! And therefore—yet she moved
No farther than a window where her mother,

Watching, saw her shiver. Yet no sound
Had entered, and no image decked the glass.

"Where have you not been, then? The world is wide
Except to you. It travels at your belt
Like something stuck there, handy." Thorsten poured
More coffee, and the sugar darkened in.
"Not to the other ocean. Or much past
The biggest of the mountains. Mostly east,
And favoritely south; the rivers there,
The woods, the running game, are all one thing:
Hunter's heaven, Timothy my brother
Told me when he gave me my first gun.
Yes, the world goes with me pretty well.
It's not so wide at that; though round enough
For something lost to swing in." Thorsten jumped.
Soon, of course, but not so soon as this.
"I have my own way, Richman, to contract
Creation. It's too big for anybody:
Me, or you, or men six times our size.
Yours, that is." "What is it? What's the way?
Don't be too sure I'll take it in, but try.
I'm not a schoolish fellow; went two years
Then skipped it, with a backside red as beef.
Liked my little teacher, but his big
Stick scared me. Should have stayed and learned my R's."
"You went to learn the world that can't be written.
And, Sir, I think you have." "Well, what's your trick?"
"I never tried to say it since the time
Our parson down the valley turned me up
And paddled me for heresy and pride.
He said I was presuming like a priest.
But it was not presumption, it was modesty.
Too much modesty. And that was why
The frog-faced parson paddled me: for pride
In nothing but my smallness. I had read
Of houses in the old days where a host

199

Of holy men collected." "Monkey houses."
"Yes, you know the word. I knew the reason."
"So do I. To dress in women's clothes
And pray all day like preachers out of work."
"Listen. It was so that they could see,
As far as wit can see it, how the world
Is one, and what the stillness at its center
Says when work is happy and high-ordered.
They worked to hear the stillness; and their hope
Was not so much to be seen as to see.
Their study was to be less men and more—
Not angels, no, nor gods, for that will fail;
But men as One defined them when he first
Looked down and saw them free of his long hand:
Condemned to size and movement, yet so minded
That the last thing they wanted was to fill
Clear space and think on nothing but closed things:
Themselves, I mean. The monkish houses, Richman,
Were so a few could feed their minds on substance,
Thinning as they did so their seen selves.
Their art, but not their hope, for they were wise,
Was to become invisible if men
Can be so. And they cannot, and these knew;
But labored notwithstanding. As a hand,
With all those houses gone, and musty-smelling,
Can labor even now, in a new world
Four thousand miles to westward; even here,
In Mayfield. For the world is here as there."
"But what's the work? Who is it pays the wages?"
"Odd that you should ask, who have no master.
Have you? Does he tell you where to go?"
"Who?" "That's what I mean." "You mean myself.
The boys, they try. And once there was my wife.
She knew more tricks. Susan could have me hobbled
In a bug's love-time. Yep. Except for her,
And now on some days them, it's me myself."
"I didn't say just that, Sir. Put it thus:

200

I have a master who can call my name
And no one hear. You also, but the sound,
If bears and birds had ears, would still be Richman.
My name, the one I listen for, is strange
To alphabets. It is the name for all:
For all that is, no matter what we think.
I've never heard it yet, for when I do
I'm dead as last year's mildew; or this morning's.
There's someone in myself who's more myself
Than Thorsten, big or little. He's the one
Who would be all that is if only man
Could be so. Since he can't, he bids me tend
My store and listen everywhere at once:
Both near and far, and now to such as you.
The monkeys, as you call them, on a hill
Or meadow built their squares of lasting stone;
And in these squares, diagonal and dark,
They ruled their orders. But the stone fell down,
And light was playing pagan games with lizards
Long before I opened my squint eyes.
It's harder now, with nothing like a square
To hop into and know myself at home.
The world must be my order: all this one,
And the still other in it; both together,
Time and out of time, unseen and seen."
With such a start, and hoping to go on,
He still could not creep nearer to the night's
One subject, Nelly dead and Seth in danger.
Nearer was no better, it might be,
Than devil-born disaster. Yet too far
Might leave the field to failure. And his thought,
Hunting within him, paused by a low branch
And aimed.
      As Nancy's did, and over the way,
The pitch-dark endless way between their cabins,
As David's and his mother's did: all staring

201

On through chance's forest for a sign
Of Richman in it, ready to be told.

"You look at me," said Thorsten, "for a loon.
Yet we are not so different. Hunters, now:
Why is it they both waste and worship blood?
Slay, yet love the slain? For what they shoot
Was target to their heart as to their trigger.
I've seen one, finding beaver in a trap,
Bend over it as over his first born;
Then thud, and it was nothing. Why was this,
Unless he had his mystery, as I do?"
Richman let the questions come and go
Like bats in a strange room, but holding his head
Stock-still pretended badly; for the words,
Though mateless to the custom of his tongue,
Yet flew within his mind's range, teasing thence
More memories than he had skill to free.
A queer old customer, this peaked Swede;
Yet something in his language gave the lie
To latter-day inanity, and dressed
Even the prairie round them in a form
No farmer drudge, no drone of the sod, would see.
He could have had it worse tonight than sitting
And trading preacher nonsense: two old noggins
Having it out with heaven, sage to sage.
"Well, but don't accuse me," Richman warned,
"Of redskin superstition. I don't hold
With heathens how an animal is someone,
God or man don't matter, in disguise:
Maybe a dead friend, come back a muskrat,
And popping up his head whenever help's
Not handy; maybe, though, a supernatural
Something that is there on four cold feet
To watch you like a son. A Choctaw doctor,
Once I heard of, piped a little song
To patients in a fever, and they slept,

And said they dreamed of mountain lions; claimed
It rid them of their weakness. Or he'd prance,
And trance, and bring a houseful in of owls
And panthers, so their voices, close and strong,
Would set a sick girl's pulse to work again.
Bird bones in a grave were meant to fly with;
But I have dug and found them still as sticks,
And the dead Indian claybound. No use, Thorsten,
Trying to make me out a redskin coward.
For that was it, they worshipped what could scare them.
Anything that moved was more than something:
Everything, it might be. So they prayed
And yelled till they was cross-eyed. I see straight."
"Of course, and no one better down the sights.
All I meant was this: you aim your lead
At something loved. You keep a strange respect,
Strange, that is, to masterless low minds,
For what must let you kill it if you live.
It isn't murder, man. You shoot to eat."
"Murder? No, it isn't. But you miss
The bull's eye, Thorsten, by a lame dog's mile.
Not that words can hit it, or thoughts either.
Shooting: that's not all of it. Or eating.
Even living, maybe, if you mean
Liver and lights exclusive. Hunting's a life
That takes two hands to do it, them and us:
Runners and chasers. Partners, that's the point;
And either of them knows it by a sign
From nowhere. So if such is what you mean,
We're not to have an argument. Each hand
Prefers the other on it, hot and hard,
To the fish kiss of strangers. What's to do
Has to be done together, in a time
Both know, and to a ballad, maybe, thrumming
Out of a bit of a pocket twixt two winds."
He paused, embarrased, having heard himself
Say something, no, not nonsense, but too near

203

What Thorsten must have meant when he said mystery.
"I've only got in mind," saving his face,
"The difference, plain as day, between him there,"
Nodding at Gard, "and a wild animal.
Wildness. There's another point: a will
Not to be whistled at or clucked to feeding;
An eye that holds its fire or lets all heaven
Have it when the time comes; and, I say,
We hear the tick together, and four feet
Fly into tune with fingers on a trigger.
High the jump and pretty; but the man
Most to admire it aims to lay it low.
Why? But it's his part, as the critter's part
Is like a heathen horse to hurdle rocks,
Stumps, logs, as if the real ground wasn't there."
"Just as I knew," said Thorsten. "You're no brute
Squirrel-barker." "Squirrel! That never was my size."
"No, there's bigger game. You're not a dumb
Bloodletter, then, or hater of tall hearts.
Hunting's a life for you, hunting's a heaven,
Hunting's a thing you do because a master—"
"Who? There's no one there but them and me."
"You spoke as if a third one called the tune,
And both of you obeyed. And that's the case
With Thorsten, save he's not a hunting man.
He lets too much live on, perhaps you think.
He lets it all. He has to listen sharp
For the last truth, and so no other music,
Least of all gun music, comes between."

A rise of half a note in Richman's voice
Lifted the hound's free ear. "A woman god!
Don't think you're going to preach me down. I pray,
I probably do; but not from rocking chairs,
With yarn balls on my lap, and hoping so
That nothing's ever going to get hurt."

A full note's rise, and Gard looked up; and the room,
Too suddenly, was quiet.
                              But Nancy ran,
The very stillness here commanding there
A whirling where the vortex had its edge,
And whipped her scarlet cloak about her, crying
"Wait!" as the doctor warned her. Then, in the darkness,
Pausing past the cabin's moonless door,
She felt the slabs beside her, gathering strength
To go at last and say it. For no man
Moved anywhere in Mayfield: not a sound
Of any fire but that one whose red shadows
Raced, in the mantel's corner, up dull steel:
A tube of it, so dozing on its stock
That the least noise might wake it. So her breath
Lessened, and she pressed the slabs again
For caution, sister there of sight and courage,
While time passed unmeasured; and while David,
Coatless, pushed another door before him—
Slowly, but his father hiccupped loud,
And one of Ben's eyes widened; only Clara,
Gently, and just as slowly, watched him out—
Pushed, and disappeared. Even to her
Who followed when the hinges ceased their sighs,
Even from Clara's whisper he was gone,
As if no man moved anywhere in Mayfield:
Man, or maid, or woman; for all three
Stood frozen in their places, hoping hard
For dumbness in a fourth one if he too
Stood frozen, staring with them towards the south
Where a small smoky window hid two heads,
Two old and stubborn talkers by a fire.

"Still, Gard!" Thorsten muttered to those ears,
"Still! Our guest was right if any unction
Sounded in your master. Sir, forgive
A brabbler. There was nothing in my thought

Of worse or better music; or if so,
Of mine as being nearer the sweet truth.
There is a goodness lurking in your lead:
I know it, as I feel the ritual faith
In your two forest partners, mutual thus
In a wild shrewdness, counterpointing death.
I only sketched a difference; and admitted,
Maybe, a childish weakness that fears change."
"I was too hot," said Richman, letting his eyes
Drop elsewhere. "Now forget how loud I hollered.
You are my host, and kind; and what's the loss
If two old strangers, straddled from the start,
Have missed each other's trails? The truth's the same."
"Yes!" And Thorsten, eager at the cue,
Hopped upright. "Still, Gard, still! Yes, yes! The truth's
The same, no matter where; no matter, either,
Which of us misses worst. I only meant,
It masters you as me." "I guess it does."
"By your own word it does. Through my own fault
You find me foreign too. We say one thing
And signify two others." "Oh, not always.
Supper: that's the same for us. And sleep."
"So. And moon and fire. And man and girl.
But what of this one: death? And this one: deer?"

At last he had the word out. And at last,
Shallowing, the eyes of Richman shot
Blind lights of recognition round the room.
But Thorsten must not falter. "When I say it,
Deer, I think of venison. Or beauty
Bounding for its life as here I rot,
A stationary stump of ugliness.
No more than that. So when a deer is dead,
The deer, my friend, is dead, and I think on
To other things, and later. This from one
Who never pressed a trigger in the name
Of truth or trouble. You, now, that have slain

206

Your thousands, can no more forget the death
Of one, if it is death—" "I think it is,
And think you know it, Thorsten! Look at me!"
But Thorsten sat again in his carved chair,
Motionless, and did not lift his gaze
From Gard, who twitched to stand and yet was still.
"Well then, I know you know it. Thorsten! Who!
And where's the meddler now? The boy, the man,
The fool that wouldn't look? Or looked and let
The rules of my own game go bloody hang.
A little time will tell me if you won't.
Sit there, nubbin; I can see you won't.
Sit, and let me finish my deersay.
You had it fairly right. The hearts we stop
Are those we think the beat of is the best.
Or put it backwards: those we listen to
Most loverly, most long, we have to kill.
And I have killed my thousands, as you say;
And with no woman's horror I have heard
Close neighbors here tell how in wintertime,
When snow was belly deep, and foundered bucks
No more than fawns could fly, the bobsleds filled
Faster than carts with corn; their carcasses
House-high as home they slid to feed the town.
Crude, but there was sense in it; and some
Could boast a little, even, when the crust
Thawed off, and famine died. Oh, I have shot
My thousands, and my last gun lies as proud
Along the ready shoulder as my first.
Yet all the while no animal has more
Bewitched me, little Thorsten, than a doe
With four clean legs. And so when she was found,
A fawn that you could almost fold inside
A coonskin, she was delicate and small,
I let the business work; I named her Nelly;
I raised her like a man's last daughter, born
Through miracle when warmth and wife are gone.

207

I brought her up, I think, to take the place
Of all those other thousands; and with eyes
Like hers, and with that dancing step, she did.
Three early springs I've plowed for her, and planted
Lettuces she liked. For her, that is,
I've made myself an old fool of a farmer.
Not that my sons would say so; in their minds
I'm useless, or at best I'm ornament,
I'm trumpery out of old time, good to keep.
But as to Nelly: Thorsten, you are wise
In a cracked way, and you can guess the rest.
So you won't be surprised if what I said,
Yesterday, when they forced me to, I meant.
I meant the last loud word of it, by God,
And you nor any other little man,
Or big one if the bullies come, can change me.
Look at me, Thorsten, look!"
                                        But none of those
In darkness, by their houses, knew that now
His very lids were lost in a wild stare,
A look that clouded walls and cleared the broad
Far night of every blackness save his own.
Their eyes were on a window still unchanged,
Unshattered, as their feet past one another
Started on three journeys: Nancy's dark
By David's, and his mother's following soon;
All of them toward Richman, realms away.

Thorsten kept his eyes on Gard, as on
God's sleeping witness. "Anger, my sent guest,
My column of cold fire to light the road,
Hath something of divinity: that's written,
And so it must be true. But anger strikes
For one of two known reasons, and the worst
Is farther from the best than I from you.
It strikes to save the good from hurt again,

Or strikes to hurt the hurter. Which is best?"
But Richman if he listened scorned to choose.
"And if to hurt the hurter, then is good
Advantaged? Who can say that this is so?
A hunter has been hurt, and so presumes
To vindicate the good by hunting on
To murder." Not an echo in the room.
"To murder, having proved his private hurt,
Yet having still to state the good it threatened;
Whether, too, the hurter is less fit
Henceforth than he for champion; and whether—
This is the last—the hunter himself, becoming
Hurtful, shall not be the hunted then."

Quiet still. But now there was change, was difference,
Suddenly, past the door, and Gard's old ears,
Familiar beyond Richman's, named the sound.
Seth.
        While Nancy, nearing that same door,
Saw nothing in her darkness, and those others
Nothing in theirs; rehearsing only "Sir,
Listen to the best that we can say,
Then bide the rest!"
                        "Lie down, Gard!" Thorsten shrilled,
Innocent of a cause. But Gard was up
Like whirled wind, and Old Richman, twisting round,
Had something in his hands that clicked as the doorpin
Clicked.
        And there was Seth, with three faint faces
Past him in night's mirror paling his.
His cap was on the threshold, where his feet
Trampled it, and his lips, dry with decision,
Parted to no end; until the three
Behind him lifted voices like one voice:
"Seth, come back!" and Thorsten with his arms
Waved "Back" and Gard, agreeing with low growls,

Threatened a stiff leap. While Richman's gun
Steadily, steadily lowered.
                                    Heard or seen,
So much of sound, of motion, was the sign
For Seth to raise his right hand, as he did,
And stop it all: except the steady gun,
Lowering as the lips undid their drouth.
"Sir. You never saw me. But I know
Your errand, and I am the end of it.
I am the reason that you need no longer
Look for her, for Nelly. She is dead.
Days ago I did it. Why, I'll never
Know too clear myself, Sir, nor will say
This evening, when the fact is ampler sound.
If I could bring her back with band and bell
I'd climb the sky to do it. Since she's lost,
I cannot have you looking any more,
And listening, and calling. I won't keep
A silence any longer that is truth's,
Not mine. Not even yours. Not even, Sir—"
But his breath failed its function. He had met
One wave too many in the sea of wills.
There was no further stroke. And his eyes closed
Just as the heaven's silence he had dreamed of
Opened and let him in, and drew him down.
And as the earth's, wrinkled beyond reshaping,
Tore with a single shot, and Richman stepped,
Head up, across the threshold where a cap,
Forgotten, was revisited by curls
That never again would wear it save as now:
Thrust into it, nudging its wool awry.

VI

The hunter himself had judged, and for an ending
Syllable had spoken sharpest death;
And altering thus the order that no man

Administers, the silence no man owns,
Had disappeared in darkness, from the several
Voices that at last by Thorsten's door—
After the numbed recoil, the nothing felt—
Broke upward.
    "It was my fault," David groaned,
The first of them to separate clear sound
From the half sound of horror. "Maybe so.
As soon as I had guessed what Seth was sick with,
As soon as the old puke was poison too
In my own mind, I tried to snort him down
With snicker hawhaws. Damn me for a loon!
Pardon, little Ma, if I swore then."
But Clara had not listened where she lay,
Her breath unwelcome as it wandered back,
And where the hands of Nancy, shunning Seth
As something still too precious, still too strange,
Fluttered in the doorlight to revive her;
Where Thorsten, stooping too, fumbled at laces
With the one paw that Gard's throat left him free;
For, strangle-held, Gard lunged as if to follow,
And his choked cries, accompaniment to David,
Only with effort ceased. "I bull-roared so,
Last night in the barn, the poor boy lost his intellects.
When the time come, he wasn't healthy scared,
He didn't keep himself off like I cautioned.
Read him all the lecture I knew how,
But the horse laugh was louder." All this while
His mind remembered Seth as the small comrade
Who slipping from a teaser flew one day
And wept against his forearm; which at first
Was rough, for David still despised the rare,
The woman arts of comfort; but they ended
Humming random choruses of hymns.
That was the good beginning, that was how
The chain between them tested its gold link.
Not that a Mayfield elder would have known.

211

For he was vain, was bully; and once more
He groaned, desiring memories no lie
Could muster: even recollected mirth
In neighbors who had nudged each other, saying:
"Seth and Dave are thick as two hung thieves;
Ought to be more proud and show it less."
But that had never happened, as on marches,
West of here by mountains, it was heard
Of two that in their war paint walked as one:
Two stripling braves, compacted in a June
When peace hovered the lowlands. Now in fall
They climbed to bloody ground; but each would blow
His signal to the other up the file,
And halting, had no mind for elder music.
Then one of them was wounded, and must wait
In a white cave till victory brought again
A serpent line of warriors winding down.
His mate, commanded onward, never ceased
His whispers night or day, in rest or motion,
To an invisible, a listening forehead;
Sharing his meat and berries with a mouth
That no one saw devour them, though they vanished.
When the new moon was sharper than a shell,
And the tired troop, returning, scaled the rock,
He was the first to clamber and embrace
A youth too gaunt for gladness: only joy,
Solemn as death between them, while the chieftains
Nodded beneath their war paint and scuffed on.
Nothing like that for David to remember;
And a third time he groaned, but now for shame
That Seth lay thus untended: all their thoughts
Yet not their hands upon him, all their grief
As if for one untouchable. "By God,
There's Sethie, and no stump of us has stirred.
But then it's plain enough. Sethie is gone.
Here! I'll run for Doctor." And if ears
Were in them they distinguished his great boots

212

Beating the dark cold ground toward Nancy's house.
While Nancy, still at Clara's head, stroked softly
And held her face away; and Thorsten, pulling
At Gard, and gritting his teeth in a grey anguish,
Waited for the right word that would ring,
Continuing, their lamentation's chorus.
"Boy," and he began in such a voice
As locusts in a far tree faintly use
When August, sick of summer, can endure
No fuller sound, and muffles even this;
"Boy, the best of men can no more tell
Time's ways than angels can the acts of him
Whose all is act, whose all, before and after,
There as here, above us and below,
Forever now is being done: forever
Now, now, now, and not when reason,
Limping from the rear, sits down to say
This, or this, the cause. Was mine the fault,
Beguiling what was left of his old soul
With pitiful philosophies, with brags
Of how we both were heaven's grey-haired children,
Bred to a brace of rituals; and if his,
Why not redeem it instantly with fire?
Was I the one that set his mind in motion
Just when it would be still? I do not know.
We thought you lasting; and the lightning fell
To show us in a flash that nothing is.
Richman was the bolt; and may he burn
Even as faggots do, that in their pride
Forget they are but instruments of change:
Material, not mind, of sacrifice.
No, not that. I may not right his wrong
And judge him. Let him smolder where he is—"

"Where is he!" someone bellowed. It was Seth
The elder, come with Ben at his loud back;
And both of them were crouched above the doctor,

Whose lenses, when he reared his head at last,
Caught Thorsten's fire full on them, and declared,
As owls declare, nothing but doom and quiet.
Clara was the first of them to read
In the two depthless tokens what she knew,
And Nancy knew, and Thorsten knew, already.
Then she was gone again, in a wide silence
That held them all as bound; till the grey doctor,
Shifting to her side, and tenderly taking
Nancy's hand, that faltered, from its place,
Ministered to grief on grief's own ground;
While Nancy knelt, and three men over her
Stared helplessly at Seth, whom not to save
Was not to have a function while time lasted.

"Who, where's who?" droned Thorsten. "You mean
        Richman?"
"Richman! Hell and hoppergrass! Where's David?
Come by like a bull loose; pawed the door
And bawled at me; it fairly shook the bed:
'Go over! He's at Thorsten's, and he's hurt!
Sethie's hurt!' Well, here we be. But David's
Off again. And where? For there's a danger—"
"Yes," said Thorsten. "David must be found.
Only wandering, maybe; but the worst
Is likeliest. Hush, though; don't wake her yet
With a new worry. See? The doctor wants
All quiet that can be so."
                                And her husband,
Bending his heavy head to where she lay,
Saw her for the first time in her stricken
Smallness, and his own loss spoke aloud:
His own loss, such as western fathers once
Had burned their tents for, and their counted goods,
Their robes, their painted weapons, and all moving
Creatures they had tamed to follow fire.
"Lord, O Lord, give me the little language

214

A fellow in trouble needs, the lightfoot word
That travels till it reaches the true place,
Then sits, and sorrow opens the big door
And says to it: Come in, for we be friends.
Lord, let me mourn him as I might
If the black cat they told me got my tongue
When I was kitten high had ever kept it.
Delicate's the language Sethie calls for,
Or maybe none at all. I swear I'm humble
Hogtied by this misery in my mind.
Sethie was a good boy, and he's gone.
Sethie—"
          "Don't!" said Clara, bending up
Straightly with all her strength, and with the doctor's
Arm for more behind her. "Don't you try.
It's terrible, this trying. Not for us,
Or you. For Seth. There! I have said his name,
And instantly my mind is a cold house,
All dark between where my door was and where—
But he has gone clear through it, and it's closed.
His door is heaven's door."
                    The doctor, clearing
His throat, and thrusting his face into her vision,
Said: "Help me with your hands, and we'll go home."
"Home!" She pushed him from her and got up.
"Home! But who goes first? Who needs my bed
Before I do, and hungers to lie straight—
Go, why don't you all, and rest the poor
Tired boy? You gawking simpletons, you ganders!
David! Where is David?" And she squinted,
Counting the other faces. "He should be
My help in time of trouble, my good wall
Against all future weather." "Little Ma,"
And Ben's hoarse voice came closer, climbing slopes
Of strangeness, "can't I help? Can't I for once?"
She reached for him and held him while the tears,
Merciful in their plenty, flowed at last

And melted her false anger. "Ben my dear,
Forgive the things I called you, and ask these
In his name to forgive. But where is David?"
"We don't know. He went to get the doctor.
Me and Dad, too: here both of us are."

"You!" But it was fear, not anger now,
That brought the shrillness back. "Another gone!
My next best, and the nearest to my life.
David! Listen! David!" Three still men,
Glancing at one another in the half-light,
Passing her presentiment along
As if a turning lantern slowly swept
Their faces, stamped as if to follow: dim
Their purpose, but the end of it was David.
"Doctor, what are they doing?" And for her
He stayed them. "Thorsten, let me have a blanket.
Ben, you be here ready with your father
To carry what I wrap. I'll walk ahead
With her, with your poor mother. Thorsten, help
Me turn him. Nancy, take her in awhile.
Find her a low chair, and talk to her
Of anything. Of him." For Clara leaned
Too close above their working.
                                    And he thought:
Nancy has been quiet now so long,
I doubt if she can do it. But the stir
Will steady her if only—"Father! Here!"
And Nancy, never moving, made him look.
"Don't you see? The reason, first and last,
Was vanity, was me. I wanted something—
Something—oh, so silly!—and he dared
To get it. In the woods. In pretty woods
That never will be that way any more."
"Nancy." He was gentle with her name,
Yet doctorwise to coldness. "Go in now,

216

And wait for her, and talk—why, even talk
Of this."
        "No, not of this. And I can go
Unguided. But I won't," said Clara, altering
Everything at once with an odd smile.
"Come in with me. You are the weaker woman,
Suddenly. Come in." And both their tears
Went with them, friendly now to their free woe
As round the blanket's corner they limped in
To firelight; where they sat until the sound
Of four still men at work grew bearable.
"Nancy, dear. My daughter if the world
Had lasted." "But you never would have liked—"
"Yes, for he did." "Then you knew he said it:
Sweethearts?" "So, my child, I say it too."

"Doctor!" at the door, in a scratched whisper,
"Why not here, with Thorsten? It's too much,
Maybe, for a mother to sit through:
The sight, among so many living sounds—"
"No!" And Clara, nipping him to silence,
Darted from her chair. "His place is home,
And I'll go on before you to be sure
All's ready. Nancy darling, your good father's
Waiting. Not for me, child. Take his arm,
Then lead me on as far as to the store.
After that we part. And may you sleep
Forever. There is nothing to be done
Till Doomsday. Be his sweetheart still, and dream
Even as he would dream. Oh!" and her bravery,
Buckling under a burden so unnatural,
Broke. And so the doctor, nodding sidewise,
Ordering the march, went on as prop
To Clara, not to Nancy; who at his heels,
And never glancing backward where the open
Door still shed its dusk on bending men,
Followed all of the way through Mayfield's night:

217

On to the store, then eastward over ruts
To the slow-waving curtains in a window
No one's hand had fastened, so that tapers,
Midway of the mantel, tossed blear light
On muslin, and were guide to moving woe.

"My little room, our little room, is ready.
It will be his tonight," said Clara, feeling
The door frame as she entered. "I can sleep—
Why, anywhere. That corner there is kind—
See, where the couch is?" "Lady, it is good,
But come to us tonight. Or go with Nancy,
Now, before they—nothing's to be done
But what my skill can do it." When he frowned
She trembled. "No, I never would forgive—"
"Then this is what I say. Lie down at once—
Here, Nancy, you must help—here!" And against
His coolness she could offer only tears,
That washed her first with rage, but then with a rinsing
Weakness. "Well." "I told you so. Now, lady—
There, now, are you listening?" "Not for long.
I am so tired. As he is. Did you say—"

"Father, they are coming." "Then it's time
For my good girl herself to be in bed.
Tell Mother that, and slip on up to sleep."
"Please. I'll wait outside. I can't go home
Without you. Now they're almost—I'll keep warm
And wait." She went; and heard how Thorsten groaned
And stumbled. But it might be for his burden,
Come now to its threshold seeking rest.
The first sound of her father on the path
Was a low word to Thorsten, whom she saw
As something small and doglike following near.
"Here she is. So you go on to Gard
And give him our goodnight." "Goodnight." And Thorsten,
Edging beyond them both, was soon a soft

218

Lost particle of darkness. "Did he mean
Goodnight to me too, Father? Does he forgive
My sending Seth away?" "Hush to your nonsense,
Darling. No one here sent Seth away.
But come along, my girl, and in the lamplight
Show me your color, show me yourself again.
Nothing could be so happy to remember
Up north of here tonight." "Tonight! You wouldn't!"
"Wouldn't? No, but must. I promised her.
She turned as I was leaving; then I knew
The woman hadn't slept one pitiful wink;
She turned, but just her eyes, that caught our tiptoe,
And begged me with them, saying David, David.
How she knows he followed you can guess.
And she does know. I'd swear it. But her hope
Of finding him and changing his big will:
I haven't that. The chances of his dodging,
His ducking, while I pass him are as good—
As you are. Yet I'll try it. And your trick,
After Mother wears out her worst worry,
Is meanwhile, dear, to sleep." "Impossible.
I'll be with you." "Nancy, no! You won't,
Of course not! Here we are, though. In with you.
Nonsense time is past."
                                    He thrust her in
Before him, sending a glance to the strict eyes
Wherein a solemn terror kept itself
With difficulty silent. "Well, my dear:
The worst. But she is cold—dead cold—and tired."
"You say it was the worst?" He nodded, frowning,
And took his glasses off to rub them clear.
"But now I must be gone. A call, of course,
Just in the prime of evening. Nolan's boy
Drove by and said to hurry, and I said
I would, and then forgot. It may be long.
Don't look for me till morning; if old Nolan's
Halfway like he sounds it might be later."

219

Lantern light, fringing with hay shadows
Bin-door, stall, and buggy, fell on the dappled
Necks of Prince and Peter, and on their bald
Slow-blinking faces, hung there in a doze.
He slapped them: "Peter! Prince!" and let his gloved,
Affectionate hand slide down to stroke their noses.
Sometimes he would come and only that much
Happened: stroke on stroke until he chuckled,
And both heads clumsily tossed, and then the under
Lips of his great slaves slobbered a shoulder.
So they would wait and see, and meanwhile soak
More darkness in, as flanks of horses do
When lanterns leave them, warm in their deep rest.
But this was no such night, the bridles said,
Clinking as he brought them; and the bits
Clicked upon teeth that set, resisting his will
Through liberty's last moment; yet in vain
Beyond it, for the buckles in their places
Tightened, and the rest, the rearward harness—
"Peter! Prince!" They backed away, obedient,
And soon the doctor, settled in his seat,
Was off, with not a sign of Nancy waving
Luck to him from any lighted window.

He sighed, reaching the road and turning north
In the high darkness, trusting his horses' feet
With all that lay below: crisp rut on rut
As far as Colebridge corner, then right on,
After the little jog, due north to the store
At Ambraw Bend where this road forded the river,
The looping line that, done with its eastern bulge,
Came in again just there and wandered on
Northwest to Nolan's acres; and past those,
Three rough miles perhaps, or four, to Richman's.

Not a star stood over. And he thought:
David should be with me, as by day

He used to, finding reasons as a bear
Finds honey, pawing any bush around:
Turning up excuses for a trip
With Doctor. And the horses. It was Prince
Who charmed him; and the clatter of his driving
Echoed even here, upon the walls
Of this most woeful world. For David drove
By yelling, not by leather, and his joy
Was all in watching flesh fly under song.
"Hi!" and "Yipayandy!" "Prince, boy!" "Pete!"
The syllables were close about here, sounding
Perfectly like David in the sun;
As if last June were now, and at this rise,
Where Beckwith's view was coming, and the horses
Slowed to a tired walk, a cheerful voice,
Acknowledging the change, dropped into tune,
And even sluggish Peter sloped his ears.
The doctor checked himself. It was November,
And late, and sullen cold. Nobody sang
This side the dashboard, and no floating chant
Brought David in above it; though he stood,
Conceivably, and stared through darkness now
At his four-footed heroes, hearing them
As he the doctor did: their iron hooves
Still thudding up the rise, and their thin nostrils
Shaping into trumpets of forced breath.

A giant, loud with grief, was on the way
To vengeance. On the way to death again.
Death. It was a thing a doctor knew
Could never lose its strangeness. Yet it came,
Some years, in gentle guises, yielding good
With terror; mercy tempering its black.
Death could be a greyness, spreading rest;
Rippling on to peace. Not this one, though.
He pressed the horses, scolding their dumb hope
Of rest beyond the rise, and drilled the dark

221

With fierce and futile glances; it was vain,
This driving on and on in a blank world
Of someone else's wishes, even hers
The weak one, who had tried to roll her head
And could not. "David, David!" came again,
In smallness, the clear voice, as if a bird,
Untouchable by whirlwinds, yet knew best
Thin premonition's note, pain's roundelay.

No force but that faint calling kept him on
To Colebridge, where one lighted cabin window
Tempted him; yet warned him, as he paused,
Of what a curious tongue might toss abroad
Tomorrow. It was not a public woe
The eight feet here were pounding to prevent.
Richman's blood or David's, like the last
Warm drop of Seth's: it was a thing of Mayfield,
Something to be labelled in the phial:
Poison, yet our own, and in its way
The life of all, elixir to our story;
Not to be ever tested on the lips
Of strangers, even just ones. He must look
And pass. So on to the Bend, where no man's boots,
Not even David's, leagued against delay,
Would beat him to the turning, he beslaved
His horses, with a hope that grim despair
Made greater in its intervals of flight.

But west of him and Colebridge lay the footways
Of David and Old Richman. Separate there
In thick and saving darkness, still the paths
They lined across the prairie would converge.
Morning, and the web would have its center,
North and west of here where Dandy slept,
And where the doctor's arc, and the slow river's,
Ran in a wider time. Old Richman's front
All night had never weakened, nor had missed,

222

Magnet-sure, the straightest cable home.
From Thorsten's door and Seth, from duty done,
From past and present trouble he had stepped
And studied how a short cut over fields
And fences, over sloughs and weasel runs,
Would bring him home to Dandy, who was right
And waiting to be told so. Dandy right!
And Nelly by that token nowhere now.
So in the prairie blackness, three sore miles
From David, he kept on. While David followed
No man where from Colebridge he had turned,
Anticipating horses, and had cut
His own short way to Richman's. There he trudged;
And Richman, if he pondered on pursuit,
Sent up no sign of heeding. Richman tramped
In the bleak truth of victory, naked now
With triumph over doubt. And if he staggered
No one sighed. The battle in his heart
Was over, and the badge of it he wore
Was a huge loneliness till he came home.

VII

Peter and Prince, interpreting too well
A sleepiness of leather, a slacked rein,
Paused at Nolan's gatepost. This their last
Known landmark west or north; and water spilled
From a long trough their mouths, alert, remembered.
Dozing at his whip the doctor nodded
Lazily, acknowledging no death
Of fixed familiar motion, and still suiting
The pitch of his tired shoulders to a jolt.
Then the stillness woke him, and the stamp
Of Peter's thirsty hooves; then, suddenly,
A sense of Nolan there, as if his lie
Had looked at him through darkness, in the form
Of an old Irish beard and a blue nightcap:

Nolan, sore of sight, accusing him.
He cleared his throat, rebuking the two beasts,
And backed them. Now the roadway on from here—
Yes, this was how his eyes at Nolan's gate
Had seen and yet not seen; as if the senses,
Huddled there to save the weakest one,
Had drawn a barn and cabin in black lines
On blackness. Thus he knew that it was Nolan's;
And thus, along these windings he had never
Travelled, he was seeing: rut by rut
The road was greying on, and the few trees,
Feathering into vision, showed a west
No more than he was willing for new day.
The doctor shivered. Business, needing light,
Should love it; but the dark that must be left
Was in its own way warm, and clearness comes
Like loudness: ears and eyes too soon awake.

He shivered, and the robe across his knees
Slid to a new shape, shield against the sun,
That still unborn behind him still could pale
All darkness with a thought of coming death.
In front of him the country was as strange
As those five stars there, fading into pearl.
Richman's house, the sons, the father in it,
And the brown Ambraw gurgling in its bed
Somewhere beyond and downward; barn and crib,
And, westward in the oak woods not too far,
The deer close: all were legend, all were dream.
Would that it all could sleep there, and last night
Be nothing. But the river, adding silver,
Suddenly, to sound, was double guide,
Was conscience. There its current, that by dark
Had voices, hushed them now to a swift stillness,
Washing the roots of sycamores like blissful
Slaves at the feet of kings, nor wanting song
To say it. So the river in its pride

Slipped onward, and the road with a rough clearness,
Parallel and faithful, ran ahead
To Richman's, where perhaps the horses' ears
Already had forseen themselves at home.
For Prince's traces lagged, and the four wheels
Jolted, and the tires rang out the clods.
Then it was there. The last jog being rounded,
The long, low house of Richman, with its porch
Of cedar posts and clapboards: there it was,
Silent in the first sun. But the smoke
That smiled above the chimney sent no sign
Of David or no David come to kill.

The three late sons of Richman, scraping chairs
And rising from their coffee cups to listen,
Looked at one another. Horses' hooves.
A team. And from the east. And buggy tires.
"Lordy, boys, the old one's done surrendered.
Coming home in style! And so, of course,
No Nelly." Paul the youngest, lover of horses,
Scrambled to a window. "What do you see?"
George, with eyes on Dandy, and as still,
Stammered: "What do you see? Who is it with him?
Getting out himself? Or is he lame,
And carried? Can he walk?" Paul waved a hand,
Impatient. "No, it's not him after all.
Stranger, and alone. A beaver cap
And glasses. And a yoke of spotted greys:
Beauties! Boy, they're beauties, and as big
As steamboats. Now he's tying them. I'll go."
"Let Dandy go," said George, the middle son,
The gentle. They arrived so close together,
Three of them, the summer gifts of Susan
To an autumnal husband, she had said:
They'll be the same in oldness, equal brothers,
And luxury to each other when we go.
But Dandy had been oldest from the first

In brotherly decision; and so now.
"Let Dandy go," said George. And Dandy went
Between them to the door, beyond whose grain
They heard the doctor scolding his high steeds
To patience.

    When it opened, and the sun
Swung in upon them, low from the cool east,
There was the stranger, halfway up the lane
And hesitating; yet he came straight on.

"I'm Doctor Emerson, of Mayfield. No,
Not lost exactly. I am here in search
Of one of our best citizens. He's lost.
Dave Golliday. You know him?" "Golliday."
Dandy rehearsed it absently. "We wondered,
Hearing your horses there, if you had brought
Our father. He's not lost, he couldn't be."
"Your father." "Then you've seen him?" But he rubbed
His eyes, from which the glasses had been lifted,
Wearily. He wanted further time,
And took it with a question. "Have you corn
For my two hungry horses?" Dandy brightened,
Happily conspiring. "And yourself—
Paul, unhitch and feed them while the doctor
Samples what we had. It's bacon, Sir,
And coffee, and hoecakes the southern way.
Hang your coat up here, and while you scrub
I'll rummage. Do you trust your team with Paul?
He isn't used to—" "Left horse bites a little.
Better tell your brother. It's in fun,
Though few would know till after." But the door,
Opening to his hand, showed Prince and Peter
Patient in the sun as two curved arms
Moved over their worn harness. "He'll be safe.
They know him for a horseman. It descends
By birth, and it can skip two generations."
Noisily pouring water, now he rolled

A wrist free of its cuff and called across:
"That one?" "George." "And you?" "I'm Daniel Richman.
Dandy, here with us." "So? In the den,
Not Daniel? You are very kind to me."

The time for both of them went on as slow
As palms could rub each other, contemplating;
Slow, and elsewhere stopped. Outdoors, in the cold,
In the newborn light, a minute missed its beat
As Richman's ancient eyes, threading the hazel
Down and across the road, saw two white horses
Led by his happiest son, and heard the "Hi!",
The "Here, boy!" of authority's fresh lungs.
Horses. And a second minute shied
From passing; and the old man lost an inch
Of last night's fierce erectness, when he swore—
But who was here? With horses? So it stopped,
The ticking, while an old hand on a gun
Loosened and tightened; loosened again and slid,
Bewildered, down the barrel.
                    Far away,
And none but he could know it, David leaned,
Stalking the old head still with tireless eyes,
And listened. Since the dawn he had not lost
One motion of those fringes. On and on,
Guarding his distance, he had stamped and glared,
Exulting. But the interval between them,
Guarding itself as well, had checked him now,
Here in the very sight of sons and home,
Here at the sanctuary. So in doubt
He halted, and his mind went swift ahead,
Calculating dangers. Why not now?
Never a soul was looking. Why not now?
Fifty leaps, and the hazel brush would help:
Two in a thicket wrestling, then one falling,
Falling; then a wand to wind him with.
But the barn there: someone, finished with his chores

And loitering; looking back, and stepping slow.
As soon as he was in then, David said.
So both of them, unmoving, held their breath
While no heard minute struck, outdoors or in.

"The other one, my cheerful groom, is Paul.
So now I have your names. And a duke's breakfast.
Yet I must tell you—" studying the lean length
Of Dandy's face, with temples early streaked,
And deep between, importunate black eyes—
"I haven't in your kindness, or in Paul's,
Or George's, for I think he too would serve me,
The key to your lost sire." "He isn't lost,
Nor could be. He's a hunter, and the world's
One place for him. You mean we aren't hunters?
No, but we are his." "And a strong mother's,
Happier in her silence than John Richman
For all his piping is?" Dandy withdrew
His gaze and let it wander to the gold,
The little oval frame where Susan's eyes,
Black as his and still, ordered the room.
"We're like her more, they say; except that Paul,"
And now the groom himself burst whistling in,
"Is sudden, and except that all would walk
To the land's end to find him if he fell.
Sir! Has he been seen? And on which day?
And where? And did he lead—" "The deer is dead."

David, staring forward, blinked and freed
His vision from its trance. The brown old man
Was moving. His gun lifted and his shoulders
Ducked as he went sidling to the left
Through sparser brush and followed the rail fence—
Not home now, David saw, but up the road
In a wide arc whose end would be that grove,
That stretch of copper darkness where the oaks
Still slept in their late leaves, and whence the river

228

Sounded even here, falling above
Some pool or rapid rare in its long course.
The barn, the house, a low shed, and the grove:
From right to left the line went roundabout
To safety. So the old hawk must be thinking:
Back way home is best. Well, go on fooling
Wrens and turtle doves; the big wing's here
Behind you, and a talon set to tear.
So now he moved with Richman, swift to the grove.

"Dandy! Did you hear? The doe was—" "Paul,
Nelly's not the thing now. Then you mean,
He found her: so?" "He found that she was dead.
Where Nelly is, who knows? Except the one—"
"Then someone?" "Yes." "Dave Golliday, I guess
You mean—is he the one? He knows the place?"
"I doubt it. There are other Gollidays.
Or were."
          The youngest Richman, rising still
And staring, was the wild one in the room.
"Dandy! Don't you see? He's done it, sure.
Ask him if he's done it. Then we'll know.
Hell and peppered devils! Have it out!
I can't stand this." "Paul, be still awhile."
"No," said the doctor, resolute at last,
"I'll tell you what I must. Your father's errand
Ended in our town. Last night it was.
Dave's brother Seth, six days ago or so,
My daughter's lost the count, the poor girl says
The poor boy was her beau and did her bidding,
Shot—" "No!" Dandy cried. "He must have known."
"I don't know what Seth knew. Nor ever will."
"He must have seen." "I'll tell you what I saw;
And my bad eyes are none the better for it.
Last night it was. David ran and woke me,
And so I went; and so, in Thorsten's door,
Lay Seth. And David Golliday, his brother:

No one saw him after, no one's seen—"
Dandy had little voice, but standing up
He used it. "Father, too. Nobody's seen—"
"I never did. Before I got there, Daniel,
The beast's king was—" "Careful, Sir! The name
Is lovable here still." "And so in heaven,
Doubtless. Don't mistake me. I am but heaven's
Deputy. Saving David's saving him.
I came, if you insist, to stop the blood;
And if one vessel's fairer than another,
I am not called to judge. Except I say,
A third, more nearly gold than either, spilled
Last night. He was a valuable boy."

"He's dead, then, he is dead," from the dry throat
Of George. "So Father's hiding. But it's day,
And he'll not be afraid. He's coming home,
I see him." "Where!" "I see him as he'll be:
Not looking back, just coming in the door
And wiping his old gun, grandfather's gun."

But Dandy's agitation where he paced
From chair to window, shuffling as in chains,
Muffled the low stammer. "Doctor," he said,
Reaching for his coat, that from a hook
Hung carefully, its ample folds in order,
"There's coffee still to pour, and there's a bed
To rest in. George, you stay and show him that,
And turn it back, and be three hosts in one.
Paul, the horses. Help him out to them
If I'm not home by—" "Daniel, I am tired.
But time the villain isn't, and an hour's
Eternity if lost. I'm going too."
"As you would have it, Sir. But not with me."
And the door cried behind him on its hinges,
Forced to a final turning, oak on oak.

The doctor and his groom, unevenly
Advancing, uncommunicative now,
Went over frozen leaves and the packed earth
Of barnway paths till there in the dark entry
Prince and Peter lifted their long faces,
Mutinously blinking, robbed of rest.
"Pretending you don't know!" the doctor mumbled,
Smoothing Prince's mane with a slow glove;
"Pretending I'm a stranger, and this hall
Your home, and no good reason now for wetting
Fetlocks in a waste November world.
Out with you, my handsome! And you there,"
Drawing a sudden thumb down Peter's nose,
"Be my horse this morning and don't bite."
In the far gloom the oxen stood and watched them,
Stupefied with hay, not caring much
Who moved in forward sunshine that a window
Narrowed to four shafts the doctor watched.
"A barn that Mayfield men should come and study.
Even our women might. It's kitchen trim.
And the curved bins: who cared to have them so?"
"Dandy." "Even hayseed doesn't drop.
And there's no dust to sift—where's Dandy now?
He went to look, but where? Is there a place—"
Paul jerked the dangling reins until they flapped
And Prince's head flew up. "I didn't mean to.
Maybe to the grove. That's been the deer-place.
George and me should be there too by now.
Maybe not, but Dandy—" "You go on.
I'll finish here. Go now, and thanks for this."

Now where? He saw the quick turn, then the grove.
But Dandy would be there, and Dandy wanted
No one at his side, not even Paul.
Dandy would be entering it now,
Russet under oak leaves, flushed as they
With the year's end, with rumors of red death.

231

The doctor scowled: "The river and the road:
They both go in. Which then am I to wait by?
Dandy went the low way, by the bluffs,
And George and Paul have followed. They are woodsmen.
I am not. Prince! Peter! Do you hear?
Prince! Peter!" And they left the house behind them,
Trotting till the oak grove walled them in
From west; when with a whispered whoa they stopped
And, standing, heard the crows cry: only crows,
And, deeper in the shade, the bells of jays.
No huntsman and his hunter, no rash tongue
Replying, no bull voice of David there.

Even now, in a clearing where long shadows,
Lace on the brittle ground, on the bronze leaf-cover,
Said it was early morning, was late fall,
Was thinning time for the burr oaks, was this grove's
Climacteric, mid-moment unto barren
Slumber; half its bravery still high,
Still clinging for the sun to cool with fire;
Even now, by a low bluff, rim to the river,
Back from its edge a way, on the table's top—
The rumor of swirling water, and the plunge
As playfully it fell, came cautious up,
Over the rim and over, then went again—
Old Richman kneeled, and with his hunting knife
Dug leaves, dug mold away till the earth was bare:
A circle of it, wide as three men's hands.
Then, since the frost was in it, and his fingers
Failed of a deeper entrance, steel descended,
Chipping and picking flint till a hole was done,
A rounded hole, as big as three men's heads.
And now his fingers, raking the rubbish out,
Patted and smoothed the lining of a grave
He lingered over, lengthening some deed
For love's sake, or in fear lest it be seen.

And it was seen. David, with a double
Oak trunk for his shield, stood scowling off
Ten paces, haggard pale; for he was tired;
And galled that he was tired; and bitter-tongued
That now he had grown curious. For the grave
Bemused him, and he balanced, leaning low,
Spying upon an old head that in shame
Looked round. But Richman, sure at last of stillness,
And glancing for good measure where his gun,
Its butt and muzzle spanning two low stumps
Behind him, lay for solitary guard,
Pulled something from his belt and let it be there,
Flat on his palm awhile, before the fingers,
Flexing, meditated what they held.

The turkey bone, said David. What he called
His deer with. He is burying it, by devil—
Hush! the moment said, and simply listen.
For now the hand had risen, and the lips,
Finding bone between them, blew three small
Half doubtful notes, "Hi, Nelly," that the air
Took into it as nothing. But the more
Came soon that it demanded. Standing straight
And bracing his thonged ankles, Richman blew
"Hi, Nelly!" loud and slow, and each note long:
"Hi, Nelly!" and each syllable in its pride
Went on, its waves disturbing the brown wood
Till crows responded, brawling, and the jays,
Metallic in the middle distance, shrilled.
No other sound but that; no bounding hooves;
Not even breath, restoring the musician
After his heart's expense. While David pondered,
Rueful, as the purpose in his blood
Ran pale, and like a leech upon his will
Exhaustion drained its liquor. Yet again
He groaned, remembering Seth; and so his eyes
Returned to their slack duty; and they saw

233

How Richman, with a sudden angry start,
Flung the object from him, letting it fall
Like any other stick in a found hole;
Then, kneeling, how he scratched the rubble in
And the torn mold, and pounded a few leaves
As if in hatred, careless of last cover.

Now, said David, now it could be done:
Now, while he is deaf with his fool's fury.
Now! he said. And still, as if a guard
Laid hands upon him roughly, there he lagged
By his twin pillars, aching to advance
Yet ignorant of north and the first step;
And would have stood so always, or till doom
Descended in the guise of falling trees,
Had Richman, reared again to his known height,
Not moved to take his gun; and as he moved,
Extended his long joints, said David, shifting
Like an old mountain cat, a lithe old varmint
Stiffened a little, maybe, and top-grizzled,
But scarce enough to cancel being cat;
And had he never, turning for one more look
Behind him, from a lynx fear of spaces,
Exposed—as once before, beside a bonfire—
The worst of his eyes' wildness, their high stare
At nothing, their inhuman and unlidded
Legend of mistrust and hot contempt.
Dandy, being by, could have resummoned
The part of him not animal, the piece
That in an hour, if all of him should live,
Would pat three heads at home and send a look,
When no one saw, toward Susan's oval presence:
Small in the room yet there, and therefore great.
But Dandy, elsewhere still and white at the lips
With looking, was not by. So nothing stopped
The leap of David's legs, the lift of his hair
As the ten paces tumbled into one

And the shy musket, patient on its rests,
Lay from that instant evenly in reach
Of him and his dreamed victim. Whose recoil
Only was for the instant. Half alert,
Half slouching, for disdain was in his grace,
He answered David's eyes with a blind dare
That all at once some bitterness reduced
To seeing; for a wrinkle of his lids
Confessed it, and a curling at his lips.

"You saw," he said, "you stood somewhere and saw
A certain thing I did, I buried? Well."
"A thing for certain! And for sore eyes, too!"
David's voice, more slender than a slingshot,
Still could find a forehead. Richman squinted.
"You don't know what it could have been I buried."
"Buzzard bone? A big thorn knitting needle?
Toothpick? Ram's horn? Pizzle of an ox
From Iceland? If I don't know, then I don't.
But I was to an auction once in Mayfield—"
Could it be terror, yellowing those eyes—
"And who should pop along but Panther John
In war paint? Frills aplenty. Shawnee slippers
And a belt stuck with butcher knives, meat axes,
Skillet handles, skewer bones. Or bones
With songbirds in them, maybe; couldn't keep
True count of all them tricksies. There was one
We didn't see, though, till he slipped it out—"
No, it was hate now, jaundicing a whole
Bright forest, breeding fungus in the sun—
"And tooted it three toots. You might have thought
A toy stagecoach was coming, but he said
He blew it thataway for Nelly Richman:
Panther John, his pet. Seems like this doe—
Well, out she lit. And so he takes his bone,
A turkey bone, the best he says for tooting,
And wanders. And he ends up by a bonfire,

235

Talking mighty talk of what he'll do."
"Be still, boy. There is limits to a laugh."
And the hawk face had drawn them, even then.
"Who's laughing? Who by Golliday is laughing?"
Richman backed away an eyelash length.
"You're one of them," he said. "But if I wasn't,
Still," said David softly, "I'd have guessed,
From being at that bonfire, what you buried."
"Let it be, the bone. You're one of them.
You're brother to the brat." "Be still yourself!
By God, Sir, there is limits to a lie!"
"Lying? Who's a lying? That's the word
He went by in my best of understandings.
That's the word he goes by till you wash
Your tongue of its own filthiness, and find
A decent name or two for her and me."
"To hell with her!" "Be careful, boy." "To hell
With all the does and roebucks in the brush!
They're nothing to me here. And as for that,
They didn't have a hand in what you done.
It's what you done I'm here for. Decent name?
For that? It was the dirtiest cold killing—"
"Killing, was it? Well," and the lips clamped,
"I couldn't wait to notice. But no more
It was than I had give fair warning of.
You say you saw me. Then you heard me too.
I promised—" "Hell's hot harness! Why, I've promised
Murder in a whipstitch. But I never
Done it. That's the difference. And my brother—"
"Brat he was for doing what I swore
I'd shoot to kill for doing." "Man, the word—"
"Is brat. The deer had marks. A fool would know.
The settlement's all fools, one way of thinking.
Honor's been plowed under. But the prince
Of all a prairie's fools would be the one
That couldn't hear a bell or see a band
As red as measle rash." "You said a prince.

236

He was, for fair. As clean of harm and hate
As someone here is dirty with his death.
Death for a doe! That anyhow was done for
Days before you come there with your traps
And fouled him. And it don't upset you now
Hearing me say you did! Like a caught dog!"
The weariness long since had gone from David,
Whose every sentence blazed: and both his arms
Hung rigid from his shoulders: rods to swing.
"Like a deer-killing dog. You hit the truth
Your ownself, without aiming. Like a hound
That's lost the smell of rightness, of the rules.
Such critters can't be cured, and it's a pity.
Sometimes they're a loss. Your brother was,
You say. I could believe it. But I swear,
By God and what I've buried in this hole,
I'm no more shamed than you of being here,
And who I am, and what I had to do.
I killed a killer. Well, you told yourself
Last night you'd do the same. So here we be.
Do it, boy. But what's the difference then
Betwixt your tale and mine?" "A dog? A man?
No difference?" David struggled with his breath.
"Seth? A hound? And you're not sorry?" "No.
And sick I am of saying it. Get out.
Get off my land. Go back to your fool Mayfield.
Here! I'll say it plain." And with a cat's
Decision, and a quick unearthly grace,
He wheeled a quarter turn and had the gun
Once more in his two hands, that closed upon it
Slowly, and did not lift it. "See?" he said.
"Maybe it ain't so anxious, but it's willing."
And the slant barrel stiffened among the shadows,
Tilting a subtle inch. "Now get, now go!"

But David's only going was a stallion's
Plunge, straight on and down, before the sights

Could level, and before the palms could shift;
And now they wrestled, panting all at once
Wind-loud, as if the first work of their strength
Were last, and this an end. But there was more,
And long, before the hands of David, whitening,
Wrenched the weapon free and flung it off
Like a raw splinter, broken as beams fall.
They heard it where it thudded on the leaves,
And listening was truce for a wild second,
Separating glances. Yet again,
As if a signal came, they crouched and wrestled
Horribly. Their heel prints in the mold,
Multiplying, wounded the cool earth
As if shod herds had trampled it, or bolts
Of thunder had descended, hissing scorn
And envy of such coolness, of such calm.
Unevenly they wrestled, youth and age
Ill yoked; and David felt it; and his heart,
Furious now with conscience, loathed afresh
This cause of it, this snarling grizzled man
So weak between his arms and yet so strong,
So brittle and so unbreakable. Then more,
Said David. More, not less; letting his strength
Come out of him at last like something vile,
Something to be used once in the world,
Then never. All, not half. No justice now.
To spare the frailer thing is to be punished.
Free it, and it plagues us. Beat it down,
And something's gone forever. So his madness,
Mixing with his strength, knew what it did
Only upon the dry edge of the bluff,
That crumbled as they reached it: crumbled and slid,
With four disordered ankles, into the river.
Now it knew, his madness; for the knee-deep
Water, cold and terrible, awoke
Worse images of weakness: Richman there,
Knee-foundered in the mire, unfree to rise

Till David's hand should help him; Richman there,
His breath all spent, his eyes high in his head
And rolling; Richman there to help or strike,
To extricate or strangle. David struck,
And missing, struck again, for the head rolled
Obedient to the eyes. Then madness knew
Its master, and the hands that could have helped
Came otherwise together, one brute thumb
Lapping the other's hatred where a windpipe
Wanted to be forever; and forever
Failed, as now the shoulders slipped the hands
And the brown Ambraw took its hunter in.

VIII

"Who's that?" For Prince's ears had picked the one
Thing moving in a wilderness of rest:
Of massy woods, sloped weeds, and buried road.
"Who's that?" For Prince's eyes were drawing here
A thing as big as wasp wings where it staggered,
Stumbling, out of shadow into sun
And, hesitating, crawled; and grew to man.
"David!" said the doctor; not as calling,
Not to urge him nearer, but for sound.
The hulking stare, the great uncertain legs,
The hung hands: he waited on them here
Like one who never saw them in their giant's
Grace when height was young and might was free
And yesterday was yesterday; when Seth—
But this was David, walking in his sleep:
Sun-stupefied, death-slow. And still the doctor,
Fingering his whip, could not descend
And meet him; still must watch him as he came
And stopped without amaze at Peter's head
And stroked it: with a stiff hand found the ears,
The foretop, then the long familiar nose,

And smoothed them, playing absently with warmth
That pleased him; till a nudge from jealous Prince,
And the blown speech of nostrils, startled awake
Some double recognition, so that his tongue
Said "Prince," said "Peter," sluggishly; said "Doc."
For there the third one was, he seemed to whisper,
Just where he ought to be, and nothing strange:
The dashboard and the spectacles, the cap,
The ready whip, the stillness.
                                        "Hold your horses,
Don't go yet," he struggled, half his voice
Gone from him, "don't go yet," the louder half
Lost out of him for good, the doctor said,
Buried somewhere, living and remembering,
"Don't you stir a stump till I be back
From telling. There's a house not far from here.
His. And they'll be looking for him. His
No more, though. Not this morning. Not for good.
I got to tell them fair. Then I'll be back."
"No, now!" the doctor shouted, hoping to bring
That louder part, still living, from its grave.
"Now! Get up here, David, and be driver.
Hi, there! Yipayandy! Pete, boy! Prince!"
But David, once so reachable, so ready,
Balked; and an alien cunning, born in his eyes
Since yesterday, since sunup, softened again
The answer. "Hold your horses. Then there's him:
I got to fix him better. He's half out,
Half under. Got to lay him up on leaves
And straighten what they'll find of him, by Wherry!
Back in there he is," a thumb assisting,
"Back in there, in water up to his belt.
Got to lay him straighter, else they'll think—
So don't you go. Set easy. Hold them tight
Till both my jobs is over. Won't be long."
And round their heads he started, moving slow
Past Peter's rump, nor heeding the switched tail;

Nor glancing into the buggy, whence again:
"No, David! We'll go now."
                              Dandy and Paul,
With George a pace behind them in the shadows,
Searched as one, crisscrossing the brown grove
And calling half in fear lest they be heard,
Lest silence's uncertainty be shattered.
Even now they rose upon a slope
And mounted the last clearing, the leaf chamber
Where Nelly sometimes sauntered, showing herself
To voices and returning a bell's tone.
Even now, as David in his thought
Went triple-jointed, lumbering, between
And through them to the rubble of the bluff;
And as in Mayfield Clara's startled eyes,
Parting their lids painfully, looked off
And saw what dawn was doing in another
Room, a little room, where something showed
Which night, the nipped eternity, had hidden;
And as a ladder, bringing Nancy down
To breakfast in the fatherless cold waste
Of memory, creaked and lengthened its worn rungs;
As Thorsten shut his door and pulled at Gard,
Impatient, for the nose had not forgotten,
And the stained threshold stopped him; as on roads
And bridges, by canals and over mountains,
Wagons started moving, and the million
Houses of the land sent forth their smoke,
Their people; as the oxen of the Buells
Swung westward, and a boy upon a seat
Skipped stones across a river, saying Seth,
Goodbye till summers age us and our children
Meet, and we remember; as the dogs
Of Indians hunted bones where still in night
The tipi flaps were laced and the tribe slumbered;
Even now the three of them stared long,
Stared silently at gashes in the mold

241

Where feet had shallowed furrows; and as one,
Tracing the print of battle to its end,
Found the hurt bluff, the falling-over place.

"David," and the doctor's gentlest voice
Dishonored nothing now in the shrunk shoulders,
"David, we can leave now. Come with Prince
And Peter, you can drive them all the way
To Mayfield; Mayfield, David, and your mother.
She it was that sent me." "Little Ma.
That's someone else to tell, Doc. But you wait.
Hold them till I finish laying out
Our old one, he's a sight the way he is.
Then there's his boys to notify. It's like
I went to a new country after work
And there was more than one fool head could do."
"That country," said the doctor, "is this world,
And many have been lost. But you are lucky.
Someone's come with orders. So be spry.
Home!" "Is them the orders?" David listened,
Blinking. "That it, Doc?" "But hurry, boy.
I'm here to tell the time, too." David listened,
Hopeful. "Then it's ticking? The same sun?"
"The same. And it is higher than you think.
It's in your mother's window, it's in Thorsten's;
Nancy will be yawning; Ben's been up
A worm's age; all the town is turning out
To look for us. We're late." But he was one,
Still tethered, who awaits the final tug,
The sharp one. "If you're sure, and if you say so—"
"Clown! I have been saying so! Climb in!"
And the spent bulk, obedient, doubled itself
To enter, and as it did so crushed the springs;
And Prince and Peter, tossing their white heads,
Whirled at the doctor's cry; and now the grove
Was gone with all the other west behind them,

And the road home was ready: down, then up,
Then level on to Ambraw Bend, to Mayfield.

"There!" said David. "That's the house! That's where—"
"No one's in it, though. They all went out
When I did." "Who?" The finger ends were working,
Suddenly, at the cushion, and the face
Had twisted hard away. Yet I was right,
It's better, he can feel, the doctor said.
"You know who. They're looking for him now.
And with my luck they'll find him." "But he's half—"
"No matter." "And I won't be there to tell.
But I can tell you, Doc. We had a wrastle."
"So! And he went down. You said enough
Back there about the end of it. I know.
And Dandy Richman knows who came last night—"
"You told them." "Yes. But not to give away—"
"So they know who to look for besides him."
"They're out about it now." "But Doc, I don't—
It ain't right-minded, running away like this.
Figgered I would tell them how it happened.
Figger even now I ought to let them
Find me, so as they can learn I meant
To lay him more like proper on dry ground.
Never aimed to leave him thataway.
Better let me down. You say it's Dandy
Richman? Will I know him? Does he favor—
Better let me down, I won't be long.
Dandy. Does he favor him—the old one?"
Till the low porch was past them, and the ruts,
Bending at the rise, went level on
By prairie, and the Ambraw hushed its fall,
Meandering through mud in the old way.
Then silence. But the head was still as one
That forceps hold askew; the neck still turned,
Self-tortured. So the doctor, glancing down,
And seeing how the hands, unskilled in rest,

243

Worked awkwardly at nothing, ventured again:
Parted the broad thumbs and laid the reins
Like thread between the fingers, like black thread
With messages. And while he watched they came.
As the bent sapling answers to the pull
Of custom and cool sun; as dented turf,
When the heel leaves it, levels itself slyly,
David's handsome head with its bear's wounds
Responded, and authority's sleek leather
Bound him once again to his great friends.
He saw them in their grandeur that was once
A wildness in his throat; but he drove gently,
Miles away through silence and recovered
Trust; he let them pound in their own rhythm,
Pulling him with the doctor where they would
Through a still world with all the fences down.

The sons of Richman, laboring up the bluff
With a sagged weight, a water-blinded burden,
And coming forth at last on level leaves,
Midway of the standing burr oaks, midway
Of the ringed cries of jays, of crow alarums,
Laid their father down; and Dandy knelt,
Reordering the raiment of a man
Whom none before had seen except in hunter's
Neatness, in a thonged and belted pride.
The tomahawk was straightened in its loop,
And the sheathed knife; and now the powder horn,
Whose dripping point drew Dandy's gaze away,
Suddenly, in search of a thrown gun.
There it was, so close to them that George
Cried out against it, serpent-struck, and Paul,
Pouncing, would have claimed it save that Dandy
Hushed them. It was there, and in good time
Its iron would be remembered: so the pause
In his still muted movements seemed to say.
The brothers watched him then as he probed on,

His fingers not too willing, not too brave,
For something else he missed. The turkey bone
Was nowhere, Dandy whispered to himself:
Nowhere on dry land. The river had it.
Even now the rapids past the fall
Were washing it to merest hollow brown,
The tune gone with the lips, the message changed
To such as waters murmur to themselves
At a sure depth, all surface chatter silenced.
Nothing we could hear; and had she lived,
Nothing Nelly's feet would ever come to,
Snapping through the forest. And he thought:
It might be calling now, but the smooth whirlpools
Muffle it, the current drowns the name.
His hands abruptly pressed at the bent knees
And firmed the heels together. Then they traveled
Lengthwise of his sire, to such of the locks
As water snarls had tufted; and at last
To the wild eyes he should have tended first,
Shutting the stare away. But Dandy's touch,
Malingering, had loitered; and his brothers'
Glances had been everywhere but here.
Now it was quickly done, and Dandy knew,
Lifting his own glance, that George and Paul
Had seen what he saw: tigers in the earth,
Trapped awhile and trying to be free,
Then lidded over. "So it is the last,"
Standing again he said, "except for something
Level to go home on, something carried.
Paul, you cut a pole. I'll cut another,
And George can bring a blanket from the house:
One of his, the white and turkey-red one.
Anything. And hurry." But he said it
Slowly, in the way a mind, musing,
Cons again the overheard commands
Of alien armies thicketing the dark;
And neither of his brothers moved an inch

Toward deeper shade, acknowledging with Dandy
Something still to do here in the sun's
Oval, in the gold that slanted down.

"Remember, on the Ohio, how he cursed
That sawyer with its underwater root?
All of us were little, or I was;
But I can still see bullets in his eyes,
Spitting at what would sink us, I can hear
His anger sizzle past me," George announced
To no one. "I can feel our fear of him
When a sheep bawled and like a rat he shook it,
Terrier that he was and tartar-strong.
He mortified us too with his laments
For the man's freedom he had thrown away:
Hunter that he was, to have been bogged
In woman slime, crawled over with slug boys!
And yet we helped him out of it: we hauled,
We sang till we were breathless at the sweeps,
And heard him say 'Good young ones!', and heard Susan
Shame him. Then he sat at the blunt prow,
Forgiven, and he said he searched downstream
For more, for coming danger; but we knew,
Or I did, that he studied the low west
For any sign that five could be as free there
As one had been on mountains, among trees
That showed across a valley, ridge from ridge,
Pure blue, as he himself was, deep in his eyes
When the cat-yellow parted, the fire faded.
We knew, or I did, watching the sharp way
He rested, with his shins against the rail,
That nothing like a sign, no splash, no bird,
Betrayed the truth to come, which we have known
Our lives long: he adored us and despised us.
Susan, too. For all that she could wrap
His fever in cool gauzes, he fell short
Of loving who could do it; or at least

Of loving what was done." If Dandy stirred
And shuffled the torn mold with bitter feet,
If Paul looked up and scowled, and Susan sighed,
The middle son, oblivious, simply ceased
And waited—not on Dandy now, but Paul.

"He was a wild one. Recollect? Who wouldn't?
Time he took the tow rope and beat off
Them river bandits. Didn't leave them free
One minute to bring down their double guns
And blast him. Off they tore; and Shawneetown
Is laughing yet, and pointing to the cave
They made for and went into: all one welt
They was, and licked each other like sore dogs.
That was a man they boarded. They found out.
We knowed it from the minute he caught Dandy,
Back on the Kanawha, taking aim
At shore bucks when we didn't need the meat:
Only would have left them to the flies
And buzzards if he'd hit them. Which he didn't.
But that was when he learned us how a gun
Was business, and a deer was king of the woods
Till someone had to live that ought to live.
Not every fool, he said. And then he changed,
And chuckled to us all that we was such,
And grabbed at Susan, whistling the first dance
He thought of; and they capered round the stern,
Knocking someone down at every pass,
Stamping like it was at their own wedding.
That was how it went with our old man:
Nick's old blazes suddenly'd go out
And leave him cool as peppermint, as kind
As water in a well. We had them both,
The trouble and the cure. And both was cut
From heartwood that ain't found in common trees.
There's no such other man. You mark my word,
We'll never see the least of him again

247

In them that God lets walk. His later days
Was different. He would stray in on us sometimes
Like an old animal without a name.
We thought we didn't know him. Then we did,
Better than our own selves. For he could bring
Her back, and all them rivers; he could grow
Big woods around him only by standing there
And being like he was; he had it all
Close to him all the time, the way the world
Once looked. He never lost it. But we did.
And now we've lost the only one could bring
Her back, and all them colors, all them horns
A farmer never hears. Pa Nolan's she-mule—
That's our prettiest music. Godamighty!
Who could a told how different he would lay
From the old duke that carried Nelly home,
One morning like to this, and called us round
For counsel how to raise her; and he reared
High dander when we doubted she could mend.
He never let us touch a hair of Nelly.
Him it was that messed the milk and greens
Together in that butter-bowl of Susan's;
Him it was that got her on her pipe-legs;
Him it was that saved her. And for her
He's this thing here." He stopped, and seemed to listen.
"Golliday. And Mayfield. Never been
To Mayfield. So I'm going. Clear the wind!"
But his first motion died in Dandy's gaze,
That lifted coldly.
           "No, not yet. Not you.
I was the last to see him. I could have said:
'You mustn't!' and it might have turned him home.
I am the one she left him with, to shame
And shield him when the hate was in his legs.
That morning it was sorrow; it was fear
For Nelly. But I might have understood.
Hate can be son of those. And we are sons

248

Of a dead man, of John Richman, since I failed.
How could a hand have done it, how could a heart
Have left him where he was, a thing to find
As we find sycamores in swollen creeks:
Tops under, and the branches done with breath?
And yet I know. A Golliday might whisper:
'How could a man have done it? But you there—
You killed a boy for Nelly, and for him
Another boy came here to strangle you.
It is a kind of close.' " He waited, shuddering,
The wreck of his still self, before he shouted:
"And yet it is no close! For all our fear
We loved him, and we have to say so, loud.
Here!" And while they gaped at him he left them,
Feeling with a hand for the gun-barrel
He touched instead of saw; for coming back,
He kept his eyes on them, and George discovered
Tears, or starting tears, where cold had been,
Where blackness.
           "Dandy. No. Put the gun down.
Give it to Paul, to Father. Even to me."
But Paul, excitement beating at his ears,
Stepped across Old Richman and took hold
Of Dandy as if to shake him. "Let me do it.
We've no horse for quickness, but I'd find
A short cut, and my legs is used to lather.
Brush don't stop me, creeks and froggy sloughs
Is natural steady going when I git.
Let me, Dandy. Give me the persuader.
Horses, though! I'd give a red-gold ramrod—
Horses, like them two the doctor drove!
Where's he now, you reckon? Sneaking home,
He'd be about at Nolan's place. By thunder!
Nolan's! That old rabbit-ears of his!
She-critter with a shavetail, Jenny Lou!
I'll go and beg her bones. I'll get to Mayfield."

"No," they heard. "He's nearest to me now.
He was an old-world man; he told his first-born
More than he told you. When I was small,
In the deer woods one day, while with his knife
He carved my bread, I promised, if he died
This way, I would remember. He was wrong
To slay a boy in Mayfield, as that boy
Was wrong to slight the warning of a bell,
A neckband; and his brother, hurrying here,
Was wrong in triple measure. Do I then
Forget? He said remember. There was a day—
But this one is another, and we stand
Like shot towers! George, the blanket. And the axe.
Stir yourself, and meanwhile we'll go pick
Two burr oaks of a size. And bring us cord
For lashing. When he's home I'll let him rest—
But one of you there always—and be off
To Nolan's, where I'll borrow that bay mule
And catch the doctor's buggy; if I can."

The slim trunks, toppling, fanned the sober air
With their spent plumage, brown as Richman's garb
Yet tamer: autumn-tarnished and sun-dried.
And while the branches fell beneath the blade,
George in the clearing, stooped at his father's feet,
Unfolded the gay bed, uncoiled the cord.
Then all of them were busy; scented poles
Sweetened their task; the body sank in place
Resistless; and the white hair started home.

Down a mown hill emerging, Paul and Dandy
Bore the old sleeper straightly, reaching at last
The yard fence and the grass that frost had laid,
And over it the steps of the verandah.
Then in; and there was sun on Richman's bed,
The bed that filled the little eastward room
Where Susan gazed, noting each morning's light

250

As now. They turned and hushed her as they passed,
Hoping to close the eyes. But nothing stilled
Or stopped her: witness then of the blunt way
They shifted what they bore to better rest,
And laid the hands together, and brought the poles,
The blanket forth to stand in her own corner,
Folded, while she sent across the room,
And Richman's room, welcome to bright windows.
Dandy, seeing patience in her face,
And pity, looked away. No more of that,
He whispered. "Now to Nolan's. And remember,
One of you here always. I'll be soon.
Jenny Lou will jog me there and back.
Don't leave him, sun or dark. I should be home
By midnight, for tomorrow is the time.
We'll take him back up there, I think," lifting
His free arm toward the grove. The other held
The gun, that now he hugged to his stiff side
And went.
      So each by a pillar saw him march,
Head up, toward where a she-mule switched at flies
Still buzzing in a warm November barn.
Paul shivered; it was cold here, out of doors;
And wondered if the tricksterish old wit
Of Nolan would decipher Dandy's errand.
And what a mount, if Dandy should prevail,
For one who while his brothers languished here,
Mourning all their loss, rode after justice.
Justice! But he shied from the great sound
And only thought of Dandy, humbly set
On God's least noble animal, on man's
Last slave before he loses what of pride
He strangely still possesses; and he wept,
Unknowing why the tears that had not come
Fell now, and for no father. Then they both
Remembered, and went oddly in to stand

With Susan by the bed of him whose loss
Was nothing if another stayed away.

IX

Down from the north, the sun of afternoon
Preceding him and falling where he gazed—
On Seth's house and the band of people there,
Expectant, though in weariness they once
Had ceased to look, and now had ceased again—
The doctor glided, letting the reins be still
Small threads that tugged at David's hands and told him:
Here, it will be home for you at last;
There, and then you tumble into sheets
Not talking, for the world is dead away.
Then one of them, with scarlet at her shoulders,
Motioned; and the others at her back
Ran with her, quick or slow as fear lay on them:
Burden, or a whip. But she was first,
And had his only eyes, that watched her paleness
Parting under speech.
                        "Dear God," she whispered,
"Both of you"; and trembled as the boy
Stared past her; but the most that Nancy saw
Was the abstracted forehead, the fixed hands.
"What is it? Why is David as he is?
Father, was he there when—" "Nancy, Nancy!
Gollidays have ears!" "And so have I
A desperate, tired tongue, from soothing her."
"How is she then?" "You'll know. But tell me first."
"No, later. If at all. When the time comes—
But here! They have caught up with you. Hello, Sir."
For David's father, panting, peered this way
As at a wild boar captured in the wastes
And brought home bound; and lo, it was his own
Son, silent. "Hello, Doc. By all that's hogtied,
Where'd you pick him up, the rascal shoat?

Dave, where was you? Dave!" But then the silence
Clubbed him, and he staggered, looking round
For Ben; then back to the doctor. "Is he hurt?
Knocked out of his true lights? By Lor and Godfrey,
Who will give me tidings?" But the wheels,
Indifferent, turned again, for Prince and Peter,
Knowing their lane before them, moved away
With no care but for corn; and the doctor lifted,
Skilfully, the threads from David's paws,
That lay as listless still on the gaunt knees
As if no voice had spoken. Then they knew;
And groped; and, holding nothing, raised themselves
For shade to the too soon awakened eyes,
That took their own house in, and Clara standing,
Helpless, by the side of little Thorsten;
And Gard was rushing toward them, teasing Prince,
And Peter had his head down, pulling the reins
And blowing.
                    "David! David! My own David!"
"Who's that one? Little Ma!" And David leapt
Unthinking to the ground, whose iron, whose black,
Crippled his feet an instant with blear pain,
That stopped him. But he stumbled on and found,
Familiar, the caress. "Now, little Ma,
I'm here! The Doc, he brought me. How's my dime?
And how is—" "David, David! That you're home
Is everything. I'm well now." "Was it bad?"
"Was what bad?" And she waited. "Missing you?"
"No." His head was down. The doctor listened.
"No, Ma." And the doctor frowned at Thorsten,
Bidding him be ready. "What I done.
Back there. The Doc, he knows." She let an arm
Fall slowly; but the other one had strength
To tighten at his coat; and she could turn
Her face as far as need be, searching this one.
"Doctor! What does he mean? Back where? Did David—
"What is he trying—" "Only what you guess.

That he is tired almost to madness: mumbling
Madness, lady. He means nothing. Thorsten—
No, I want you later. Ben and his father:
Those can take him off and see that he sleeps—
There, Ben, you guide him in. And Mr. Golliday,
Help if you will. Now, Nancy, while I drive
With Thorsten to the barn and put these stampers—
Pete, you fool!—where both are dead to stay,
Be my good daughter for another hour
And keep her where it's quiet." And he waved
For Thorsten to ascend and sit beside him.

"Nancy, one more thing," as Peter backed
Unbidden, and was checked upon the turn.
"Darling, here! Come close." And Nancy clung
To the side bows, and the long scarf whipped its flame.
"He's worn to dumbness, though hallucinations
Startle him sometimes. You understand?
You don't? Yet soon you will. I pledge,
I do, that I will tell you. But not now."
Pressing both cheeks, she let the buggy go
And hurried to her station, yet her eyes
Were still upon the horses as they turned,
Right by the store, then left; then left again
Where the fences drew them home: so slowly home,
So dwindled at a quarter-mile's remove,
So slow, like sleepy toys, that she could doubt them.

"He did it, Thorsten. Mortal that I am,
I found him a fool's hour too late. John Richman's
Dead." "So Thorsten thought," sending a sigh
At Gard, who on his haunches watched the heels
Of the white monsters, wondering why they dozed.
"Furthermore, he's head and shoulders drowned
In Ambraw water; thrown like baggage there."
The grey one at his side, groaning a little,

Begged: "No more! I'm glad I didn't see
What you did." "All I saw was David falling
Bug-eyed out of a grove, and all I heard
From him is what I tell you; except this:
He's sorry. Which is putting it so mildly,
I'd laugh had I the muscles. He's been hit
With thunderbolts; with even worse. But now—"
And he tossed his reins away on the windless ground—
"You see, there were three sons. I wasted time—"
"What are they like, the sons?" And Thorsten blinked.
"Savages? Like him?" "Like him. Not savages."
"No, he had his law. I understand.
But will they—" "One of them, yes. The eldest. Daniel.
Eldest, and most excellent. But banked
With fire I am afraid of. He could be coming
Now, and may be nearer than I think.
Go meet him somewhere northward on the road
And talk with him, and maybe turn him back.
Somewhere, I say; and hazard a cool guess
It's Colebridge. If he's mounted, though, and Prince
Came slowly while I slept, it's anywhere.
So time would be a treasure. Will you go?
Dandy Richman. Call him and he'll stop.
He's courteous, he's kind, beneath a gloomy
Forehead; and he's younger than his temples
Testify. You'll go?" "If Gard agrees.
He does—Gard!" And a hand, dropped to the ruff,
Calmed first of all himself. "But who will tend
My counter? Ben?"

           "No, me." And Nancy pushed
Past Gard who knew her there, past Thorsten's gaze,
To her father. "Please. I heard. I couldn't sit—
I'll keep the store for something sane to do.
She's stronger now. Forgive me if I heard."
"It may be best at that," the doctor sighed,
Accepting her swift kisses. "When I swore

I'd tell you too, I doubted I could manage.
Now you know that David—and that Dandy's
Coming; or that I believe he is.
He wouldn't let it rest. So he'll be here,
Murdering our peace, before we mend it."
"Father!" And she hid her face in him.
"I am the murderer, I am the cause."
"Hush! Or sleep will hear, and in its wild
Way walk; and then where are we? Causes, dear?
Dozens of them rivalled what you did,
And some of them are boastful, and declare
There never will be comfort any more
In Mayfield. But there can be if we hold
Our places. Then the world is what it was.
Your place is clear. Thorsten surrenders it.
He lives no more by merchandise than I
For sleep, or you for sanity. Yet I'll
Go sleep, and you'll go sit, and he'll go north,
Pretending to be pleased." He smiled; and Thorsten
Answered him, grimacing; then the three,
With Gard a merry fourth, for through his hair
Ran rumors of a journey, and he jumped,
Waiting his master's lead, rejoined the sun.

Where Seth had walked but yesterday, and Richman,
Days on end ago, had wound his horn;
Where David and the doctor night and day
Had run, had ridden, joyless; where the autumn
Birds now hugged the fences, holding court
On summer's death, absolving the weak wind;
Where all the north, huge in its empty arcways,
Hunched and threatened winter, Thorsten pushed
His smallness, peering bravely over Gard:
A mite in the immensity, yet sharpened
Craftily with purpose. Not with hope.
His heart was back in Mayfield. But his wit
Went on before him, lonely, thin with fear.

If Daniel—and these oxen were not his,
Swinging down the rutways. Such a wagon:
No, it would be Gunderson, the bearded
Savage—yes, it was; his whip had waved,
And rods before they met he stood up yelling:
"Hi there, Thorsten! How's a man to git
God's sugar when you gallivant away?
Come for that I did, and here you be,
You and your hyena. Call him off.
One ox is mean, and I'm not telling which."
"Gard! But I'm not gallivanting. Sugar?
Say how much; and she will chalk it down."
"She who?" "The doctor's daughter. Goodbye, Gun,
I've business where I'm going." And he thought:
The beard is riding backward; and it will be
So long as I'm a speck; but I'll not wave;
I've business where I'm headed. My hyena!
Gard! And the scout, returning, trotted abreast
Till—here! a horseman! Dandy? But the hat
Was eastern, and the saddlebags, the greatcoat:
No, it would be some august contriver
Of treaties, or a peddler of brown land.
And so it was, for the high nose, scorning custom,
Tilted away from Thorsten as it passed,
And the whip hand, the elbow, twitched imperious
Challenges to Gard: who with his master
Turned and stared, and all but smiled at godhead
Mounted on a roan, dispensing prairies.

Then on again, but slower. If the sun
Seemed tireless, he was not; and even Gard
Suited his paces hence to an oldish man's,
That shuffled now and then, recovering strength
By negatives of effort scarcely made.
And now the sun was halfway down from noon;
The day's last quarter quickened; and no head
Of man or horse came over the horizon;

No one there to halt with wisdom's word:
Wisdom's if he had it. And fatigue
Fed at his heart, and set his wits awander:
Following those oxen into Mayfield
Where Gunderson the mad one even now
Was loading the white sugar, and was turning.
Yes! But here was someone. Ready, Gard.

Only a mule, though, flap-eared in the distance:
Indolent, ill swung, and bearing hither
Someone not in war paint; someone gaited
Leisurely, and gauchely, as for peace.
Itinerant? Rain-maker? Parson's son?
Huckster without wagon? Wastrel? Saint?
Thorsten's wit, relaxing, spun the list
To spider thread, and let it ravel on
Till the stranger stopped, and Thorsten watched his eyes,
Abandoned once to musing, come awake
Between the silver temples, under the gloomy
Forehead. Gloomy. That was the doctor's word.

"You're Daniel Richman." And the tensive sound
Laid back the ears of Gard until they flattened.
"Aye." And was that all? Was no surprise
To break from him when solitude said names?
"Aye. The doctor sent you. Is he well?
Is everybody well? He had a patient:
One of your best citizens, he said.
I found our best this morning. But a river
Keeps no count of rank; it can insult
A noble if it pleases. So it did
My father. And I've come to find—" "Your father,
Daniel, was my guest, and I agree.
A monarch." Dandy frowned. "You call him that?"
"A king, but not my own. For mine is mist,
It may be. So he said. Or something worse:
A subterfuge, an argument against Richmans.

He was my guest last night at a good supper,
And afterward we garnished every dish
With discourse. And the end of it, before
This other end, the one that brings you riding,
Was ridicule of me, was howling wrath,
Because my mist had magic, was a haze
On mountains, was a trap of woven words
To tangle his pure purpose. So, as a door
Opened, he and his king took aim together."
"So he did. And simply. Why this host
Of helpers? Mist and monarch! Heathen slaves!"

"There was no talk of slaves," said Thorsten slyly.
"Who are you? Why do you stop me when I'm bound—"
"A friend, had he permitted, of your father's.
And still of his good son. Of Gollidays,
Of Emersons. The keeper of a store,
The master of this dog; who is no slave
To prove me worse than master. Sir, my king
Is free of me, and I'm as free of him
As man can be of what his mind desires.
He is invisible, and has no power
Save such as makes me wish him what he is,
And where he is, and when. But he's all places,
Please you, and all times; and how he thinks
Is how the truth's aware that it be truth."

"Jenny Lou!" And Dandy kicked her ribs.
"He's wild with his own drooling." Yet she waited,
As he himself did: waited, and looked down.
"Truth! As if I weren't—" "All you are,
And much it is, you think you have to squander.
But truth is just that treasure, if God please."
"My father has been murdered." "And he murdered
Seth, a darkling boy who could have sat
For double to you, adding the grace of years.
But that's not it. Murder's a barren subject.

259

If you can listen, pilgrim, I can prove—"
And so he might, thought Dandy. "But you won't!
Jenny Lou! Be lively! It's a good
Mile still, and here we stand." "If you would listen—"
"Lord, I would go mad! Good day to you
And that toad hound, two warts upon the truth!"

So off he bounced, the barrel of Jenny thumping,
Miserably, with music from his heels;
While Thorsten, turning after him, and clutching
Gard, hobbled his fastest. But the mile
To Mayfield stretched already in his fancy
Hopelessly to deserts, and he whispered:
I was the last defense, and now he falls
Like armies on them, waiting to be warned.
My best was nothing. Nightmare of my failure,
Follow and overtake him. If there's time.
But time itself was nightmares over Mayfield.

Dandy rode, the long gun bouncing with him
Slantwise of the burlap while his anger
Rose and fell like breathing; charged, withdrew
Like hosts against him, for him. Now no more
Simplicity. This chirper in the wind,
This wizened nit, had changed it all. Or tried to.

It must not be, with Mayfield thus before him:
He counted the few cabins, named the store;
And with that woman watching him. For Clara,
Vigilant by her house, was the one human
Mark in all of Mayfield, and he paused,
Noticing her smallness while he reached
And freed the weary gun from its odd angle:
Dusted it with movements of his sleeve
And slung it into readiness, advancing
Now at Jenny's pace, that would outspeed
His own unless he quickened; for his heart

Strangely had grown sluggish, and impatience
Rested in him, distant from his will.
This must not be, though. Curses on that he-witch,
Hobbling hither now beside his wolf-dog.
He straightened on his mount and cursed as well
Her lethargy, her death's legs. Yet he came
As Jenny brought him, ambling, and the eyes
Of Clara had all time in which to grow.

"I'm looking," Dandy said, "for David Golliday.
This his house? Or where? I am a stranger";
Ceasing when he saw how Clara, trying,
Failed at speech's onset. She could only
Turn, as now she did, and wave within
For someone to come running. It was Ben.
"I'm looking," Dandy said again, but louder,
"For David Golliday. If you're the man—"
"I ain't." But that was all from him, and Dandy
Waited: absurdly waited while the dull
Eyes travelled over Jenny, inched the barrel.
"Then where? And will you—no, if he's inside,
Stand where you are and call. I want you here;
Want everybody here." For Ben had turned
As Clara had, and overshadowed now
Her littleness, that even further shrunk
As the hands rose to shut the menace out.
"Just call. And don't you move." But then a sound
Within was someone stamping, and he gripped
The stock with stiffer fingers. If the sound—
But Seth the elder made it, gaunt in the door
And ghastly as the oblong of his face,
With grief and liquor loosened, caught the low,
The amber sun full on it, and a palsy
Shook it like a shingle flat in the wind.
"You're not—" "No, I'm his dad. I'm Seth, I'm Senior.
Stranger, you won't stop me if I send
My one boy left astanding to fetch Doc.

Worries me, the way Dave don't quite sleep.
Ben, be off there. Wonder that the Doc
Himself ain't here nohow. He's tuckered, sure;
But nothing new in that. Ben, you go look.
Get Nancy, too. She's keeping store for Thorsten.
Don't know where he's hid. Should be a poking
Some place round. Our boys is Thorsten's business;
Was, nohow, till one of them got bad,
Real bad. Then Thorsten's shy." He leaned and frowned
Benignly. "Will you let him?" "Yes, I will."
And Dandy watched the big back as it went,
Gun-conscious, to bring witnesses; and wondered,
Grimly, why he did so. But he turned,
And Clara's eyes were opening again.
"Who's Thorsten? Some old fellow with a hound?"
Seth nodded, almost falling. "Then I met him.
Mile or so from town. The doctor's name:
It's Emerson?" And Clara moaned aloud.
"He was my guest this morning. Nancy, though:
Someone's daughter? Yours? I may have heard—"
"No, Doc's, and powerful pretty." Seth was rocking
Regularly on his heels. "But this one day's
So ailed her you won't recognize the gal.
You wouldn't anyway, though." And he gravely
Grinned at his vast error. "Would you now?"
But Dandy's eyes were narrowed on the door,
And his gun trembled. "Who is that?" he whispered.
"David?" Then he knew the ghost, for Clara,
Turning, shrieked and flew into its shade.

For a long minute all of them stood limp there,
And Dandy was disarmed. So lone a giant,
Gentle, with his hands down, such a tall,
Lost enemy was dangerous to the dream,
The duty that had drawn him. There he hung,
His fearless eyes on Dandy: unamazed,
Unshivered if revenge upon a mule

Came riding to his doorstep; even if now
The gun lifted a little, nor relaxed
When other voices sounded by the door.

"Ben's as slow as sorghum, but you see,
Don't you, stranger, David ain't himself.
Ain't no doctor needed to show that.
So, if you come to—" "Seth!" and a woman's words
Sang high, displacing his. "Whoever you are,
You've eyes. But now have ears. My youngest son
Is in there past my eldest, yet he'll never
Hear his mother say so. If he hears,
It's heavenwise, it's whispering, it's whispering.
Who you are I think I know. But listen!
One came here to Mayfield and was minded,
God knows how, to murder. So my son
Lies there; and so my other son—God help him,
David, he was guilty—stands an open
Secret here, accusing his good self.
And I can read. But listen! Is it two
For one? Can't mercy stop it? He was not,
My youngest, what you think he was; your father
Saw him in a poor light. Had the lamps
Been lit, he would have known him—oh, as I do,
Now, and seen him even as I see."

"Little Ma, be hushful. This is Dandy
Richman, and I got to say my say."
The gun lifted again, the hands upon it
Hardening themselves against a voice
As level as the hum an echo brings.
Careful now, said Dandy, he will try—
But David was not trying. "There was things
Nobody let me do. Doc wouldn't let me.
Maybe that was better, but I say
I aimed to go and tell you what I done:
All of it, God's fact. For you'd have need

263

To know it some time soon. And then I aimed
To go to him again, up there in the woods,
In the water; was ashamed to leave him wet."
"You did, though!" Dandy shouted, hearing the words
As wild ones not his own, and feeling the flood
Pour back into him strangely: not his own
Anger at all, he said; but it would do.
"You left him!" "And I reckon then you found—"
"We did." "And guessed who'd been there. It was me.
And I'd a told you fair, and helped to lay him
Straightwise; but the Doc, he wouldn't wait
Ten seconds while I pulled him out and neatened—"
"None of that! No more! I see him there
As you do, and Dave Golliday, the sight
Is what you'll take to sod with you!" The gun
Shook in his hands insanely, yet it rose;
And David never blinked; and Seth sat down
And whimpered; but his wife with her last strength
Stretched herself to anguish, straining to cover
All of her son at once with what she owned
Of flesh, of flying fingers.
      David's blink
Was not at last for Dandy; was for steps
And spectacles behind; was hope, was fear,
Was musing lest the doctor reach and stop
These quiet wheels that turned so deep inside him.
"Dandy," said the doctor, arriving and rubbing
The folds of his tired eyes; "as in the beginning,
So at the end, this day is yours to feel
Like silver in your pocket. Not to spend,
To spill, but keep for luckpiece. Therefore, Dandy,
Put the gun down and listen; and get off
That weariness of bones, that leather lady."
"Sir, I have been listening." But Dandy's
Eyes along the sights were as they had been.
"Sir, I have been listening."
       The doctor

Sighed. And then he stopped. Whose feet were these,
Running and stumbling, pounding with little weight
The floor of the cold world? Yet broken horses
Scarce could have sent more desperate a sound,
More dark a little thunder. They were Nancy's:
Turning, he saw, and saw how Ben behind her
Stared at the scarf that flowed without a fall
Between him and the toss of her black hair.

Then she was at the stirrup, the frayed rope
That circled Dandy's instep; she was beating
Fiercely at his foot and crying "Listen!
Dandy Richman, listen! I'm the one
You came for. I'm the sinner. Look at me.
I was the death of Nelly when I whined
For playthings, and her neck was the one limb
They hung from—oh, so little to have brought
Death down upon us doubly! So, if you must—"
"Nancy!" But the doctor dared not hope
She heard him; and it may be good, he thought,
Letting her say this much; for she may live
As now she does not: never since last night.

But Dandy did not hate her for her crimson
Beauty as she published her grown heart
Like some poor thing outside her; some poor thing,
Yet all at once its riches wrapped a warmth,
A redness round him. Nevertheless he narrowed,
Suddenly, his eyes to what their search
Had been for: not the world, but one man in it;
Not the doctor, not that clamorous, small
Mother, not that father on the ground,
And most of all not Nancy. Not all these,
But one alone as he was: David, there,
His target. For the time had come at last.
He found the trigger. Now.
                           But Nancy screamed

And pulled at him. "Look back of you! He's here!
Be wise and wait. A syllable from Thorsten—"

"He-witch!" Dandy said. And yet the trigger
Failed him, and he turned. And there on the path
Was Gard, escaped from his master; and as far
As scolding notes would carry, there came Thorsten,
Hobbling: in a pitiful, hunched hurry,
Hobbling after Gard, as if to save—

But who? said Dandy. Not the hound; not David—
Neither of those—nor me. Not even me.
Look at him. He is lost from his grey self.
Crippled almost with something he desires,
Crooked from that anxiety, he scuttles
And searches. He's no longer in his skin,
His skeleton, he is here where I am, sitting
And watching with me a little, hobbling person:
Himself no more than I am. There's no pride
In Thorsten. When I cursed him did he hear?
Not me, not even me. Then who is saved?

The question broke the silence as a drop
Of rain reenters water, and a spreading
Ripple is the sign the eagle sees.
Then more. But Dandy slipped from his slow mount,
And swinging one glance backward at the faces
Fixed on Thorsten's coming—Nancy and Ben,
Seth, the doctor, Clara—and laying the gun
Down softly, as if the frost and it were friends,
Strolled to meet his master.
                                                    "Sir," he said,
"I know it isn't him. It isn't me.
Nor any of these here, no matter who."
Thorsten, resting painfully, stroking a head,
A collar, peered incredulous. "You mean—"
"I mean I think you do this for no person's

Good: for his or mine, or hers or theirs.
For the world's good you do it. Am I mad?
That king—oh, but I heard—is he the one?"
But the tired tears were all, and the upturned
Poor face that peace had blinded. "Then you say—"
"I say I'm going home now. This is the end."

X

"You do me too much honor," Thorsten said.
"At best I was a busybody, coasting
An icebound hill on runners that I hoped
Would scrape the flint and spark some goodness out."
But Dandy's eyes, emergent from their cave,
Blinked; and there was David, so long lost,
So far away from rumors of himself,
That he was half at home where Dandy stood,
A stranger, and in so much light made out
Nothing at all but suns against more suns.
And neither said a word, nor did they know
That Mayfield's sun was sitting like an owl
On Thorsten's cabin, planning the plumed night.
No thought of coming darkness thickened the world
Between them which they shared; though Gard and
    Thorsten,
Shifting in their places, saw day die
On taller heads beyond them: watched a sudden
Shaft of dusk fall lengthwise over Ben,
Who shivered with new cold. And Clara, clasping
David, shivered too; but not with cold:
With calm. For peace was terrible, was tyrant,
Silencing her grief before its end
Had sounded, and usurping struggle's throne
Just as her strength had climbed to it. Yet Clara,
Drained of that strength again, could look away
Toward Dandy's eyes; could wonder what they blinked at;
Could weep; and when her tears once more came warm,

Came sweet, could all but utter the strange love
She felt for him as fourth son in her heart.
Still she was quiet, weeping; nor did Nancy,
Creeping to her father, find a name
For the half-joy she knew, the nerves that spread,
Fine branching, in her arms, her waist, her hair,
As now again Seth shone to her as always,
Brightly, and nothing dimmed him: terror, hate,
Or a long lightning row of threatened deaths.
Now he can sleep, she said, with restful thoughts
Of me in Mayfield's playtime: of the spring,
The summer, that are past and future both,
For him and for his sweetheart. I am she.
He swore it. And with all her coming days
Buried in remembrances of brightness,
Nancy slipped a hand into her father's
Pocket, and they waited with the rest
On Dandy.
          Or on David, for the first
To move was Clara's son, who put her by,
Gently, making sure that she could stand,
And stooped to the long gun, that with a grin
He laid in Dandy's arms. "It's yours," he said;
"Or his. You heard me say I meant to neaten—"
"Yes, I know you did. But George and Paul,
My brothers, helped me. Here!" And with a turn
He lashed the weapon swiftly into place
On the mule's patient hide. "And next I borrowed
This"—he rubbed her ribs, reflectively—
"And came. But now I'm going, if she's still
The standby that she was." Then with these words
For license, Dandy ventured a free smile:
Answer to David's, echo of Susan's once;
And powder train to speech in the spare world
Where death had kept decorum.
                    "That's the boys!

Shake hands, by Gee, by Jumbo. What's the use
Of young ones yelling hell at one another?
Old man's dead, and Seth: that makes enough
Misery, don't it, Dandy, for one meal?
Shake, and shuffle in. We got a sight—"
"Seth! Be still! Be stupid! David, Dandy,
Ben, and Seth—see, I can say it! Seth!
Glory that I am able. Dandy Richman,
Thank you to the stars for giving Seth
His name again, his knowledge." "Dandy Richman,
I was the death of Nelly. Don't forget.
But you gave David life. So we'll remember."
"Daniel, it's a dark way, and your she-mule's
Weary. Paul and George will be asleep.
Or one will. Not the horseman, if I know
His nature. It's a long night, Daniel. Rest."
"You did me too much honor, Dandy Richman.
So what excess I owe you I'll give back
At home, at supper. Gard, if you will guide us."
"No," said Dandy. "All of you indulge me,
And bless you; but my father is unburied.
Doctor, you must think of me hereafter
As one who would be host to you more fairly.
Come on a winter morning. There'll be fire
And welcome, as I know in Thorsten's house
Both of them this evening would be bright
And burn for me. Last evening—but it's late,
And I can scarcely see the ones I talk to:
Wearily, yet love is in the words."

More luminous than what remained of light
On the chill path made plausible, his eyes
Lengthened the day, and never while he stood there
Did his face fail them. Nancy listened. Love.
What did he mean—love—and would they have it
More in the months to come? Or would a silence,
Wrapping this moment, seal it from memory even?

Memory. For his temples and his eyes
Already were as something she had stored
In a still place. The Dandy that she looked at,
Here by the mule, was myth: as dim, as far
As Seth was, past the door there. And she shook
With a new-smitten conscience, trying to fix
That nearer face, that better. It was gone.

"I been thinking," somberly, from Ben.
"Both of us got jobs tomorrow, maybe.
Where do you plan to put him? Public ground?"
"There is none," Dandy said; "or none that's near,
That's proper." And he studied the still earth.
"There is a grove beyond us, where the Ambraw
Falls in a little gorge. We found him lying—"
David lifted a vague hand in the darkness—
"Well, no matter where. But up from the gorge,
In a burr oak clearing, Nelly would come and stand
And listen. You could see her very hair
Startle itself; his coming never surprised her.
She knew his every trick; and this was where
He fed her; where he fondled her; and told
Old stories of her kin: ten generations
Backward in bald time, in youth's Virginia.
To those she wouldn't listen; she'd be off,
Ungrateful, at the tenderness, the climax:
Just as the fawn was found. So this is where
We'll put him. He is home now, being watched.
But the last watch is his: from the dead middle
Of Nelly's quiet floor. We'll step it off
Exactly, and be sure—the very center."
"That'll be good," said Ben. "But there's no such
In these parts."
                    "Yes!" said Clara. "Yes, there is.
The sycamores where Lester used to climb
And drop into the river. Seth would say:
Don't do it; then he'd follow, and the foolish

270

Pair of them one hot noon dived together.
Nancy, you remember; for you told,
And then it was forbidden; and they sulked,
Refusing you the tree-house they had promised."
"Yes, I do remember." This was where,
Oh, covetous! the first flash of a band,
The first tone of a bell, was flame, was teasing—
No, she said, forget that. "There's a few
Fine oaks there, too," said Clara, "on high ground
This way of April water. Ben and David,
There and then—tomorrow, at the moment
Dandy's father knows it is the center—
Will you? Then?" But Ben and David breathed
And only Seth broke silence. "It's a heathen
Hole you'll be a digging. I declare!
What's wrong with blessed ground, and people hearing
Hymns across a fence rail? Drive him east
I say to Indiana, where we stopped
That year and counted headstones." But her will
Outsang him, and his words were less than locusts.
"Dandy Richman, what would be the hour
You went there? Noon? High noon? It is the best
For burying, for borning. Old and new—
Time's tail in its mouth. So your white sire
And my green son will sleep at the same instant:
One for the rest of the world, as one the feud
That chilled them. Will you, Dandy?" A long wait;
Then "Yes; at noon: I'll manage"; but a longer
Still before the tears that in the darkness
Stopped her were delivered of their load.

"What are you up to, girl?" the doctor whispered,
Feeling his pocket empty. But her hand,
Its tenant, was already groping off
Through greyness: searching the dooryard of the night
For a dear thing misplaced. Then she was home;
Fearing her mother less, and the cold tones

Of why and where, than this her pressing loss,
This vacancy that crushed her. I should walk,
Her father sighed, and help her; she is strayed
From courage; it is right that she be here,
As I am, to the end. But there was Dandy
Going, and there still was this to say
That last night he had pondered.
                              "Have you thought?"—
He hurried with it, hearing the halter tighten—
"Has anybody guessed how it will be
With strangers: with the world that doesn't know,
Yet will, that death has been here double-handed?
They were not stones; they will be missed; and then,
How shall we give it out? A pair of chances?
Two accidents of God? But there is God."
"Certainly," said Thorsten, "there is God."
But Clara's voice was stronger. "And he knows
All that we know, and more. He saw them die,
And why. And then was angry. But this hour
He witnessed goodness, too, and the wild hand
That halted. He was present when I prayed,
And heard me. So his mind is elsewhere now,
Sufficient in its mercy to be sure
That truth for men, for strangers, can be lies
In heaven. Don't you hear it there: the stillness?"
All that they heard was Jenny's bit ajingle,
And the last wandering shreds of Clara's cry.
"David my son is changed; and as for Dandy,
How could he hurt the world? The world has hurt
Us equally; yet equally it stills
And heals us. There is peace now. Let it be.
Our suffering is over." "So I tell
Myself," the doctor said. "We can be silent."

"Nevertheless," said Thorsten, "there is God.
Men cannot speak for him; nor in his name
Be silent. Shall we listen any longer?

He will not send a word. The ways of truth
Are wilder than we know: more terrible,
More perfect. I have listened and heard nothing.
That is his wont. And yet I know he is:
And pray you not to do what you must do
Pretending he is partner. What he wills
Is willed, and time may show it; or may not.
Meanwhile here we are, and our best good,
I say with you, is silence. Let it be
Two accidents. Not God's, though. Lead and water.
Thorsten will trim the truth. Thorsten is willing."
"Don't lie for me," said David out of the darkness.
"I ain't afraid no more, nor ever will be,
Of what by God must happen. If it's telling,
Tell! There ain't no lie will ever save—"
"Not you," said Thorsten. "All of us. And peace."
"And quiet," Clara murmured. "Little Ma!
To think you'd ever fib! But if you say so,
Mum's my middle name." "And mine," said Ben.
And after a little while, "It's mine," said Dandy.
"Mum," said Seth the elder, as though answering
Roll calls in his sleep.
                              "And now I'm off,"
Said Dandy; and a creaking in her withers,
As of old leather stretching, showed that Jenny
Knew him, and accepted, and was sad.
But still he did not turn her. There he lingered,
High on his dim mount, and held the cabin
Steadily in his gaze; till Clara, starting,
Said to herself: It's Seth. He wants to see—
But no. It's nothing near us. And she knew,
Watching him there, how darkness can refrain
From flooding its last object. So they all
Saw Dandy: not as lighted, but as lacking
Some of their own full night; and saw his shoulders
Listening, as for someone still to come.

273

Then she was there. Nancy was at the stirrup,
Jingling his foot again and feeling her way
To his half-open hand. "Here, Dandy Richman!
These are for you. They're Nelly's, they're your father's,
Sethie's. They are everyone's but mine."
The bell tinkled in darkness, letting a palm
Enclose it while it tinkled once again:
Farther away, and clearer. Then it rested,
And the band wrapped it: carefully the color
Hid it away from nothingness, from night,
Though its own hue was night, the flannel drained
To velvet now, to mourning. Yet it drew
Some remnant of the sun here, Dandy said;
Lying upon his palm, that opened again,
It flamed a little, duskily, and dyed
The face of Nancy near it a full rose
That his own eyes reflected, studying her.
"They're scarcely mine to give." She all but grew
Inaudible. "But take them, Dandy Richman.
These are the very end; though I was vain,
Even till now, and hid them. But they burned
My bed, and made a noise in the still night.
Now I can sleep; and they can; Nelly is home
If these are." "I will take them," Dandy said,
Slipping them into a pocket which he patted,
"And bury them with him. He used to say
The Indians stuffed a grave with more such nonsense
Than a red ghost would need. But I could tell:
It wasn't nonsense with him. What he dropped
In Susan's grave, my mother's, no one saw.
After we put her down he drove us off
Like vultures. It was terrible, his look,
His language. No one saw; yet George insists
He dropped some light thing in: something that fluttered
And fell, a handkerchief, maybe, or a hermit's
Feather, across her breast."
               He paused; and Nancy,

Noting how his fingers crept and touched
The trinkets where they lay and the wool warmed them,
Said: I see him now, he is not gone
As Seth was; both are with me till I die;
Seth is still my sweetheart, and this man,
This stranger, is my friend. And she so searched
His face that Dandy felt it like a touch,
Tingling him everywhere. Yet all the while
His voice went on, dividing with tomorrow
The musings of this twilight. "It will please him,
Having the bell, the cloth, in a safe place
Beside him. He denies it, but I know.
And I'd ransack all earth for a third thing
If it were left on land. The turkey bone
Went downstream with its music. I am sorry.
The bell and it were sisters. If the bone
Had lasted, I would lay it with your gifts
And tell him where they came from; as I will,
No matter, when tomorrow stands at noon.
Up, Jenny!"
                    But there still was David's laugh,
A little husky now from its long silence,
A little hoarse from doubting it should sound.
"Why, man! The tooter's waiting for you, dug
In leaf-dirt where we wrastled. Save you mind
Uprooting what he buried, there it lays
For fair in a filled hole. The one last thing
He handled but for me. Or the gun, maybe.
Anyhow it's there, in a pint pot
Of top soil, and you're welcome to its toot."
"Stop," said Dandy, "stop! My father's end
Was laughable, perhaps; yet not to me.
Be serious. I will listen if you do."
"That's all I'm after, Dandy. Didn't go
To gall you; honest God, I wouldn't belittle
Him or the bone or any landish thing."

"I wasn't galled," said Dandy, "and I see.
Forgive me. Now go on. You say you saw—"

"I seen your dad a digging and a chipping,
Right there in the middle of that place,
Till a round hole was ready. Then he took
His tooter, and he blew it till a big
Bird sassed him; then he buried it, a looking
All this time for fear a stranger'd laugh.
There didn't seem to be nobody there.
But I was; and I tell you I'm ashamed
I spied it, and that later on I spit
Contemption on him, burying thataway
The funny-bones of buzzards. So I said.
Fact was, I almost sorried when I heard him.
Solemnlike it hooted. The last thing
He done, and it was maybe the God's best."
"But where?" "Plumb in the middle, where you plan
To measure. Step it off and there you'll be.
Maybe, though, you'd hesitate to meddle,
Or act as if you knowed. It was enough
That I did. Well, then, dig along the side
And leave it. That's as near as he would want;
And when the ground works, all of it bogs down
To one thing anyway. A bone's a bone,
But afterwards it won't be even that."
"Yes," said Dandy. "Sounds will do for center:
Three small notes beside him, that the bell
May answer. Thank you, David; I'll report
How you and Nancy both bide in the grave,
His friends. For you have given him goodnight."

"And now," he said, "goodnight to the boy's father
Whom my own father missed; the light was weak,
As grove light was for David, and he looked
At less than God permitted to shine there.
Goodnight to Ben, who is but one of two now,

276

While I am one of three; who would have been
But one in all the world if Thorsten's pride—
Goodnight to you, Sir. It was not a mist;
I say it now for justice; it was clearness.
So it deceived my sight; but when you followed,
There it was plain around you. Not to see.
To love. For nothing's braver than no pride
When wisdom is in danger, and humility
Hobbles to save truth." "My feet were sore,"
Said Thorsten, "and I wouldn't be surprised
If hers, the mule's were sorer. What I did
Was nothing that I know; but if it helped,
You let it; you were he in whom the heart
Survived that was to save us. What I'd do
This evening you have heard, and have refused."
"There will be other evenings when my heart
Is friendly to fireplaces. Now it shuts
All warmths away but one. I am a citizen
Of Mayfield if you please, though, and the time
Is coming when I'll take my ease among you.
Doctor, you did well by me and David,
Putting the end off longer, putting your horses'
Scent between his blood and my blood, stopping
His tale when he would tell it." "When you come,
I'll teach you chess. The knight's head, the antic,
Prances two ways at once, and can prevent
More than I did this morning. But your move
Is first to come. I do pronounce you, Dandy,
A citizen of Mayfield, and bespeak
A winter hour or two when you can save me
From the poor vice of gobbling my own pawns."
"Prince and Pete," said David, "is the best
On four foot. When you're tuckered out with squinting
Sideways of them squares, I hope the Doc
Will leave me take and drive you to the Barrens.
There and back's an easy day for elephants;
For us it's hop and jump." "Goodbye to you,"

Said Dandy, "till that day. For I'll remember;
And bring my second brother, horseman Paul.
Lady, I'll not ask you to forgive
Me or my father now. I'm sorry Seth's
A stranger and must keep so; though I saw him
Once, before the sun set, in the joy
That sweetened you with his name." "Oh, my fourth son!"
"Nancy—here," and his hand caught her cold one,
Rising to prove him there. "When this is warm
I'll come again. Be wise and let the blood
Work back into it fitly. You're to forget me
As much as you may need to. I'll remember.
And when I come, let blue be in your eyes
For blessing on a stranger. Goodnight, now;
Keep warm, and never think of who said so."

They turned their heads with the slow sound he made,
Moving as if in slumber out of vision
Till the whole night contained him and sent back
The picture, not the person. Even Seth,
Propped on his elbows, saw it and was glad
For stillness; though the image that he guarded
Was no one else's there, for each beguiled
Himself with separate fancy. David's gaze
Had past and future in it: both Old Richman,
Beaten into the water, and bright Nancy,
Young again when Dandy should look down
And smile upon her blue, her red, her black.
These had been lit for Seth, and it was sad
That a strange eye should come then, not his own,
And borrow them like coals, and run with them
To a new hearth not here, not here in Mayfield.
Yet David let it be. If it was so,
Then simply it was so, and his new world
Was big enough for difference. He considered
In silence while his mother, listening off,
Saw one she could have talked with long and long

If grief had not benumbed her. Now the words
Rushed hither: words of Seth and a fourth son,
Of burial, of blessing, of remembrance;
Yet she too honored stillness. Only Thorsten
Broke it with his dry voice after sound
Had ceased upon the north road, and the night
Was his to burn away with speaking fair.

"He takes the winter with him," Thorsten said,
"Like a great stone that some day will be rolled
With all our darkness in it down to the sea:
To sink there, making bubbles that will burst
And spray our valley over with quick spring.
I think of home, where winter went that way,
Crunching the valley floor till you would think
No flower, no bee survived. And yet they did,
And buzzed and glittered bravely; till a new
Stone gathered in its hardness all the hate
That two mild months forgot. It balanced long,
High on the death-white top, the overhanging
Winter of our small life; then it too bounded,
Bruising the very slopes it fell to save,
And fountained the warm surf. I think of home;
But this too is our home, and the long dark,
The cold, will not be lasting. What he takes
He needs, and night is proper yet awhile
To us in Mayfield, mourning. But the spring
Is brilliant that I see spreading again
Its haze of diamond particles, more bold,
More beautiful, for pressures underground,
For lessons we have learned from a boy's death.
Dandy, here or there, will shine more surely,
As we shall, for this sorrow. Not that it goes.
It stays, but it will meet the April sun
As we shall, glancing. Never did I think
I'd live to love more winter than snow brings,
Than snarls of wind announce. This one is inward,

279

Needful; and I know it will grind on
Till light is thick around us, powdered fine
By difficulty's weight that we endured."

They heard him on the path, with Gard at his heels,
Going to sleep and supper. For a sign
They took it, as betokening the end
Of sound. So Clara, pushing at the door,
Passed in; and Ben and David followed after
With what of Seth their four arms could control.
Only the doctor stood with his still daughter,
Waiting upon the start that she must make.
She made none, and he frowned; but with more thought
Desisted. She would come in her own time,
And meanwhile he was weary. Such a load,
Put down at last, was memory's fiercest tyrant,
And the mind's tendons never would relax.
He smiled at his despair; it was untrue,
As death is while we breathe, as the worst is
When still the worst awaits us. Two more days,
Two months, and much of this would be forgotten:
The brain's way, the body's; and with touches
Eloquent of his tenderness he left her,
Warm in a candle's weak and spreading light
That David had made watchman. Not that he knew
It flushed her, or that she was audience now
To noise in any cabin. If she listened,
Seth was what she heard, lone in his room
And satisfied with silence.
                                        Seth was clear
Once more in her quick mind, that hastened back
And found him—yes, there—in the still days
When nothing yet had happened, nothing had hurt
Their courage. He was standing for her now
And laughing, and his thought was all of her:
Of what she next would want from him, of dares,
Of dangers. He was generous, she was bright,

And her black hair could tease him. So her hands
Flew to her head and held it; it was his
For silence, and the colors he had known,
The burning red, the burning blue, were his
For comfort in that darkness. She would live
To light him; and light Dandy if he came,
Some day, and she remembered who said so.
She would; he was her friend, and he would come
With spring if not with winter—dropping her hands
And musing as she went, the candle beams
Failing her cloak at last.
     So she would live
By being what she was, although it strained
Her wisdom, and Seth's wisdom, at the start.
Not to be were easier, Nancy said,
Imagining the windows of that house,
Her father's, boarded over. But a world
Shone through, and when she knocked it was enough.
And Mayfield seemed a moment in slow time.

MORTAL SUMMER
(1953)

Mortal Summer

I

The cave they slept in, halfway down Olympus
On the eastern slope, toward Asia, whence the archangels
Even then were coming—even then
Bright Michael, and tall Gabriel, and the dark-faced
Raphael, healer of men's wounds, were flying,
Flying toward the ship all ten would take—
The cave they slept in sparkled as their eyelids
Opened; burned as they rose and stood; hummed
And trembled as the seven, the beautiful gods
Gazed at each other, wonderful again.
The sweet sleep of centuries was over,
If only as in dream; if only a mortal
Summer woke them out of endless death.

The grey eyes of Athene, flashing slowly,
Demanded of Hermes more than he could tell.

"It was not I that roused you." Hermes pondered,
Tightening his sandals. "All at once,
And equally, we woke. Apollo there—"
The musical man-slayer listened and frowned—
"And Ares, and foam-loving Aphrodite
Yawned at the very instant Artemis did,

285

With me, and swart Hephaestus." The lame smith,
Stroking his leather apron, blinked at the others,
Worshipful of brilliance. Even in Ares,
Scowling, and more quietly in her
The huntress, whose green robe the animals knew,
He found it; and of course in Aphrodite,
Wife to him once, he found it, a relentless
Laughter filling her eyes and her gold limbs.
"It was not I," said Hermes.

                        Thunder sounded,
Weakly and far away. And yet no distance
Wrapped it. It was here in the lit cavern:
Here, or nowhere. And the trembling seven
Turned to the rock that sealed a deeper room.
There Zeus, there Hera sat, the feasted prisoners
Of a still greater person, one who changed
The world while there they mourned, remembering Ida.
Some day they too would sleep, but now weak thunder
Witnessed their remnant glory; which appalled
As ever the proud seven, until Hermes
Listened and leaned, then spoke.

                        "It was the king
Our father. He has willed that we should wander,
Even as in a dream, and be the gods
Of strangers. Somewhere west of the ocean stream
He sends us, to a circle of small hills—
Come, for I see the place!"

                        That suffered thunder
Sounded again, agreeing; and they went.
Out of the cave they poured, into spring sun
Whose warmth they yet increased, for the falling light
Was less than theirs was, moving as they moved.
No soldier and no shepherd, climbing here,
Would have discovered deity. The brambles
Hid as they ever had this stony hole
Whence seven had been wakened, and where still,
Enormous in dark chains, their parents wept.

Invisible to suns, the seven gathered
Round a white rock and gazed. The sea was there,
The Aegean, and a ship without a sail
Plied southward, trailing smoke; at which Hephaestus
Squinted. Then he slapped his thigh and smiled,
And waved for six to follow as down world
He leapt.
      They landed, all of them, as lightly
As a fair flock of gulls upon the prow
Of the tramp *Jonathan B. Travis*, bound
Tomorrow for Gibraltar, then northwest,
Northwest, both night and day, till the ocean stream
Was conquered. Not a god had ever gone there,
Not one of these high seven, in the old
Dark sail time. Now, invisible to waves,
To men and birds, they watched twelve grimy sailors
Washing their clothes on deck; and wondered still
At the two wakes behind them, foam and funnel.

But who were these arriving, these gaunt three
On giant wings that folded as they fell
And staggered, then stood upright? Even now
Michael had dropped among them, with his archangel
Brethren, bony Gabriel and lank Raphael.
From nearer Asia, lonely a long while,
They had come flying, sick of the desert silence,
Sick of the centuries through which no lord,
No king of the host, had blessed them with command.
As orphaned eagles, missing their ancient's cry,
They had come hither, hopeful of these seven,
Hopeful of noble company, of new act.
Now on the prow they gathered, and no sailor
Saw them; but Apollo did, and Artemis—
Fingering their bows—as Hermes reared
On tiptoe, smiling welcome. Aphrodite,
Slipping to lee of Ares, feigned a fear

More beautiful than truth was; while Hephaestus,
Curious, near-sighted, fingered those wing-joints
Athene only studied where she stood.

"Whoever you are," said Hermes, "and whatever—
Pardon this—you were, sail now as we do,
And be the gods of strangers far to west.
If only as in dream the vessel draws us,
Zeus our sire consenting. Your own sire—"
But the three stared so sadly over the waves
That Hermes paused, and beckoning to Gabriel
Whispered with him alone while dolphins played
As lambs do on dry land, and fishes scattered.

Alone to Hermes, while the dolphins heaved
Grey backs above green water, Gabriel murmured:
"Your sire. We had one too. And have Him still,
Though silent. It is listening for his thunder
That leans us. He is busy with new folk,
New, humble folk he speaks to in a low voice.
We have not learned that language—humble words,
With never death or danger in the message.
A star stood still above a stable once,
And a weak infant wept. And there He left us."
"Our sire," said Hermes, "—he too sleeps away
Our centuries. We have the selfsame fortune.
Sail westward with us then." And Gabriel nodded.

The steel that sliced the water swung at length,
And in three days they nosed between the Pillars;
Past which—and the ten all shuddered—monsters once
Made chaos of the world's end. But no fangs
Closed over the black prow, and mile on mile
Slid under them, familiar as a meadow
To the small men they watched amid the smoke.
Mile on mile, by hundreds and by thousands,

The Atlantic sloped away. Then lands and harbors,
And a deep whistle groaning.
                              "Now!" said Hermes,
"Now!" So nine to one they lifted wing,
Or no-wing like their leader, and went on,
High over chimneys and chill rivers, north
By west till it was there—the rounded valley,
Green with new spring, where cattle bawled in barns
And people, patient, waited for hot June.

II

Daniel was mending fence, for it was May,
And early rains had painted the drear pastures.
He walked, testing the wire, and wished again
For his old pipe. He missed it, and grew moody.
Berrien would never notice it on the shelf;
Berrien would never bring it. A good wife,
But scornful of the comforts. A good woman,
Who never guessed the outrage he had done her.
New Year's Eve, and Dora. He remembered—
And set his jaw, missing the pipe stem there.
He pulled at a slack strand of the barbed wire,
And snagged himself—here, in the palm of his hand.
A little blood came which he wiped away.
He did miss that tobacco. And he did,
He did loathe simple Dora—warm and simple,
Who with her dark head nodding close to his,
On New Year's Eve, had done with him this outrage.
He would forget her if he could; and old
Darius, her profane, her grizzled father.
So proud of her he was, and kept so neat
The mountain shack they lived in, he and his one
Sweet chick he swore was safe as in State's prison.
Daniel counted the months. Was the child showing?
Darius—did he guess? And Doctor Smith—
Would she have gone to him? Daniel looked off,

Unmindful of the beautiful May morning.
Bruce Hanna, that poor boy. Was he suspicious?
He had been born for Dora, she for him;
And then last New Year's Eve, when the sleigh bells rang
So slyly, writing ruin in cold air!
Daniel, wiping his hand again, looked back
At the wild barb that bit him.
                              Who was that?
For a quizzical, small stranger stood by the fence,
Feeling its rust, its toughness. He was swarthy
And lame, and had bright eyes. And in his hand
A pipe—for all the township Daniel's own!

"Here, have you need of this? I'm on my way
Northeast awhile, repairing peoples' ranges.
It gave itself to me, but you can have it."

Then he was gone, unless he walked and waved—
For someone did—Daniel could not distinguish—
From the far border of the field. The small
Stranger was gone, and all that Daniel held
Was a filled pipe bowl, comforting his palm.

He must ask Berrien, he said at noon,
If a lame dwarf had come to mend the cook stove.
He must ask Berrien, who wouldn't listen,
How a man's pipe could vanish from its shelf.
For so it had, into his very pocket.

"Berrien!" he called. But she was busy
With her own bother.
                    "Daniel, a woman's here—
Wants to stay and board all summer—wants
To rest. A theater woman. I've said no,
But maybe—"
            Who was the gold one, listening there

And smiling? Looking over Berrien's shoulder
And lighting the front room with little smiles?
A faded gold one, well beyond her prime,
But the true substance, glistening. Berrien frowned
And her head shook. But Daniel, fascinated,
Said he would think, would figure.
                    In the end
She stayed, the theater woman; and that night
Daniel had dreams of her. She came to his bed
In beauty; stood beside him and said "Dora."
How could she know of Dora? It was a dream,
Yet how could she know so much? And how had she fathomed,
All in one day, the longing he denied?
There was no loathing. Anywhere in his heart—
That sweetened as he said it—there was no hate
For Dora, whom he thought he saw there too,
Standing beside the theater woman and weeping,
And holding her simple hands out so he could say:
"Tomorrow, little sweetheart half my years,
Tomorrow I will tell the world about us.
You must be mine to keep. I have been cruel;
I have been absent, darling, from your pain.
Tomorrow I will put my two arms round you,
And bear if I can the—pleasure."
                       Then he woke,
And none but Berrien watched him in the room—
Berrien, who ever after watched him,
Night and day detesting this pale witch
Who came and went and charmed him.
                    So she thought,
Said Daniel, never answering her eyes.
For him there were no hours now save those dark ones
When the pair came. At midnight they would be there,
Faithful as moths; and every sunny morning,
Starting from his pillow, he would mutter:
"Tomorrow is today. Then I must go
To Dora, I must tell her." Yet he waited

291

Always upon another secret midnight;
And witnessed every noon how the gold woman,
Smiling her light smile, seemed not to know
Of Dora; was no witch at all; was no one.

III

Meanwhile a little mountain house was murmurous
With his own name—evil, could he but hear it.
Darius had discovered his sweet daughter's
Swelling, and had pressed her for the cause;
And yesterday, in terror, Dora yielded.
Now Bruce was there, with the old badger watching
How sick one word could make him. So it was spoken—
"Daniel." And the kill was on.
                                    A soldier,
Footing it home from Canada, stood by
With a gourd dipper, dripping as he drank.
He listened, lounging, and his bushy eyes
Burned at the accusation. When Bruce faltered—
And he did falter, for his hate of Daniel,
Less than the sore so sudden in his breast,
So hopeless, so beyond all thought of cure,
Was a weak thing at first—this brawny witness
Shone like a savior in the old one's eyes,
The little old one, dancing in his fury
As he repeated "Daniel"; and made doubly
Sure that Dora's corner room was bolted.
Afterwards, remembering how the knuckled
Soldier had spat curses on that name,
"Daniel," and had spun a scheme for them—
Perfection, he declared it, of revenge—
Darius called him blessed. "You'd have failed me,
Bruce, you would have wobbled like a calf
And licked this devil's hand, but for that sergeant.
Who sent him here, I wonder?"
                                    "I don't know,"

Said Bruce, his mind on Dora's room. "Is she—"
"Yes, she's in there. And stays there till we've finished.
When do we go and do it? Think of that—
Think only of that thing, my boy, that needful
Thing." Darius nudged him, and they dropped
Their voices.
            Dora, listening, heard little,
Crouched by her door. Bruce—he mustn't do it.
Bruce—he was the only thing she wanted
In the poor world. A poor one too for Daniel;
But she shut out the thought. Bruce mustn't do it,
Whatever it was. She beat on the thick wood
And cried to him; but only heard Darius
Coaxing him outdoors; then only silence.

"When shall it be, my boy? What dark of the moon
Does best for our good purpose—damn his bones!
Two shotguns—that's enough—then home, then here—
That's it, and neither knows of it next day.
We'll even shed a hot tear, being told!
When do we do it, boy?"
            But Bruce was slow:
Angry and sick, but slow. And once when Dora
Found him, deep in the woods between their cabins,
He almost lost his purpose as she held him,
Wetting his face with tears.
            "Listen!" she whispered.
"I have been down to Doctor, and his new nurse
Knows—I can't guess how—knows everything.
A beautiful, tall woman, and her friend
The teacher—she is like her. Colder, though,
With different, with grey eyes. The new nurse says—"
"What, Dora, what does she say?"
            "Oh, no, I can't—
I'll never, never tell you."
            As she ran
He followed, farther into the still woods;

293

Then stopped as she did, startled. For those two—
It must be those two new ones, those tall women—
Pondered the carcass of a fawn, a spotted
Three-months fawn that dogs had torn at the throat.

It was the nurse that knelt, lifting brown eyes
In sorrow, scarcely knowing Dora there.
The other one bent down to her.
                              "Stand up.
They both are here. The boy, too."
                                   Level voiced,
The teacher touched her friend's hair.
                               "Stand up, stand up.
The fawn is dead. These others—"
                             "Yes, I know.
I heard, I saw them. But consider death.
Consider this young death awhile, and say—
But softly—of what it is the paradigm.
Do not disdain one death, one single death;
And when we can, prevent."
                         The grey eyes cooled,
Consenting. So the sorrowful one arose.
"Come here," she said to Dora, and to Bruce
Behind her. "We were walking in the woods,
My visitor and I; we saw this sight."

But Bruce and Dora stared at only her,
So beautiful, so tall, and at the other
Strange one by her side.
                      "We had been talking,
Children, of you two. No matter if Daniel
Loves you, little girl of the dark eyes—"

"He doesn't!" Dora shuddered. "If he could,
He'd have it that I never lived on earth.
He hates it, having to remember me.

And that's all right. I want it so. But Bruce—"

"Will be, my dear, the father of your—listen,
Listen! You start away."
     For both had broken
Breath, as if with running, and only the hands
Of the grey-eyed, the firm one, held them there.
"I mean," and the tall beautiful one blinked,
Twitching the green selvage of her skirt,
"The foster father. He is young for that;
Yet he is to be, my child, the chosen one
Who saves you, and saves it—the life you carry.
Your husband. Nothing less. And not in dream."

Bruce turned his head in fear that old Darius
Listened—was it he among the hemlocks,
Stepping so lightly?
    But the foliage opened
For a fair, smiling face, and the broad shoulders,
Burdened with straps, of one who tramped these hills
By summer, following signs. A brilliance round him,
Caused by no sun, for none came through the branches,
Struck silence from all four; until the nurse,
Nodding as if she knew him, said: "Due north,
Pilgrim, is there. Your compass—have you lost it?
Well, north is that way"—pointing—"but stand here
In patience for some seconds; then we two
Will guide you back to town for better bearing.
Can you be patient?"
     "Thank you, yes." The giant
Smiled at her once again.
     "You see, my small one,
Bruce there by your side would break and run,
Fearing his sweet fate. He even wonders
Whether some partner, deep in another plan,
Listens and chides him."
    Staring, the boy blushed.

295

Then, fearful, he looked up and met her eyes,
The nurse's distant eyes, that fixed him gently.
"My friend here—she will tell you more than I can
Of the black folly born of feud. Attend her."

But the still teacher only parted wide
Her capable cool lids, and let him see
Agreement flash between them.
                  "Someone's death"—
She forced the words at last—"is cheap to buy.
A minute of man's time, and breathing stops.
The cost is in the echo; for to cease
Makes sound. So you will hear it coming home,
The rumor of that death. My friend is right.
Marry the maiden."
              But the words came strangely,
Out of some older earth, and even she
The speaker knew their failure; for she frowned.
Bruce turned his head again, fearing the hemlock
Heard. Yet no one listened there; no fourth one
Followed this lofty fellow who in patience
Folded his arms and smiled—as if he too
Had knowledge, and agreed with the grey eyes.
As Dora did, said Bruce. And yet Darius—
He paled at the grim image, and remembered,
Suddenly, that soldier; whose disgust
If the dear purpose foundered was itself
A death, along with Dora's yesterday.
Daniel. Who but Daniel was the father
Of a whole world's confusion?
                And his anger,
Running before him, took him from this place,
This glade where three, left thoughtful, were as figures
Molded of shadow. Dora was gone with Bruce,
Gasping and crying "Wait!"
              But the three tall ones
Listened to nothing human. Hermes came.

296

IV

Hermes came, and hailing his three peers,
Spoke Aphrodite's name; whose beautiful laughter
Answered as she glistened in their midst—
No woman now, but goddess. So Hephaestus
Hove into their view, and all of the others,
Manifest together. This was where,
In tulip and oak shade, they pleased to meet,
To sit sometimes and say how the world went,
Mortal and immortal.
                    "You of the golden
Shoulders," Hermes said, "bring dreams to one
Who lived in peace without them."
                                "Lived in hate,
In loathing of those very limbs he fondled—
Poor, poor limbs, so lonely!" And her insolent
Laughter shook the listening green leaves.
"Yet he would have forgotten, and his only
Danger been from Ares"—who was there,
Swelling his thick chest, as Hermes spoke—
"From the two minions, old and young, of Ares.
Such danger can dissolve, for it is wind
And fury; but the damage that you do,
Arrogant bright daughter of the dolphins,
Is endless as waves are, or serpent segments
The impotent keen knife divides. Have mercy,
Goddess." And he waited. But her lips,
Unmoving, only teased him; and tormented
Artemis.
        "The man was free of longing,
And the dark maid of him," the huntress said,
"Till this one wantoned, wooing him with dreams.
Then Ares—common soldier—fanned the fire
In those you call his minions." Hermes nodded.
"And so our plan's perplexed before it ripens.

297

Athene, Michael—tell them how we stood,
Just here, and heard the boy refuse his function."

But it was known among them even then,
And so no witness needed. Aphrodite,
Secure in beauty's pride, tilted her head
To hear, intending mockery of the tale.
But the wise one withheld it, and majestic
Michael only folded his broad wings
As Gabriel did, as Raphael.
                              Yet that last one,
Mournful of face and long, had ears for Artemis,
Nurse to all things aborning, as she mused:

"The young one when he comes in what men call
The fall of their brief year—the roofless infant—
It was for him we planned. And still we do—"
She dared the glittering goddess—"still we seek
Safe birth for the small mother, and for him
The wailing, the unwanted."
                              Crooked Hephaestus,
Clearing his mild throat, remarked in modesty:
"The man works well and silently. He loves,
In solitude, the comfort of my fire.
And so in a bowl I brought it. As for her—
He will not have her near him. I was by;
I read his thoughts of this."
                              "Absurd contriver!
Artisan of the bellows! Zeus's butt!
As ever, you know nothing." Aphrodite
Sparkled with rage, reviling him. "You saw
By daylight, and at labor in the field,
One whom that very night I made my slave.
Off to your anvil, ass!"
                              But Hermes calmed
Their quarrel, lifting his either hand in grace.
"Without our father's thunder we are fools

And children. Who decides when lesser gods,
When angels disagree? Authority absent,
Silence—a silver silence—that is best."
And like a song they heard it, and they wondered,
Measuring its notes. Until Apollo,
Lord of the muses, laughed.
                              "You heard me humming.
All to myself I sang it—with sealed lips."

"What did you sing?" said Hermes.
                              "Nothing, nothing.
My sisters round the world—a sweet wind brought me,
Sleepily, this air."
                    He hummed again,
And this time closed his eyes. "Perhaps I see,"
He said, "some silver moment coming soon—
Necessity for music. But not now."

Nor could those other nine foresee the summer.
Already, in mid June, high long days
Hovered the world, and change, like ripening fruit,
Hung ever, ever plainer. Yet no man,
No god distinguished more in this green time
Than purposes that crossed; and ever tighter.
In Daniel's house the woman who was resting—
Daily, in scorn, Berrien spoke the word—
Still did not spare the beautiful dream body
She sent to him by dark, when Dora too
Lived by his side and loved him: standing there
In the shed radiance of one who smiled
And smiled, and burned his reticence away.
For he would go to Dora—come July,
Said Daniel, lying afterwards and listening
As night died between him and the windows,
He would go there, he would, and say it all;
He would have Dora, small in his long arms,
Forever. Yet the sweetness of this thought

Exhausted him, and hollowed his wild eyes,
So that he never went.
                    And had he gone,
What Dora would have seen him come and shivered?
One whom as strong a dream—if it was a dream—
Estranged. It was of having, yet not having,
Bruce for her brave husband. For he mustn't—
He mustn't, she said nightly, shutting away
The vision—Bruce must never let it be.
The nurse—he mustn't listen. Yet if he did—
And then she wept.
                    Darius in the morning,
Seeing her tears, thought only of his purpose.
He should conceal it better. She was afraid,
Was frantic, she might go somewhere and tell.
That boy—he was so hard to keep in anger.
He faltered, and he wilted; he was a fool.
That boy, the center of confusion's cross,
For still he hated Daniel, still with Darius
Plotted the loud death; yet loved all day,
All night the dream of lying in clear peace
Forever, in dear confidence, with Dora;
That boy was whom the strangers in this valley
Watched while the moments went; while June decayed;
While middle summer dozed; and no leaves fell.

V

A hundred people coming to the barn dance,
The barn dance at MacPherson's, saw the full moon.
It hung there like a lantern in the low east,
Enormous and blood red, and stationary.
Daniel came, and Berrien, with that woman—
So fair, she seemed unnatural—between them.
She must have made them bring her, someone said;
And laughed.
          But no one laughed when Dora came.

300

She was so pitiful in her loose coat,
Concealing, healing nothing. Would she dance?
If only with Bruce Hanna, would she dance?
Too late for it, some whispered; and some blamed
The silly boy. To let her show like that!
The nurse, the doctor's nurse, and her tall friend
The teacher—no one dreamed those two, those two—
They stood by their grand selves, and no one saw
How Bruce, how Dora lived but in their glances.

Then all the strangers. When the music started,
Who but a giant—handsome, with tow hair—
Bowed to the grand ones? And to more
Beyond them? For a pair of unknown farmers,
Lanky and cave-eyed, leaned bony shoulders
Where a great upright shaded the rude floor.
From the next valley, maybe, like this lame
Pedlar; like the soldier; like that lightfoot
Traveller, the one with pointed ears,
The one with cropped hair and a twisted staff,
Who wandered in the crowd, watching and watched.
The shepherd of the strangers? Yet no word
Between them, and no look, Darius said—
Darius, who had eyes for everything;
And ears, when music started.
                    "One more couple!
One more couple!" Glendy the clear-caller
Shouted while harmonicas, like locusts,
Shrilled, and while Young Gus tuned his guitar.
"One more couple!"
            Here they came.
                   "Join hands
And circle left!"
          Darius heard the words
Above him, in the corner where by Glendy
And the harmonicas he tapped the floor.
His was the curious, the musicians' corner,

301

Whence he could see how Dora sat and trembled,
Wondering what next—why she was here.
"The dog!" he growled, catching on Daniel's face,
In a far corner, hunger and indifference
Fighting. Hunger—damn him—for my child,
My child, Darius said, whom he has changed;
And smothering this, the smoke of a pretence
That nothing here was wrong, nothing at all.
The soldier had come back. Darius saw him,
Red-eyed, drinking water by a droplight,
And his own conscience hurt him. Daniel lived.
If Bruce could only raise his eyes a little—
But they were hangdog, or were fixed in fear
On those two stranger women. Why in fear?

The music, though.
                    "Swing your corner lady!"
Darius, rocking gently on his heels,
Was lost again in that, and in the wild
Mouth organs, going mournful overhead.
"First two gents cross over!" In his thought
He crossed; he took that partner by the hand;
He swung her, swung her, swung her, you know where.
He promenaded, proudly, and he clapped
His palms, that sweated bravely. Then the swinging
Ceased. The set was over. And he sang:
"Good boy, Gus! That was calling, old man Glendy!"
They winked at him, wiping their foreheads off;
Then soon another set. And still he listened
And watched, and still he saw how Dora sat,
Trembling, and never danced.
                              But once the soldier,
Slouching to her side, made mockery signs
Suggesting that she stand. Darius started
In anger; then he stopped, for Bruce was up,

Explaining—yet avoiding the brute stare;
And Daniel, in his corner, clenched both fists.
Even the strangers knew, for one came over—
The one with such a neat head on his body,
And the curled stick—as if to beat away
Wild boars escaped here. That was good, was good,
Darius said; then listened as the music
Whispered again.
                              Whispered.
                                         For the tune
Had altered. Where was Glendy? Who was this
Where Glendy had been standing? And what ailed,
What softened so the clamor of the mouth harps?

"One more couple!"
                              Who was the intruder,
Calling in so sweet, so low a voice,
Strange orders? Yet not strange; for the hot crowd,
Heedless of any difference, swirled on,
Loving its evolutions, and no head
Turned hither.
                    "Take your Dora by the hand—"
Darius, looking up, saw how the silver
Light of the full moon, mature at zenith,
Fell on the singer. Through one gable window
It fell, and on no head but his, the silvery
Singer. He was slender, he was strange:
And the high moon—it burned for none but him.

"Where's Glendy, Gus?"
                              "Took sick."
                                         The loud guitar,
Hesitating, rallied and persevered;
But modified its note to a new sweetness,
A low, a far-off sweetness, as Gus looked,

303

Listened, and looked again at the mysterious
Caller on whose mouth the full moon smiled.

> Take your Dora by the hand,
> Your little Dora, grown so large.
> By another she was manned,
> But she is now your loving charge.

> Mercy marries you, my boy,
> And mercy—oh, it is unjust.
> But it was born of truth and joy,
> And lives with misery if it must.

Darius, and then Daniel, comprehending,
Stared at a hundred dancers who did not.
Heedless of any change, they stamped and swung,
Those hundred, as if Glendy still were here—
Old Glendy, whose thin throat still mastered them.
Yet Daniel saw how Dora, dropping her eyes,
Sat silent, deathly silent; and how Bruce,
Guardian to her, looked only down—
Looked everywhere save at the singer, singing:

> Take your Dora by the hand.
> There is life within her waist.
> And there is woe, unless you stand
> And love with bravery is graced.

> So all the world will know her wed,
> And all the people call it yours—
> The life within her, small and red;
> And wrathful, were it none but hers.

> With you beside her all is well.
> She will be tended in her time.
> There is more that I could tell,
> But Glendy now resumes the rhyme.

"Circle four!"
                    Darius, and then Daniel,
Dazed, regarded Glendy once again.
The moonlit one was gone, and only these
Had seen him—these and Dora, and dumb Bruce.
And all of the nine strangers. For they too
Had listened; bending their bodies, they had weighed,
Had witnessed every word as it arrived;
Had watched the boy's confusion; then the girl's;
Then both together, as if woe had wed
Already the poor lovers.
                    "Nelly Gray!"
The hundred dancers, heedless, went right on;
And only Berrien's boarder, the gold woman
Who stood so close by Daniel—only that one
Kindled. Then she blazed, and Daniel, blushing,
Knew she had found his thought.
                              So I have lost her—
This was his thought—have lost her. Then my love
Must die, and no man know it. He was true,
That singer. It is not my life she carries—
Dora, who was mine for that cold minute;
Dora, whom I never can forget.

The eyes of the theater woman burned so fiercely,
Punishing his own, that Daniel shook.
How could she guess his trouble? Only in dreams
She knew it, only in dreams, when Dora came.
Only in darkness. "Now she disapproves,
She probes me."
                    But the woman looked away,
Suddenly, and signalled to the soldier;
Who, nodding, went to stand before Darius.
Daniel saw him there, gesticulating,
With his feet spread, as if he meant to spring,
To throttle someone. And Darius blinked.
But music and the distance drowned their words.

305

And now the tall nurse, bending over Dora,
Whispered to her and Bruce; and the boy, rising,
Reached for a small hand. The singer had said
To take it, and he took it, and pulled up
The girl who still was trying to be free,
To save him.
    And the music never stopped.
"Kiss her if you dare!" cried old man Glendy.
And many a dancer did. But neither Bruce
Nor Dora, arm in arm, had present ears.
They listened still to what the other singer,
Gone now as the moon was from the window,
Sang and sang again, as if his silvery
Face never had faded. Arm in arm
They walked among the dancers to the big door;
Arm in arm, sleepwalking, they went forth,
Under the slant moon, and disappeared.

VI

Some whispers, like the wake of blowing leaves
When a swift body passes west, pursued them.
But Daniel never stirred.
    Nor old Darius—
Neither did he listen as the sergeant
Swore, swelling the wrath in his red eyes
Till most of him was fire. "Follow him home,
The fool. He is forgetting it—the purpose.
Tear him free. He softens in her arms
To the sick sound of 'Father.' "
    But Darius,
Lost in the same sound, was thinking softly:
"I had not dreamed of this. She will be friended,
She will not go alone. He is a good boy,
Bruce. I never coupled her with him.

306

It may be in the cards." Whereat the soldier
Left him, spitting disgust.
                            And Daniel saw
How all of the fair strangers followed soon—
All of them, as if they were a company.
They wouldn't be, of course. And yet they smiled
In the same grave degree, as if some secret
Bound them.
              And he thought the dapper one,
Who tapped the sanded floor and twirled his stick,
His curlicue of a cane—whatever it was—
Communicated thus to the gold woman
That she too must away. But she was Daniel's,
Berrien's; she was not of any company,
Wandering, like this one. She had come
Alone to them, in May, and she would go—
Would go, said Daniel, taking her dream body,
Her beautiful dream body, that was his,
Was his alone.
                And suddenly his sadness
Doubled. For the singer had left living
None of his sweet hope. Dora was gone,
A ghost in outer moonlight, a surrendered
Sweetness, and he stood there like a dead man,
A noble dead man, numbering his loss.
Now, multiplied, it smote him. This one too—
In fall—he would be losing this one too,
In fall. Or even here, while he stood looking,
Here, with that lithe one calling from the door.
For there he was, the last one to go through,
And Daniel thought the signal came again:
An elbow's twitch, a twirl of his live staff,
His vine that had the strength to stand alone.

But she had arms and eyes for only Daniel,
Worshipping her now. She seemed as near,

He whispered to himself, as lamplight must,
At midnight, to poor moths. And yet no brush
Of fingers, such as Berrien might have frowned on.
Simply her brilliance chained him, simply her arms,
Her eyes, took hold of everything in him
And hurt it.
                "So you let her go," she said.
"You shadow of a man, you let her go.
Those limbs of hers, so beautiful in light,
In darkness, and the breast you could have bruised,
Crushing it with yours—and yet you would not,
For it is white, is small, and precious to you—
Derelict! Oh, shameful! What a shadow
Falls on you for lover—disobedient
Lover of that girl whom still you crave!"

Did her lips part? Was any of it spoken?
Berrien still watched the weary dancers
Like one whom nothing moved. Then whence the words?
And why? For the gold woman's only knowledge
Was a dream knowledge, drawn to him by night
When her own body slept in her own bed.
How could she understand? And what untruth
Was working in her, making these sweet sounds?
Their honey was more false for being heard
By him, by only him. That other singer—
He had been true. And troubling. But his song
Was never to be lost now. Dora was,
Forever. And he said it must be so.

The woman, though. Her arms. And now her eyes,
Beating upon him, beautiful, imperious,
Not to be contradicted. And her lips.
Lest the unparted lips again deliver
What was so loud, so terrible—though heard
By him, by only him—he spoke of home.

308

Berrien—wasn't she tired? And Berrien was.
So with no words they went.
                              Some dancers saw them,
Picking their way, and winked at one another;
Daniel, with that artificial woman;
Berrien, with her boarder. What a household!
None of them looked happy. Three old-fashioned
People going home. The actress, too—
An old, old timer, powdered up to kill,
And painted. You could see it—Indian summer
Everywhere. Yet once a pretty world.

They could not see how beautiful she was.
Only for Daniel was she beautiful,
And for those others, strangers here with her,
Who from the border of MacPherson's grove,
In their own forms, were watching.
                              Hermes leaned
Like none but Hermes, graceful as the grass,
On a slim sapling, serpent-shaped, and said:
"She flaunts us. Aphrodite is not Ares,
She is not schooled in victory and defeat,
She is not skilful at surrender—save
The lover's kind. See? She is bent on that.
She will not let him go, the farmer there,
While any of her poison works in him.
Ares, what if some of your new wisdom—
You could persuade her, Ares."
                              But the sullen
Soldier still was sullen, though a god;
He would not lift his face as Aphrodite,
Smiling at them, catlike, kept her way
With Daniel down the road.
                              "Apollo's song,"
Said Hermes, "—it was all we needed then."
He nodded, and the bright musician bowed.
"It was a potent song. The tough old man,

The tender young, the farmer in his heart—
All four of them were changed. But now you see—"
He pointed, and they looked where Aphrodite,
Dimming with her companions down the highway,
Walked as a mortal would; though still they knew
The goddess by a smile that lingered somewhere,
Mingling as the moon did with the tops
Of trees, and scenting midnight with its malice.
Artemis, more angry than the rest,
More like the moon, declining now so clear,
So cold, beyond the body of this grove,
Remembered the dead fawn. "So with that child,"
She brooded. "If the farmer man confesses,
Nothing but grief will grow where you and I—"
She took Athene's hand—"have wisely tilled
And planted. Never then will the boy serve,
With loving care, my cause—the cause of the world,
Of the newborn things whose nurture saves the world.
The farmer would have let the maiden go—
Sadly, yet Apollo made it sure.
Or so we said who listened. Yet that one,
That laughing one, pursues him now and sings,
And sings—oh, what low song, what tale of the flesh,
What burden that may topple his intention?
Hephaestus, our contriver, you could seal
His ears, his sleeping eyelids, if you would;
Even tonight you could."
                              Hephaestus, pacing
Oddly the smooth floor, rested his leg,
The shortened leg Zeus long ago had crippled.
"The farmer—he works well, and loves the fire
I gave him. Let him be."
                              But none of them saw
His meaning, if he had one. He was lame
And foolish, and he muttered as he walked,
And turned and walked again, counting the steps
Between two oaks that limited his way.

The great angels watched him with their wings
Folded. Standing deeper in the shade,
They waited with the others while the moon
Sloped to its rest, the music having wearied
And stopped, and all the dancers wandered home.

VII

"Dora, do you take Bruce for your husband,
To cherish him, for better or for worse?"
The justice of the peace, Tobias Hapgood,
Peered over his dim glasses at the pair
Who said "I do, I do" among the dusty
Law books.
       And there were three witnesses.
Darius in a white shirt stood between
Two others, old and little like himself:
The father of the groom—roundheaded, fumbling
Miserably at his tie—and full of tears
The mother, full of shame and happy tears.

Her boy was being married. But to think—
To think—and then the rest of it was weeping;
Was waiting till the four of them were home;
Was wondering how soon she could forget.
Dora would have his baby in her house,
And then she could forget. She wiped her eyes.
Darius here—now he would be alone,
And that perhaps was harder. So "I do"
Came distantly across the room as she compared
Their griefs; and when the couple, bent to kiss,
Held on to one another, and held on
And on, as if the world would die this way,
She was content again.
       But no one saw
Nine more in the brown room, or heard the voice
Of Hermes asking Artemis, who frowned,

What further end she strained for. All but Ares
Stood there, in no space the mortals knew,
The little mortals, mingling their low words
With these unheard, these high ones. Sullen Ares
Sulked on a far hill. But Aphrodite,
Resting her fair side against the law books,
Laughed; and the green goddess answered Hermes:

"See? There still is mischief in one mind
Among us, there is insolence. The end?
She has not worked it yet. Beware of her
Who hates this thing we witness; it defeats
Her farmer, and she never will forgive."

The laughing goddess listened with her eyes
Turned elsewhere—on Hephaestus, whom she taunted,
Teasing him with glances at his broken
Foot, and at the thickness of his wrists.
"Artisan!" she said. "Infernal tinker!
You are not one of us. Then why do you creep
Each morning, crooked fool, and haunt the man?
You do, in the poor likeness of a mender—
What is it that you mend? What is the word?"

"Stoves."
          "I'll not pronounce it. Such a word!
I scorn it. And scorn you. And yet I say—
Remember my own strength, that can undo
The cunningest contriver. No more haunt
The man. By night, by morning, no more crawl—
You hear?—and charm his sadness till it sleeps.
You think to cure his longing with some lessons,
Monger, in your art. But my own art
Is ultimate. Remember, and refrain."

Hephaestus shifted crabwise on his ankles,
Refusing every glance until the rite

Was finished, and the people in the room
Departed. Then he ducked and disappeared,
Eluding even Hermes, even the sea-grey
Eyes of sage Athene. He was bound
For Daniel, whom he haunted every day
In the same likeness he had first assumed
When Daniel, missing the comfort of his pipe bowl,
Got it again, and wondered.
                Bruce and Dora,
Heeled by their elders, one of whom still wept,
Went home another way; and the inaudible
Deities went home to the green hilltop,
The high glade where Ares, though he heard,
Sent down no shout of welcome. Aphrodite,
Following to where the mountains forked,
Deserted there; dipping away and flying,
Like one of her own doves, to Daniel's house.

But Daniel stood with someone in the barn
By the new anvil he had bought, considering
Hot and cold; and how a hammer's blow
Can bend the iron, not break it.
                      "When you came,
That day, and brought my pipe—I still am puzzled—
How did you do it, man?"
                  "Look here! I take
This strip of ten-gauge, and I heat it thus—
Pretend the forge is going—then I twist it,
So, until I have a perfect handle
For the fire tongs you need."
                No other answer.
"See? Now when you have the bellows going—
Watch me—this is what the draft can do."
No other answer. So the pupil bent,
Considering.
        And neither of them saw—

Or Daniel did not—bright eyes at the door,
Brimming with alien purpose.

"Your good wife,"
The woman said—and Daniel, starting round,
Saw how the gold one narrowed her long lids
Toward him who held the hammer—"sends for you.
She tells you this is wasting time, is wearing
The day out; is pure nothing. And she says,
Dismiss the tinker. Let him go his way.
He is not wanted here."

The hammer dropped.
But Daniel shook his head at her.

"She wouldn't
Know. It isn't woman's work. Besides,
It keeps me safe from thinking certain thoughts.
She wouldn't know that either. Or would you."

He flushed, remembering how much she knew
If dreams had body, and if at the dance
It was her own live lips that so rebuked him.
But no, that couldn't be. He said it again,
And turned to the lame tinker.

"We'll not stop,
For her or anybody. Tell me now—"
Whereat Hephaestus grinned, and Aphrodite,
Stamping her white foot, that all but showed
Immortal through the slipper, let them be.

Yet not for long. The lame one in his room,
That night and every night, was pinched awake
By fingers he well knew; and knew as well
How in the darkness, sweating, to endure.
For he was steadfast—like his tossing pupil,
Daniel, in the bed where Berrien lay.

Hour after hour, that night and every night,
Berrien strove to riddle his strange words,

314

His mumbled words, that stubbornly kept on
Refusing what was whispered. What was that?
Or was it anything? Was someone by them,
Whispering to him? She lay and wondered,
Doubtful of his mind, that so could mumble,
Endlessly, at nothing, maybe nothing.

But it was never nothing. Aphrodite,
Going between Hephaestus' bed and his,
Was a changed goddess, bearing every charm
Of beauty she possessed, that he once more
Might madden. Dora came there too, he thought,
And wept in her first figure, the demure one,
The thin and still one, that was his again—
"It is, it is!" the whisper at his side
Said tirelessly, "whenever you will reach
And take it. Be the lover you were then,
And take it, take it, take it. Go and be
Her lover; speak the truth as winter once,
As warmness, spoke it for you. Is it late?
Is there a foolish thing that now deforms her?
And for that thing a father? Is it published
That he is the thing's foolish, foolish father?
Have none of it. Forget these moments since,
And take her. She is yours; see how she weeps
And wishes she had Daniel's hands forever—
Forever it could be, if you were bold
And shouted without shame the burning truth—
Forever, Daniel, ever down her small
Smooth sides; or where her breasts, that breathed for you,
Might breathe again."
                    He moaned and turned away,
Tormented. And sometimes the whisper died,
So that he looked again. It was an artful
Death, increasing torment, for the two
Shone there as always. They were never gone,

315

Those two, while August lasted; and while summer
Saddened on the stalk.
           For rust had bent
The hayheads while he dreamed, and far to north
The feet of fall were coming. Daniel rose
Each day a wearier man, yet not apostate
Ever to his black anvil, where with the smith
He lost himself in lessons hot and cold.
And still the woman came to call him in.
And still he could refuse her.
              So September,
With speckles on its back, slid like a serpent
Over the cool slopes; and lucky houses,
Filled with a winter's wood, sat where they were,
Complacent; while upon the homeless highways
Wanderers appeared.
           So Dora's time
Came slowly, slowly on, with few to know
Or care when it should come; except Darius,
Who prowled each afternoon to Bruce's house,
Consoling himself there for being lonely;
Except the little roundhead and his anxious
Wife; except those strangers up the mountain;
And Bruce himself, awaiting it with Dora.

VIII

It came, the time of Dora, when no man,
No man of all her three, was home for messenger.
Darius snored in his own house—a ball
Of skin beneath the bedclothes—and the night
Was early yet for Bruce, who with his father
Tramped the low road from Brownlee's where they worked,
And working, thought of Dora—all day long
Of Dora's time, next week or the week after.

But it was now, and none of all the three men
Home to be her messenger! The doctor—
How could he be told the time had come
For pain, for crying out? Then Bruce's mother,
Moaning, was so helpless at the door,
Calling, calling, calling: "Bruce, where are you?
Go and get the doctor! Hurry, boy!"
But Bruce was on the low road, and the only
Ears that heard were scattered up the sky.
Artemis, on top of Silver Mountain,
Heard; and woke Athene; and the others,
Knowing it was time, went with them both
Like falling stars—all of them, like stars,
To drop and stand in darkness by the door
While Bruce's mother, moaning, called and called:
"Where are you, boy? Hurry! Get the doctor!"

And still another heard. But Aphrodite,
Listening while Daniel sat, could smile
And wait; could think and wait. It was the time
For punishing this man who in his dreams
Refused her. She could wait and let it work—
The punishment she planned.
                    For she had looked
Last night along the valley, and seen coming,
Hapless on the highway, two small wanderers,
And said: They shall be mine.
                    She heard the moaning
Cease, and knew that Artemis was there.
The nurse was there, and Dora would be crying
Softly: "Save me, save me! Send for him!"

So Aphrodite, gathering her sly strength,
Waited no longer.
                  Where were those poor wanderers—
That pair? But she had seen them, and she knew.
She saw them even now at the abandoned

317

Chapel down the old road, trying doors
And windows, and forlornly turning in
Where nothing was but darkness; and in darkness,
Nothing but cobwebs.
              Smiling a last smile,
Vindictive, at the sitter, she uprose
And scented the whole night, the outer night
Of fields and barns and houses, as she flew
And flew, tinting earth with a false dawn
As in her brilliant singleness she flew
And flew to be the first where Hermes came.

For even now the tall nurse—goddess again
In the dooryard where they clustered—told her peers:
"The time! It is the time! Go, two of you—
Hermes, shall it be? With Gabriel?—
And bring him here, the man of herbs she cries for.
I could do all alone, for I am skilful,
I am the green deliveress. Yet go—
Gabriel, with Hermes—while I soothe
And ready her. The horses that he drives—
You hear them now, drawing the tired one home.
But have no pity. Hurry and intercept him.
Say it is the nurse—say anything—
But bring him here, the mortal man of herbs,
Between you lest she die."
              The feet of Hermes
Glistened as the staff in his right hand
Touched Gabriel on the nearer wing; then lightly
Touched him again. And so the pair departed.
Before the goddess turned they were a rustle
In the far woods; and Artemis went in
Where Dora lay.
           "The doctor—he is sent for.
Child! What are you staring at?" For Dora
Shuddered, and alternately her eyes
Opened and closed in terror, as at brightness

Impossible, brought near. But then she smiled.
"It was my own mistake—the way I am.
You were so different. You shone in the door
Like candles, you were like a statue lady—
Different from us. I didn't know you.
Now I do, though."
                    She permitted hands
To smooth, to cool her as she lay in fever,
And as the pain returned; while Artemis
Looked gravely, out of eyes she kept in shadow,
At the small face whereon the truth had fallen;
Looked, and wondered fearfully. Had Hermes,
Had Gabriel heard the horses? Found the man?

But Aphrodite was there first—an ancient
Gypsy, rising out of the dim road
And shrilling between wheels:
                    "Doctor, Doctor!
Come to the dead church—the one they don't
Sing songs in any more. A poverty fellow
And his sick queen—not my people, but I pity,
Pity them—they lie in the carriage shed.
Or she does, the queen. In all the world
No friend, and both afraid. They have walked miles
From nowhere, and no house would take them in.
She whimpers with the young thing in her belly,
The babe she has to bear. Come with me, Doctor,
And help her. Be the one man in the world
To help her."
                    "Who are you?" His glasses peered
Through the poor light the buggy lamp cast down.

"Romany."
                    "And what's this? You mean the church—"

"The old one."
                    "Even mice won't go near that.

319

Mischief—you mean mischief. Out of the way,
Granny!"
        But she seized the reins and said:
"Good doctor! Be the one man in the world—"

And why it was he knew not, but he went
Where she did, down the sod road toward that moldy
Building where no hymnsong had been heard
Since war days, and where beggars—did she lie?—
Might be or not be.
        So when Hermes came,
And Gabriel, there was silence on the highway—
Soft as they listened, never the good sound
Of hooves, of whirring felloes.
        Long they looked
And listened; then were back in Bruce's dooryard,
Signalling their presence; so that Artemis,
Stooping at the window, saw them desolate,
And knew herself defeated.
        "Aphrodite!"
She only thought the word, but Dora stared
And begged of her: "Has someone—has he come?
The doctor? Bruce? Where's Bruce?"
        "Be patient, dear.
In time, in time. The doctor was not found.
But there is time, and I myself have medicines—
You trust me?"
        Dora nodded.
        "Then I'll go, child,
For certain things—for such help as I need.
Be patient a few minutes. She is here."
For Bruce's mother, torturing her hands
As if they were another's on the rack,
Stood by them, bent and weeping.
        All were there
When Artemis, the doorlight shut behind her,
Shouted. Even Aphrodite smiled

And innocently listened, fair as ever
In the fine light that clothed her—no more gypsy,
And no more theater woman. Even Ares—
All of them were there, with lame Hephaestus
Filling his low place among the pear trees,
When the green goddess called.
                              "Her breath is going.
Enemy of all"—to Aphrodite—
"I shall waste none on you. I only say,
The girl inside is going. Which of you
Can help me, and help her? The middle angel,
Second of you three, immense of wing—
Raphael—have you knowledge?"
                              There was mournful
Music in the answer.
                    "I have mended,
Green one, all the wounds made here on earth—
Or there—by deed of angels. In the old days
They fell—not such as we are—and their fall,
As of dark stars that burned, corrupted the sons,
The daughters of frail man. If this is such—"

"It is. Come in with me, shrunk to the likeness
Of a lean passing farmer. I have herbs
And needles. You have strength, and a strange art.
Between us—but come quickly!"
                              And Darius
Snored in his own house. And Daniel sat
Late by a brass lamp, reading.
                              And the doctor,
Bending to ask the name of the new mother,
Heard "Mary."
                By the half light of a low
Fire she lay on straw and let her weak hand
Wander.
        "But my husband—he is Joe.

321

There was no work for him. So we went on.
Thank you, Doctor."
                    "Quiet. No more talking."

And Bruce's father, panting on the low road,
Wondered why his son would never rest.

IX

The risen sun, sparkling upon their bridles,
Hastened the roan horses; and brought Bruce—
Brought even the stiff doctor—beams of hope,
Of something like belief; though Bruce remembered,
And groaned as he remembered, how the nurse,
Weeping, had looked afraid when he came home;
How she and the dark man she had for helper,
Bending above the sufferer, grew sad,
Grew guilty as he came, hearing with him
His little mother's whimpers, and the cry—
Sudden, as if death were in the room—
Of Dora when she saw him. And his father's
Feebleness—now he remembered that,
And groaned.
            "But couldn't the nurse—for she was there—
Wouldn't the nurse have known?"
                                "I tell you, boy,
I have no nurse. Something is stranger here—
Giddup!—than God is ever going to tell me.
Nurse? There was no such."
                            And the horses galloped,
Jingling their bright bridles, till the dooryard
Darkened them, and Bruce's mother stumbled,
Her apron at her face, among the plum trees.

"I am alone," she cried, "except for him—"
She pointed where her husband, on a stone
As grey as he was, sat and held his forehead—

"We are alone now, my boy. Too late,
Doctor. Even the nurse is gone. The child,
The dear child, is dead. They both are dead—
Dora, and the other one that never,
Never, never breathed."
                        She clutched at Bruce,
Feeling the doctor brush them as he passed,
Then feeling not at all. She only nodded,
Nodded, as her son repeated: "Dead.
Dora, she is dead." And bore her in,
A limp superfluous bundle.
                        "Oh, my boy!"—
Perceptibly her white lips lived again—
"Beautiful! One thing about her going,
Oh, my boy, was beautiful. She saw—
Or thought she saw—ten angels in the room.
She counted them. But only three had wings.
She counted the big wings. And said the nurse
Was queen above all others."
                        "Nurse? What nurse?"
The doctor in the doorway shook his head,
Frowning, as if to free it from the cobweb
Sound of that false word. "There was no such—"

But the small mother never would believe—
He knew it—and Bruce never would believe.
Who had this tall impostor woman been?
And why? And who the other one? Bruce had said:
"A teacher, too—her friend." There was no such—

The doctor shook his head. Shame on those bunglers—
Butchers of girls—who with their knotted
Grass roots and their needles—natural thorns—
Had poisoned the sweet blood, the delicate place.
Where were they, vagrants, now? Could any law
Catch up with their coarse hands, and cleanse the world
Of meddlers on the march? For they were somewhere

323

Still, the doctor knew; and looked at Bruce
Bent dumbly over Dora. In good time
The boy would feel. He was so quiet now—
An animal, playing dead.

        Then Daniel stood there—
Daniel, with Darius at his heels:
An old hound whom giant grief had gentled.
Yet he could move, and did, to where no daughter
Welcomed his hard hand; which nevertheless
Hovered and touched her—touched her, so that tears
Followed, and streamed his face.

              "I brought him here,"
Said Daniel. "I was told of it by one—
By two—but they are gone. They do not matter.
Both of them are gone. They said they knew—
My lodgers—then they went. But that's no matter.
I told her father, and he came with me.
Look at him now. And her. We are not enemies.
Who is my enemy?"

        "I was," said Bruce.

"You were. And I was Dora's. What I did—"

"You did. But never tell it. As my friend
In sorrow, never say it. There are ears—"

He went to where his mother, staring up,
Saw none but that dear face.

        Then Daniel's stillness
Reigned in the room.

        Even the doctor, going,
Went as a thought does, thinly; but his mind
Was more with Mary and her living child,
In the lost church, than here.

        A living child.
He must go back to that small son; must listen
To the soft mother's voice. Why had he stopped her?

"Quiet. No more talking." Was even then
This mystery in his head, this hazy mirror
Of a much older birth? Who was it? When?
What torment not to remember. Just like this,
Yet where? He drove and thought; and was the image
Of a whole people, impotent to see now
The one god it had.
                    So three old friends,
By death remade, stood looking down at Dora.

X

Already, in this moment before silver
Morning, ten were on their way to sea.
Already, over mountains and rock rivers—
Tawny with high autumn, yet no sun
Uprisen had revealed it—Hermes sped
And spoke not. At the center of his band,
Encircled, he was thoughtful as he flew
And flew to where a smoking funnel waited,
By a smooth prow whereon the ten would ride,
Would ride the waste Atlantic.
                            "They were small,
These people, they were pitiful and small,"
Said Hermes, half aloud. "Yet not unworthy,
Nobles, of our regard."
                        "They did not guess,"
Said Artemis, "how small."
                          "They could not measure,"
Flashed the grey eyes of swift Athene, flying,
"Difference. They were lonely. They had nothing
Past them to compare. They do not move,
These persons, among greater persons still.
The knowledge of the difference is all.
Mortals with art to measure it are never
Pitiful."
        "I thought," mused Aphrodite,

Beautiful by night as her own star,
Her morning's mirror, up now in the east,
"I thought I met a presence in that musty
Stable. Felt a power. Yet all so quiet—
Not even the black beetles crept away.
Queer, if it was a god—their only god,
And none of the fools knew."

                              "It was your own
Mind's darkness," Ares muttered; and Hephaestus
Laughed—at Aphrodite he could laugh,
Now that his limbs were free.

                              "Was there a song?
Even a musty music? Where a god is,
Surely the air will sound." Apollo hummed,
Remembering the barn dance and the moon.
"Did you hear anything to prove a presence?"

Artemis, her green robe gilded suddenly
By the first beams of sun, was angry still.
"She heard but her own hatefulness, that plotted
Death."

               "I left the living in your hands—
Yours, and the mighty angel's. If you erred,
Darling of fawns and virgins, I regret,
As you must, any faltering of skill."

"Regret!" The speed of Artemis redoubled
As fury filled her. "Lying, laughing word!
You poison the whole dawn with it, as then
You poisoned—for I know you did—the thorns,
The rare leaves I used."

                      But Hermes cried:
"Peace, peace between you, daughters! What is done
Is done. There the ship rides that we take—
As one we take it, homing to those lands
Where sleep is our best portion. Only sleep."

326

He sighed, and the archangels echoed him:
Those three whose sire, unknown to them last night,
Had dreamed again—a star above a stable.
"Not even sleep," said Michael. "No, not even
Sleep," droned weary Gabriel. But Raphael's
Sadness was for Artemis to see,
And seeing, to have pity on, that no word
Henceforth could express.
                           For now the ship
Whistled, and the spires above the harbor
Glistened, and the hawsers, letting go,
Dangled in salt.
                  So easterly they sailed,
And sailed; then south a little. And the crew
Thought only of the Pillars, of the inland
Sea where waves were smaller. But these ten,
Prone on the prow, disdained the autumn danger
Of storm, of the dark swell. Their daily vision—
Common to them all, since reconciled—
Was the long night ahead; or over Asia,
Centuries upon centuries of flying,
Flying where no desert, green with the Word,
Blossomed and blessed them.
                            Now as in a dream
Never to be redreamed the hills behind them,
Huddling that valley, muffled its fine cries
Of people trapped in sorrow. Even its glad souls,
Silenced, were obscure as drops of dew
Hung in the wild Antipodes. No mortal
Summer would be given these again:
These deities, these angels, who as the dark sea
Heaved went on themselves as waves do,
Wearily, yet smiling as in a dream.

ANGER IN THE ROOM
(1964)

Anger in the Room

The hills of little Cornwall
Themselves are dreams.
The mind lies down among them,
Even by day, and snores,
Snug in the perilous knowledge
That nothing more inward pleasing,
More like itself,
Sleeps anywhere beyond them
Even by night
In the great land it cares two pins about,
Possibly; not more.

Or inward ugly, also like itself;
As when in the old time
Two sisters, brothers,
Or a farmer and his wife,
Sat down to hate each other hard till Sunday;
Went on a second week,
A third,
Then months, then bitter years,
Then death on both sides, if not death already.

The mind, eager for caresses,
Lies down at its own risk in Cornwall;
Whose hills,
Whose cunning streams,
Whose mazes where a thought,
Doubling upon itself,
Considers the way, lazily, well lost,
Indulge it to the nick of death—
Not quite, for where it curls it still can feel,
Like feathers,
Like affectionate mouse whiskers,
The flattery, the trap.
The mind that dozes there becomes itself
Twice over; does not change,
Nor suffer truth;
If fair, more fair; if foul, more foul;
The sweet thought, the hideous,
Swell equally, and care not
What civil growths prefer the soil beyond.

"John Westwick, if you sell that woodlot
I'll never say a word to you again."
John did, and Hannah's lips,
That seldom parted anyhow,
Closed over like the grave.

The woodlot was her father's once,
Who lovingly picked trees to cut
But saved the fringe of sassafras,
Witch hazel and viburnum,
Inside of the south wall: a thicket
For thrushes, too, in June.
It was her dowry, all she brought,
With the old man nodding somewhere in it
And saying: Leave the pretty fringe.
She walked there, childless,

And chanced upon all sorts of wonders
She never shared with John.
She did, though, with her first love,
Her father. They had an understanding
Among the fern leaves; they listened
To the same birds at sunset,
The sad ones.
                    Then one day:
"McGilpin wants our woodlot."
"Ours?" "He offers a good price."
"Ours? What for? What does McGilpin—"
"You know, he owns around it;
So now he wants it too."
"What for?" "His business.
But I think, more pasture."
She almost died that minute.
"Cut it, would he? All of it?
The big trees, the little?"
She almost died again.
"John Westwick, if you ever—"
But the next week he did; and so
For years—now it was seven—
Silence;
While alien heifers romped unseen
In sun that had no business shining there.

She cooked for him and served him standing,
Arms folded, till he finished.
She made his bed,
She mended his torn clothes,
She baked and scrubbed,
She made him relishes he liked,
She was a wife in all the ways
There are, excepting three:
She slept alone, she never spoke,
And after a while no company came.
The evenings were the hard part.

They sat not more than ten feet,
Honestly, from each other,
Reading and rocking; measuring
The spread hands of the clock;
Then, earlier than used to be, to bed.

A third one would have wondered,
Seeing how Hannah sat,
If there were never twinges in her:
Doubt in her bones,
Chilblains of repentance; rusty
Needles and pins of pity or desire.
But there was no such person,
And anyway she gave no sign,
No hint that her own mind
Was here at all, unchangeable
Forever, maybe;
Or maybe not.

The stranger was there before she knew.
Odd that she saw him and John didn't.
They both were in their chairs,
And his had not stopped rocking.
But hers froze, as she did,
Extreme upon the backward tilt
As if it saw too, and was outraged.

"Ha!" said the stranger;
And still John didn't hear.
"So you don't know me—
Yet. I'm Wrath.
I'm everlasting. I'm Himself,
And you don't know me—
Yet. You will.
I mean to show you, woman,
Now, right now. That man—
Watch him. I'll be quick.

I won't take seven years.
See now. You want the worm destroyed—
Well, listen to my lightning.
And look—my arm—
Watch it, Hannah—
There—as he goes forward—
His bare neck—the back of it—"
A cape rustled;
A right arm, hidden in it,
Rose;
And Hannah screamed, louder than even lightning,
"John!"

And if John kept on going,
And fell like heavy stone,
Head first, to the floor,
It was no bolt that did it.
There was no bolt. At least there was no stranger;
Unless a door that banged—
Where?—that was him,
Thought Hannah, hearing laughter
Like horses in the night wind—
No! Her own. She couldn't stop.
"John!" She said it over and over,
Laughing like a girl, a crazy girl,
And couldn't stop.
Even John, dazed and getting up
And staring, was no cure
For this queer thing that ailed her.
But then he too began,
And he too couldn't—
John, her husband—John,
John, John,
He couldn't stop.